The Whistleblowers

THE

WHISTLEBLOWERS

Exposing Corruption in
Government and Industry

MYRON PERETZ GLAZER

&

PENINA MIGDAL GLAZER

Basic Books, Inc., Publishers

NEW YORK

Library of Congress Cataloging-in-Publication Data

Glazer, Myron.
  The Whistleblowers.

  Bibliographic notes: p. 258.
  Includes index.
  1. Whistle blowing—United States.
  2. Corruption (in politics)—United States.
  3. Corporations—United States—Corrupt
  practices.   I. Glazer, Penina Migdal.
  II. Title.
  JK468.W54G55   1989   353.009   88–47896
  ISBN   0–465–09173–3

For

Fay and Terry

Yudis and in memory of Sid

Estelle and Itz

Ayala and Yudi

Marcy and Joel

Sisters and brothers

Earliest friends

We could make no greater mistake than to be lulled into a sense of false security by believing that some disembodied force called the government will act like a beneficent big brother and make certain that the special interests will not predominate. If the general welfare is to be protected, it will be protected by the actions of people, not the government.

—Dr. A. DALE CONSOLE

The reason that there are very few Serpicos or Roses is that the message is too clearly out in this society that white-collar crime, or nonviolent crime, should be tolerated by the public at large, so long as the conduct brings a profit or a profitable result to the institution committing it.

—JOSEPH ROSE, lawyer

I know it may sound like a hackneyed phrase today but I believe it: *"The only thing necessary for evil to prevail is for good men to do nothing."*

—Dr. MARY McANAW

Contents

Preface

For six years we have traveled throughout the United States, interviewing men and women of conscience who disclosed lawless acts in the workplace. We have also spoken to their husbands and wives who stood by them, to journalists who investigated their stories, to legislators who heard their testimony, and to public-interest activists who defended them in lengthy judicial hearings.

We uncovered the cases presented in this book in several ways. The experiences of a few whistleblowers had been recorded in previous academic studies. Others appeared in journalistic accounts, and the Government Accountability Project, a major whistleblower defense organization in Washington, D.C., recommended a substantial number of ongoing cases. From these sources and from whistleblowers who called us as they learned of our research, we sought to encompass a range of employees in government and industry, including professionals, managers, police, and white-collar and blue-collar workers. As we compared the responses of our group of sixty-four with those reported by other investigators, we confirmed that the experiences reported in this volume are representative of hundreds of other employees who have challenged illegal and unethical behavior in government and corporate organizations.

The whistleblowers were receptive to our request for extended interviews even if it meant recounting the most difficult periods of their lives. They also agreed to our plan to monitor their experiences over a period of time so that we could study the impact of their public disclosure of corrupt practices on their families and careers. We are indebted to them for years of cooperation and for the insights they provided into the possibilities and costs of dissent in a society dominated by large bureaucratic organizations.

The testimony of their spouses was invariably forthcoming, even when it required them to uncover old emotional wounds and relive moments of great family stress and disruption. Their responses deepened our under-standing of the emotional fortitude necessary for employees to confront powerful superiors and fight a long battle for vindication. As our study unfolded, we became ever more convinced that these struggles could be waged only with the active intervention of the press, legislature, and public-interest organizations. While whistleblowers come forward alone or in small groups, they can survive only with the help of strategically placed allies who appreciate the significance of the problems they expose. We thank all the whistleblowers, their families, and their allies for their unflagging help with our research.

Since 1982, we have benefited from the encouragement of many other people who believe that a detailed, long-term study of the lives of whistle-blowers would make a contribution to understanding workplace ethics. Several congressional staff members, including Andrew Feinstein and George Kopp, became our earliest guides. Michael Walker merits our appreciation for his intelligence and friendship. Dina Rasor and Danielle Bryan-Bland at the Project on Military Procurement and Loeb Julie and Janice A. Rio of the Coalition to Stop Government Waste offered helpful information about their efforts to work on behalf of whistleblowers. Louis Clark, Tom Devine, Billie Garde, and the entire staff at the Government Accountability Project deserve extra recognition for their contribution at various stages of the research.

We have also learned much from colleagues who have studied freedom and dissent on the job and who encouraged our research: Michael Baker, Alan Westin, James Bowman, and the late Frederick Elliston. Miriam Slater, Paul Slater, Gail Perlman, David Schimmel, Aaron Berman, Marcy Migdal, and Joel Migdal are colleagues who read the manuscript in its various stages and provided important criticisms. We offer special thanks to Bob Rakoff and Michael Lewis for their willingness to read several drafts and force us to confront some of the limits of our analysis. As always, Terry Lichtash has read every word of our volume with the "eagle eye" of the trained attorney and the tenacity of a self-made editor. We are grateful to him. Fay Lichtash provided a crucial last reading. Eugenie Gavenchak gave us the benefit of her wise legal counsel.

Two assistants, Joshua Glazer of Brandeis University and Daniel Rosen of the University of Michigan, came to our aid during the final push to complete the book. They checked sources, ferreted out new material, organized the files, and brought a fresh burst of energy to two weary authors. They gave us "nine good innings." Jessica Glazer always reminded us that family responsibilities are a delight, even during the most demanding stages of a research project. She also assisted in the painstaking task of checking endnotes, as did Laurie Yarworth. Ayala Rosen, Jordan Rosen, and Fay Lichtash were consistent sources of articles on whistleblowing. Bill Bush, a whistleblower who has become the informal archivist of the integrity and accountability movement, was a steady source of clippings and letters. We thank him and his faithful collie, Beau, for their good information and good humor. Walt Harrison of Gehrung Associates has always believed that our subject is one of great interest and significance to the American public. Maria Moszynski for almost two decades has helped keep our two-career family thriving. She holds a special place in the affections of all the Glazers.

Our literary agent, Carol Mann, brought us to Basic Books. It was a wise choice. The editors at Basic Books have more than lived up to their deservedly high reputation in the publishing world. Judy Greissman and Richard Liebmann-Smith guided the development of the manuscript; Phoebe Hoss turned her remarkable skills to sharpening it; Linda Carbone managed the transition to the printed page, remaining calm in the face of the multitude of changes and corrections. We deeply appreciate all of their efforts.

Our two colleges have provided a working environment that sustains both teaching and research. Indeed, our study had its origins in a course first taught at Smith College over a decade ago. We applaud the many students who have helped us analyze the process of whistleblowing. We are indebted to Agnes Shannon, Norma Lepine, and Kay Worsley of the Smith Social Science Office for their continuing good cheer and secretarial help. We thank Tom O'Connell, Tom O'Connell III, and Marty Bimbane for setting up the equipment to record scores of interviews, and Joyce Wiernasz for transcribing hundreds of pages of those interviews. Tracy Gates was an able research assistant, and her graduation from Smith College coincided with the completion of the study. Jennifer McGowan, Louise Rockey, Julie Dobrow, Denise Penrose, Susan Stoneham, and Lucinda M. Williams were most helpful as student assistants in earlier stages of the project. The members of the library staff helped us in countless ways. They include Janice Daily, Vicki Hart, Robin Kinder, Elaine Miller, Bruce Sadjak, and Pamela Skinner. At Hampshire College, we are pleased to acknowledge the contribution of Kelley Piccicuto and Jackie Tuthill of the Dean of Faculty office. They have provided assistance throughout the various stages of the study and were assiduous in protecting Penina Migdal Glazer's research hours. We could not have completed this work without them.

We thank the National Endowment for the Humanities for a 1984 summer research stipend to Myron Peretz Glazer and the Smith College Committee on Faculty Compensation and Development which provided funds for student assistants. We are grateful to JAI Press for permission to reprint material from our article "Pathways to Resistance: An Ethical Odyssey in Government and Industry" in *Research in Social Problems and Public Policy*, volume 4 (1987), edited by Joann L. Miller and Michael Lewis. We also acknowledge the *Hastings Center Report* for its publication of our first article on this subject, entitled "Ten Whistleblowers and How They Fared," which appeared in December 1983. We recall the encouragement of our late kinsman Steve Reines. A committed high school social studies teacher, he passed along scores of pertinent articles to us. We sorely miss his caring and his devotion to building a more humane world.

The Whistleblowers is dedicated to our sisters and brothers, with whom we have shared joy and sorrow across the years. We are blessed by their comradeship and love.

The Whistleblowers

Introduction:
A New Tradition of
Courageous Dissent

BUILDING dangerous nuclear power plants, dumping toxic wastes, marketing unsafe drugs and cars, camouflaging huge cost overruns in the development of weapon systems, misusing public funds: these and other scandals have been legion over the last several decades. Such lawless acts are too often perpetrated by policy makers in large organizations. These bureaucracies, which employ thousands of people, are organized hierarchically, and their leaders demand complete conformity and loyalty from their employees.[1] Most workers do what their superiors require and assume that someone up the line will take responsibility for the safety of the product and the legality of the organization's actions.

But some employees have been unwilling to be so compliant. A few have dared to take an active and vociferous stand against practices they have witnessed that threaten to defraud or endanger the public. By following the path of protest, these men and women have forged a new tradition of dissent during the past quarter of a century. In refusing to succumb to the easy path of conformity or to be dissuaded by the retaliation of management, employees have risked their lives, their careers, and their families' security in order to "do the right thing." The media refer to these protesters as "whistleblowers"; we also call them "ethical resisters," to denote their commitment to the principles we all espouse—honesty, individual responsibility, and active concern for the public good.

Ethical resisters—employees who publicly disclose unethical or illegal practices in the workplace—are a recent phenomenon in American history. In the 1960s, the psychologist Stanley Milgram undertook pioneering research on the issue of obedience to authority.[2] He analyzed the propensity of Americans to obey the commands of authority figures, even when ordered to inflict pain on innocent victims. In our study we focus on precisely the opposite issue: What leads some people to act in accordance with their ethical principles against the explicit instructions of management? Why have more workers protested in the last two decades? What impels such dissenters to pursue their definition of appropriate behavior at great cost to themselves and their families? What happened to them after they contacted the press, a local legislator, or a federal agency? Who helped them in their fight for vindication and reform? Did they believe the outcome was worth the price they paid?

To answer these questions, we interviewed a group of sixty-four whistleblowers over a period of six years and followed many of them from the early stages of their resistance through the final outcome (a process by no means finished, as even now the cases of some of these whistleblowers are being decided in the courts). We chose resisters who were impelled to speak out because they had witnessed a serious violation of legal or ethical standards. To be included in the study, each resister had to have persuasive evidence to corroborate his or her personal observations—most often organization records, legal documents, newspaper accounts, and testimony by other workers. Those engaged in a personal vendetta or those who had made a deal when charged with improper conduct by a prosecuting attorney were omitted.*

We studied ethical resisters in government and industry, who were

---

*All of our cases meet Norman Bowie's ideal requirements of justifiable acts of whistleblowing: (1) that the act of whistleblowing stem from appropriate moral motives of preventing unnecessary harm to others; (2) that the whistleblower use all available internal procedures for rectifying the problematic behavior before public disclosure, although special circumstances may preclude this; (3) that the whistleblower have "evidence that would persuade a reasonable person"; (4) that the whistleblower perceive serious danger that can result from the violation; (5) that the whistleblower act in accordance with his or her responsibilities for "avoiding and/or exposing moral violations"; (6) that the whistleblower's action have some reasonable chance of success.[3]

professionals, white-collar, and blue-collar workers.[4] Although the professionals tend to predominate, comprising over half the sample, workers in industry have been particularly significant in bringing to light the dangers of poorly constructed nuclear plants. Welders, pipe fitters, and quality-control inspectors have shown clearly that the phenomenon of whistle-blowing cuts across both class and gender lines, especially where health and safety are concerned. Women have been involved in some of the most important cases in the country. In our study, there are six women among the thirty-six professionals, three among the thirteen white-collar and technical workers, and six among the fifteen skilled workers, police, and secretaries.

Two thirds of these resisters were in their thirties or forties, and eleven in their fifties at the time they blew the whistle; only a handful were either beginning their careers or were nearing retirement. Forty-four of the whistleblowers were government employees, and twenty worked in private industry. The largest concentration—nineteen—were government workers who lived in Washington, D.C. Several other small groups worked together—five in the Chicago regional office of the Environmental Protection Agency, four in a Kansas Veterans Administration hospital, eight at the Comanche Peak nuclear plant in Texas, and five in a county hospital in San Diego. The remainder were scattered throughout the country in the states of Maine, Washington, New York, Ohio, Utah, Massachusetts, and Alabama.

In addition to extensive communication and correspondence with the whistleblowers themselves, we spoke to twenty-five of their husbands and wives. These spouses provided insight into the emotional and social effects of the protest and helped us to understand the individual whistleblower's determination to endure what usually turned out to be a long, difficult, and costly fight. We also interviewed the journalists, legislators, and public-interest activists who have done more than just substantiate the resisters' stories. They themselves have often become central actors in the struggle, demanding investigations and reform. They have brought to public attention such issues as defective consumer products and contaminated meat.

Whistleblowers, we discovered, are conservative people devoted to their work and their organizations. Those we studied had built their careers—whether as professionals, managers, or workers—by conforming to the requirements of bureaucratic life. Most had been successful until they were asked to violate their own standards of appropriate workplace behavior.[5] Invariably, they believed that they were defending the true mission of their organization by resisting illicit practices and could not comprehend how their superiors could risk the good name of their company by producing defective products, the reputation of their hospital by abusing and neglecting patients, or the integrity of their agency by allowing their safety reports to be tampered with or distorted.*

The practice of whistleblowing emerged as a significant social force in the 1960s, as we discuss in chapter 1. Public concern about nuclear accidents, dangerous drugs, and toxic wastes led to government regulation of private industry, spawning a host of new laws that explicitly protect workers who report lawless actions in the workplace. In this same period, there was increasing suspicion that many of the accepted practices of government and industry officials were insufficient to guard against the dangers of the new technologies and, in some cases, actively threatened the health and safety of workers and consumers. Some employees concluded that when their superiors neglected public safety, they themselves would have to speak up—in order, as one resister said, to "sleep well at night."

We examine three cases of pioneering resisters in chapter 2: Dr. Arthur Dale Console, who exposed unethical practices in the pharmaceutical industry; James Boyd and Marjorie Carpenter, who disclosed the abuse of office by Senator Thomas Dodd; and Frank Serpico, who fought corruption in the New York City Police Department. Console, Boyd, Carpenter, and Serpico had to convince themselves and others—peers as well as superiors—that illegal and dangerous practices required them to place the common good above loyalty to the organization.

Professional ethics impelled many resisters to speak out. Thus, in chapter 3, we show how engineers and physicians relied on their judgment to confront the Nuclear Regulatory Commission, the Veterans Administration, and the Ortho Pharmaceutical Corporation. In chapter 4, we examine the power of religious belief and community ties among whistleblow-

---

*These findings are corroborated by Frederick Elliston and his associates who believe that "whistleblowing is more likely to occur if individuals are (a) committed to the formal goals of the organization or to the successful completion of the project, (b) identify with the organization, and (c) have a strong sense of professional responsibility." In another analysis, James S. Bowman states that the majority of whistleblowers are not "malcontents, misfits, neurotics, nor radicals."[6]

ers who exposed illegal practices in the General Services Administration, the Department of Education, and the Comanche Peak Nuclear Power Plant in Texas.[7]

However well justified these whistleblowers' charges—and independent investigation has subsequently borne out most of them—management in both industry and government moved quickly to retaliate. In 1965, for example, General Motors hired private detectives to spy on Ralph Nader because he had evidence from a whistleblower condemning the safety of the Corvair;[8] in another case, the federal government has spent the last twenty years trying to expel or isolate the Defense Department analyst and ethical resister Ernest Fitzgerald.[9] Many government and industry officials have, as we discuss in chapter 5, implemented a consistent pattern of harsh reprisals—from blacklisting, dismissal, or transfer to personal harassment—in the effort to define the dissident employees as the source of the problem, to undermine their credibility and effectiveness as potential witnesses, and to demonstrate to other workers the high cost of nonconformity.

Ethical resisters often have significant allies in the press and national television, in local, state, and federal legislatures, and in public-interest groups. In chapter 6, we examine the role of the *Seattle Times* in helping Casey Ruud press his allegations of severe dangers at the Hanford Nuclear Reservation; the actions of a congressional staff which exposed the poisoning of the rivers by Dow Chemical Company and the cover-up by the Environmental Protection Agency; the efforts of a crusading California state assemblyman who initiated an investigation in response to several whistleblowers who reported patient neglect in a county mental health hospital resulting in unnecessary deaths; and the far-reaching programs of Louis Clark and the Government Accountability Project in defending hundreds of whistleblowers.

Husbands and wives have been central in helping resisters survive the emotional and financial repercussions of their protests. In chapter 7, we examine the ways in which whistleblowers and their spouses re-created their lives, recovering from the career disruption and personal abuse they suffered. The routes to developing new careers vary, and resisters' assessment of their new jobs range from true satisfaction to chronic frustration. For some, the long journey concluded with the establishment of new and satisfying work roles. For others, like Maude DeVictor who helped publicize the suffering of veterans exposed to Agent Orange, the whistleblowing experience led to career dislocation and the inability to obtain a job commensurate with one's training.

In the final chapter, we examine whistleblowers and their role at the heart of a new social movement, devoted to the goal of assuring accountability by corporate and government bureaucracies whose leaders make decisions affecting the vital interests of millions of citizens. Ethical resisters and their allies insist that a respect for laws regulating worker health and safety, and consumer and environmental protection, are consistent with productivity and profit in a free enterprise system. They are equally committed to the integrity of public officials and will not tolerate collusion between government and industry, waste of public funds, or abuse of vulnerable people.

The efforts to destroy ethical resisters have not silenced them. On the contrary, there are encouraging signs of society's readiness to support those of its members who are willing, even at personal risk, to defend its long-term health and interests. In confronting corruption, lawlessness, and threats to the common good, whistleblowers and their allies provide models for all of us and offer hope for a future where industry and government are accountable for the consequences of their actions.

Chapter 1

The Beginnings of
Ethical Resistance

ON 28 JANUARY 1986, millions of American citizens watched in horror as an ostensibly sophisticated and safe space shuttle exploded, killing six astronauts and the first teacher ever to fly in space. Up to the moment of the *Challenger* disaster, most Americans believed that the National Aeronautics and Space Administration incorporated the country's finest qualities: presumably, the best scientists, engineers, and managers had developed the world's most advanced technology to explore the new frontiers of space. Suddenly the safety systems collapsed and the infallible technical expertise failed, leaving in their wake mourning families, stunned political leaders, and citizens searching for an explanation. President Reagan immediately appointed a blue-ribbon commission to investigate the events leading up to the disaster.[1]

In the hearings that followed, witnesses gradually revealed that major technological problems had been known for years to highly placed administrators. NASA engineers had recognized defects in the crucial booster rockets as far back as 1979. On the very night before the disaster, several engineers from the Morton Thiokol Company, the major contractor responsible for construction of the rockets, had clearly warned that the seals in the booster rocket could malfunction in the cold weather forecast for the day of the flight. Their recommendations to postpone the launch were, however, overruled by Thiokol's own executives and by NASA officials, all of whom were determined to go ahead. Previous successful launches had lulled them into believing that the defects were not as serious as their engineers believed. "Not one engineer or technician, however, supported a decision to launch."[2]

Engineers had not alerted Congress or the press because they believed that voicing any public dissent from the official policy would put their careers in great jeopardy. Even when technical personnel made "in house" disclosures of safety problems, their concerns were stifled in the nearly autocratic work environment that characterized NASA's Marshall Space Flight Center in Huntsville, Alabama, as well as in Thiokol laboratories.[3]

Even after the disaster, when the engineers Allan McDonald, Arnold Thompson, and Roger Boisjoly testified before the presidential commission about their strong objections to the launch, they were unceremoniously "stripped of their authority, deprived of their staffs, and prevented from seeing critical data about the investigation of the *Challenger* disaster."[4] The commission members, outraged by this blatant retaliation, forced the management to reconsider. In his letter to James Fletcher, the NASA administrator, Chairman William Rogers wrote:

> During the course of the Commission's investigation it came to our attention that certain employees of Morton Thiokol, who gave valuable testimony to the Commission, believed that they were being punished by management for cooperating with the Commission.
>
> The Commission was most favorably impressed by the courage of Mr. McDonald, Mr. Boisjoly and Mr. Thompson in presenting their views to the Commission, as they did to the management and to NASA prior to the launch of 51-L [*Challenger* space shuttle].
>
> The Commission believes they should be commended for their perception and good judgment. Retaliation of any kind for the assistance persons have given to the Presidential Commission in its investigation of this tragic accident would be reprehensible and inexcusable.
>
> Reports also were received that certain NASA engineers who testified or gave statements to the Commission with views contrary to NASA management may in the future be discriminated against.
>
> I know I speak for all members of the Commission when I urge you to make certain that nothing like this happens either now or in the years ahead.[5]

The commission may have been shocked that such reprisals were being enacted even as the whole nation watched; but employees at NASA

Thiokol saw in these actions verification of their own concerns about any public criticism or disclosure of poor practices.* Corporate and government bureaucrats would retaliate against any employees who dared expose their faulty decisions to the American public—even in a time of great national introspection, as occurred after the *Challenger* crash. And yet by 1986, despite the likelihood of serious retaliation against dissenters, many Americans had come to hope that some courageous employees in both corporations and government would speak out before lethal safety hazards caused tragic loss of lives. Models for such behavior had already surfaced among nuclear workers, big-city police officers, Defense Department personnel, automobile design engineers, and many others. The term *whistleblower* had entered America's vocabulary; and a few—such as the New York City police officer Frank Serpico, the nuclear worker Karen Silkwood, and the Tennessee state official Marie Ragghianti—had become familiar names after famous actors portrayed them as heroes in Hollywood films.†

Whistleblowers, or ethical resisters, are a historically new group. No doubt there were earlier workers who exposed practices that would harm the public, as there were thousands of workers who went on strike to improve their own wages and circumstances. But only in the period since the 1960s has there been a continual stream of employees who do not act primarily out of self-interest but concentrate on exposing policies that could endanger or defraud the public. Several interrelated social and political factors have allowed such individuals to surface as staunch defenders of legal and ethical standards. The most crucial were the struggle over the new regulations of the private sector in the 1960s and 1970s, widespread disillusionment with government and industry's ability to control technological hazards, and the increasing public cynicism about the integrity of federal officials that grew out of the Vietnam War and the Watergate scandal. Taken together, these factors created an environment of distrust among employees who witnessed indifference to dangerous and illegal practices condoned by their superiors. But alienation alone, no matter how justified, does not produce ethical resistance. Also required was a belief that something could be done to rectify the illegal or unethical

---

*In a letter from Col. Richard L. Griffin to John W. Young, Chief, Astronaut Office, the colonel bluntly informed the chief that those working in the astronaut office are fearful of expressing an opinion that does not agree with his.[6]

†The films were *Serpico* (1973), *Silkwood* (1983), and *Marie* (1985).

situation. In this chapter we shall describe the basic changes that encouraged some resisters to believe in the possibility of reform. We shall focus on the enactment of new laws and the creation of regulatory agencies, the development of public-interest groups dedicated to government and corporate accountability, and the growing attention by Congress and the media to the prevalence of corruption.

The Battle over Regulation

As major corporations grew in size, wealth, and influence after the Second World War, public-interest groups and an array of citizens' organizations pressured the federal government to regulate the worst abuses of a private-enterprise system that could have a damaging effect on the lives of millions of workers and consumers. Sparked by the victories of the civil rights, peace, and student protest movements, social activists sought to overcome corporate objections and extend the national agenda by pressing for expanded legislation to protect the rights of consumers and workers in dangerous industries, and to safeguard communities facing environmental degradation from industrial discharge of toxic wastes.[7] Reformers like Ralph Nader mounted national campaigns to win support from Congress on issues ranging from required safety devices on automobiles to protection against flammable fabrics in children's clothing. Environmental and health issues became crucial battlegrounds in election campaigns and evoked sophisticated lobbying efforts on both sides.[8]

As public consciousness reached an all-time high, environmentalists and consumer groups challenged the safety of DDT, cigarettes, Firestone tires, saccharin, the DC-10 airplane. The gathering momentum for public intervention into industrial practices marked a changed relationship between business and government. Congress passed extensive new regulatory legislation and created a series of federal agencies to administer the new laws. The Equal Employment Opportunity Commission, the Council on Environmental Quality, the Environmental Protection Agency, the Occupational Safety and Health Administration, the Consumer Product Safety Commission, and the Mining Enforcement and Safety Administration were all formed between 1964 and 1977.[9] Economic decisions that had previously been controlled by private enterprise were now subject to regulation.

In an unprecedented action, Congress also established protection for workers who publicly exposed safety hazards. For the first time in United States history, there was legislative backing for a person coming forward to report legal violations. A new role had been created and protected by the federal government. As Congress enacted this new legislation, its members believed that implementation and monitoring required the active assistance of knowledgeable insiders. In defending an amendment to environmental protection laws, one legislator voiced the need for protection of whistleblowers: "The best source of information about what a company is actually doing or not doing is often its own employees and this amendment will ensure that an employee could provide such information without losing his job or otherwise suffering economically from retribution from the polluter."[10] If an employer retaliated against a worker who reported violations, the new legislation established remedial procedures by the Department of Labor, authorizing it to order reinstatement, back pay, and possible compensatory damages for illegal firing.[11]

Not surprisingly, the resultant regulation of consumer products and the related issues of health and safety became highly politicized. Some observers have argued that the conflict between business and the public-interest groups was comparable to the struggle between management and labor over union recognition in the 1930s. By the mid-1970s, there was unprecedented regulation of the private sector and a brewing reaction by industry which had never fully accepted the premises of, or the limitations imposed by, the new laws.[12]

While regulation of business had been established with the creation of the Interstate Commerce Commission in 1894 and had increased substantially throughout the twentieth century, there was a decided shift of purpose in the 1970s. The earlier regulations had largely been industry-specific, establishing one set of rules for railroads and another for the oil industry. Often these requirements were developed and negotiated with industry leaders who provided the expertise necessary to develop industry-specific codes. Management often supported this process and benefited from the stable and predictable economic environment it created.[13]

In the 1970s, the emphasis shifted to general social regulation that applied to all industry. The greatest number of these new regulations came from the Occupational Safety and Health Administration, the Equal Employment Opportunity Commission, and especially from the Environmental Protection Agency. The growth of these new agencies provoked suspicion and hostility. Corporate executives saw the EPA's budget rise from 232 million dollars in 1974 to 522 million in 1979. OSHA and several other agencies had similar rates of growth, while the old regulatory agencies that worked with specific industries, such as the Civil Aeronautics Board, grew at a much more modest pace.[14] Corporate leaders estimated that the new environmental, health, and safety regulations cost anywhere from 58 billion to 100 billion dollars annually. As these costs could not all be passed on to consumers, they resulted in a reduction in profits.[15]

Under the new regulations, many traditional business practices were now illegal, making it unacceptable to continue doing business in the usual way. Yet many corporate executives were unwilling or unable to incur all the costs necessary to meet the new environmental and safety requirements. They believed that some of the new laws were so complex that no enterprise could be in full compliance and still remain profitable.[16]

Opposition to regulation went beyond cost. Many business leaders also believed that the new agencies had too much political power and not enough balance. They were convinced that everyone in the EPA was a "rabid environmentalist," and that industry's views were seriously underrepresented. The agency personnel, they argued, had the power to choose when and where to enforce rules, ignoring violations by political supporters and punishing those who opposed regulation or who failed to support the winning presidential candidate.[17]

The combination of the economic burden and the potential for political manipulation led many corporate leaders to define state regulation as oppressive.[18] To them it marked the end of private enterprise, foreshadowing a move toward government control of the private sector. Michael Useem quotes one banker who articulated the resentment of business executives when he said, "Why spend the money to nationalize when you can absolutely control through regulation."[19] This position was also articulated by Ronald Reagan both before and after his 1980 election. In 1978 he referred to OSHA as "one of the most pernicious of the watchdog agencies" and, a year later, argued that "through things such as OSHA, the government is trying to minimize the ownership of private property in this country." During his first term as president, Reagan appointed agency directors who were dedicated to deregulation at OSHA, EPA, and elsewhere.[20]

As early as 1976, the business community mobilized a broad coalition to oppose legislation for a new Consumer Protection Agency and to mount a more far-reaching campaign against regulation, arguing that it lowered profits and thwarted American competitiveness in the international arena. As American dominance in the world markets receded due to a series of complex causes including the high costs of the Vietnam War, the rising price of oil, and the extraordinary success of Japan in penetrating new markets, business leaders insisted that deregulation would provide the necessary correctives. Lobbyists undertook extensive efforts to reverse congressional and public support for government regulation of industry. They focused on undoing the general regulation administered by EPA, OSHA, and other agencies, while continuing to support traditional regulation of airlines or utilities. Individual corporations and federated groups like the Chamber of Commerce, and especially the Business Roundtable, began an active drive for deregulation through expansion of their lobbying activities, through organization of political-action committees to support candidates with pro-business views, and through decisions to evade and ignore rules that they considered burdensome.[21]

The opposition of corporate executives to this regulatory legislation set the stage for a new level of corporate lawlessness which, in turn, spurred ethical resistance. While actively promoting deregulation, executives found they did not always have to wait for legislative changes or administrative decisions that benefited their interests. They often disregarded many of the laws on the books. They continued to dump wastes in violation of the clear-air and clean-water acts and to expose workers to unacceptable levels of vinyl chloride, which facilitates the production of plastics but increases the incidence of cancer or chromosome damage to unprotected workers. Managers learned that it was relatively easy to conceal deviance for long periods of time, especially in large organizations that employed retinues of lawyers and accountants. Even if the companies were prosecuted for violating safety codes, many corporate executives believed the benefits of avoiding regulations frequently far outweighed the risks. Rarely would high-level managers be held personally liable, and the corporate fines were defined as another expense of doing business.[22]

THE REJECTION OF REGULATION BY FIRESTONE AND HOOKER CHEMICAL

One of the most egregious examples of the decision to ignore the new safety regulations was the policy of the Firestone Corporation to continue producing and selling a defective tire in direct violation of the Traffic

Safety Act. Only after the failure to recall the Firestone-500 tire series led to over forty deaths and hundreds of serious injuries did the National Highway Traffic Safety Administration assess penalties of $500,000 against the company. The corporation had been warned in 1973 by its own director of development about the serious danger for consumers— "We are making an inferior quality radial tire which will subject us to belt-edge separation at high mileage."[23] Firestone's management ignored the warning and continued to market the tire long after it was clear that the 500 series suffered from defects and blowouts. The development director who had dissented took no further action, and the company marketed over twenty-four million of these tires.*

An equally telling case of corporate rejection of government regulation occurred in 1975 and 1976 when engineers at the Hooker Chemical Company plant in California apprised their superiors that the company was creating a serious public danger by violating the pollution limits and dumping toxic wastes. Management was involved in a cost-cutting effort and chose to do nothing, until the Love Canal tragedy erupted several years later in Niagara, New York. Negative publicity emanated from the discovery that hundreds of homes and a school had been built on a chemical disposal site that had been owned by Hooker. When the residents suffered a disproportionately high rate of miscarriages, birth defects, and cancer, Hooker became ensnared in a prolonged debate about the responsibility for a major health crisis in the community.[25]

Shortly afterward, there was another assault on Hooker's reputation. One of its former engineers, who had been fired a year earlier, released a secret company report which documented that workers had been exposed to highly toxic chemicals in violation of federal law. The engineer publicly apologized on television for having waited a year before acting to inform workers of the hazards they faced.[26]

These actions were not peculiar to the Hooker Chemical Company but simply illustrate the decisions many corporate executives made to suppress data that documented noncompliance with federal laws, even where it presented grave dangers to the work force and to surrounding communities. From management's point of view, disclosure of their evidence exposed them to the potential of extensive liability suits, while remedy of

---

*The Firestone Corporation came under heavy attack in the press for its decision to continue marketing the Serial 500 tire despite overwhelming evidence that it was a dangerous product.[24]

the problem could cost millions of dollars without any benefit of increased productivity.[27]

This is not to say that companies never benefited from the regulations. At times, management seized the opportunity to order new equipment and redesign old plants in order to modernize the enterprise and put the company in a more competitive position, while also solving long-standing health and safety problems as required by the new federal laws. In his study of contemporary corporations, Robert Jackall interviewed one group of managers who admitted to mounting a public campaign against OSHA regulations that required cleaning up cotton dust in order to minimize the dangers of brown lung disease, while privately recognizing that the federal regulations solved a host of business problems. Even in such cases, however, management was concerned only with obeying the law to the extent that it suited other more pragmatic needs. As one executive explained to Jackall, ". . .this is the typical corporate response pattern—to hedge, dodge and try to avoid the issue in every possible way. You know [use] the old line: 'Nobody has conclusively proved that. . . .' . . . And all this when anyone who has ever been in a cotton mill, especially back in 1958, or spent some time in the mill villages, knows goddam well there was a problem."[28]

Although many corporate leaders were convinced that skirting the law was warranted and possible, others within the organization, who were instructed to carry out these decisions, were confronted by a clear personal dilemma. For most employees, such as those in Firestone and Hooker, the tension was resolved by following the lead of their superiors or by filing an internal memo detailing their objections and then remaining silent. Those concerned with future employment learned not to define business violations in moral terms; rather, they accepted their participation as part of a struggle for management to maintain its prerogatives and maximize its ability to earn profits for the company.[29] Jackall illuminates managers' rejection of moral formulations of pragmatic problems: "Managers know that in the organization right and wrong get decided by those with enough clout to make their views stick."[30]

A far smaller number of managers, professionals, and workers rejected this formulation as self-interested rationalization. They felt an acute need to weigh the potential harm to consumers and the financial costs to the public before blindly following orders to avoid regulations. These employees were also concerned with their company's reputation should injury and death occur. Equally important, many of these dissenting employees believed that they might be held personally liable if they participated in violations, and did not share the confidence of many of their superiors that only corporations, not individuals, would be prosecuted.[31]

FRANK CAMPS AND THE FORD MOTOR COMPANY

A prime example of this attitude occurred in the early 1970s in the automobile industry. The major automobile producers had long fought against proposed safety regulations that they considered costly and unlikely to increase sales. Frank Camps, a senior design engineer, worked on, and later protested, the unsafe design of the Ford Pinto. He was unwilling to endanger Ford users and also steadfastly refused to risk the possibility of indictment for production of unsafe goods, which he considered a distinct possibility under the new legislation. Camps explained Ford's reactions:

> To meet federal safety standards concerning windshield retention we came up with a clever engineering ploy. We intentionally channelled some of the kinetic energy generated in the crash away from the windshield and transmitted that energy via the driveshaft to the differential housing, causing contact with the gas tank. The corporate reasoning was sound. Windshield retention was a federally mandated area of certification. Fuel system integrity, at that time, was not.[32]

Camps, who had worked at the company since 1953 and had helped to rebuild its reputation after years of decline following the Second World War, fully believed that management would rectify the design. His manager's reaction was the first sign that he was wrong about the company's intentions. Camps described his disillusionment:

> We were still in the development stage. I had a certain degree of resentment; these people were not listening although we were having problems with the car. I can remember I went into my manager's office. He said, "Look, we're in the business of selling cars and every time we barrier crash a car and it causes problems, then we have one failure. If we get another car to crash, to see how the first failure happened, we may have two failures. This could compound itself until my bonus would be reduced." Now this was the kind of thinking—the corporate attitude—that my immediate superior had. He didn't say anything

about crashing for occupant safety. He just didn't want his bonus to be cut down. I said to my wife, "This guy is a bad actor. This guy is going to get me in trouble if I don't start documenting and protecting myself." This was colossal arrogance, callous indifference toward the safety of people. It bothered me even if only one person should die or be disfigured because of something that I was responsible for.[33]

In interviews about another comparable case of industrial dissent, Jackall found that most managers would have both disagreed with Camps's position and supported his superiors' disdain for his moral qualms. The managers believed that industrial employees cannot define technical questions as "a matter of principle," and insisted that "authority has the prerogative to resolve technical disputes."[34] These arguments rest on a clear definition that corporations are not organized democratically and have limited tolerance for dissent. Camps ignored the prevailing stricture that his boss would not want to hear objections requiring expensive and time-consuming actions which might harm the company's goals to produce an inexpensive and energy-efficient car to compete with Japanese and German models.[35]

After going up the corporation's hierarchy and urging redesign for several years with no success, Camps sued Ford to limit his own potential liability as a design engineer and resigned in 1978. While Camps agonized over his responsibility, he described how his colleagues were coerced or bribed into going along with management:

I can recall, right after I filed the suit, other engineers said—"Go get 'em, we wish we could do it, there goes a man with brass balls." While I had tacit support, I was looking for an honest man to stand with me. I found that these guys were suddenly given promotions, nice increases in salary. Next thing I knew, I did not have the support any more.[36]

At that point, Camps felt compelled to put his concerns in writing and move beyond verbal protests to his managers:

Although I had previously made my views known in conversation with my immediate superior, I now felt that I had to put my feelings on paper so that there would be a permanent record of my concern. At about this time, the concept that negligence in design is a basis of liability was taking hold in legal circles, and I was fearful of the consequences. Therefore I wrote to management in order to allay my fears that at some future date I would be held personally liable for a Pinto fatality, as well as to assure myself that I had done whatever I could to abide by Public Law 89-563, section 102, which informs me that as a citizen and as an engineer I must take care "that the public is protected against unreasonable risk of accidents occurring as a result of the design, construction, or performance of motor vehicles and is also protected against unreasonable risk of death or injury to persons in the event accidents do occur."[37]

Camps's prediction about the danger to Ford's reputation as a reliable auto maker proved prescient. The Pinto came to symbolize corporate rejection of safety regulations in the drive for a more profitable market position. Within a few years, the company paid out millions of dollars to settle scores of suits resulting from severe burn injuries caused by gas tanks that exploded on impact. In one instance in 1978, Ford was even indicted on criminal charges by an Indiana prosecutor for the death of three teenagers. Although a long, contentious trial finally resulted in Ford's acquittal, the national publicity from all these events branded the company with an unenviable reputation which stayed with it for years.[38]

Industry-Government Collusion

The incentive to avoid regulations and the ethical resisters' response to such lawless behavior were not limited to the private sector. Many officials in government agencies themselves shared these business perspectives. Some had come to public service directly from executive positions in the companies they were now negotiating with and supported the political ideology of their business colleagues who advocated minimal control of business. Other government officials developed strong ties with particular industries and hoped to obtain a position with one of these same companies after retiring from federal service. These excessively close connections often resulted in poor oversight and negligence by officials who might be seeking lucrative consultancies in the foreseeable future. The Pentagon was one breeding ground for such collusion, especially as military budgets grew dramatically in the 1960s, providing large sums for purchasing new equipment and weapons in an atmosphere that emphasized national security over concerns about cost. It was no accident that Pentagon employees turned out to be among the best-known and most significant ethical resisters. They had directly experienced the peculiar pressures placed on government personnel when dealing with military contractors, and were willing to expose the relationship that made collusion possible and attractive.[39]

Dr. Thomas Amlie, a former engineer for the U.S. Navy who was instrumental in developing the Sidewinder air-to-air missile, cogently explained the temptation of military personnel to go along with a system that breeds lax oversight of defense contractors:

> The major problem with having a military officer in charge of procurement is his vulnerability. It turns out that not everyone can make general or admiral and our "up or out" policy forces people to retire. The average age of an officer at retirement is 43 years. . . . At the age of 43 he probably has kids in or ready for college and a big mortgage and can't afford a large cut in his income. Besides, he is at the peak of his intellectual powers, is emotionally involved, and doesn't want to quit. . . . Many of these officers . . . do not have the skills which are readily marketable in the civilian sector. This nice man then comes around and offers him a job at 50K–75K per year. If he stands up and makes a fuss about high cost and poor quality, no nice man will come see him when he retires.[40]

Military officers also had other reasons to tolerate excessive costs. They knew their careers could advance if they were credited with overseeing the development of a new weapons system from contract bidding to implementation. The exposure of cost overruns could easily be defined as an impediment to program completion with potential harm to their futures. Should the issue become politically hot, most military personnel believed they could explain their relative lack of concern with price by emphasizing that national security, not cost, was the crucial variable.[41]

ERNEST FITZGERALD AND THE PENTAGON

The pressures to ignore cost overruns also affected the civilian employees, who were quickly socialized to the advantages of large contracts for both the defense industries and their Pentagon counterparts. For example, Ernest Fitzgerald was told early in his career as a Defense Department cost analyst that Pentagon civilian and military officials wanted defense contractors to earn high profits. These would not only ensure attractive opportunities for retired officials but also create a long-term relationship with a favored list of large corporations that employed experienced lobbyists to assist in obtaining congressional approval for large military budgets. Overlooking excessive costs and even concealing faulty equipment may have been acceptable to many high officials in the Defense Department; but for some federal employees, this cozy relationship between government and industry was a serious ethical breach and a massive waste of government funds. Fitzgerald was one who refused to go along.

Fitzgerald and others were deeply troubled by the excessive cost overruns in the construction of the C-5A cargo plane. In voicing his objections Fitzgerald believed he was simply doing his job. He had been hired in 1965 because of his background in cost cutting and was appointed as deputy for management systems in the office of the assistant secretary of the U.S. Air Force. Fitzgerald's GS-17 rating and his $31,000 annual salary indicated his high-level appointment. He took his post seriously and was among the earliest to write internal memos alerting superiors that the Lockheed corporation was experiencing heavy cost overruns during the early stages of development. Others working with him suspected that Lockheed had intentionally submitted an unrealistically low bid in order to get the contract. Lockheed officials had probably counted on the fact that the air force would cover their extensive overruns since the government had seldom cracked down on corporations in the past. They knew that the civilian undersecretary in charge of the operation had come from the aircraft industry and was sympathetic to its business needs.[42]

Fitzgerald met with high Pentagon personnel in order to develop a more efficient and cost-effective method of evaluating contractor performance. He understood from their reaction that cost overruns were anticipated and actually built into the contracts. Surplus money was hurriedly spent at the end of each year. Fitzgerald was unsuccessful in reforming a deeply entrenched system. By 1967 he had offended high officials by his persistent criticisms of various weapon systems and he no longer received excellent evaluations for his work. Nevertheless, he continued to correspond with the office of the secretary of defense about his findings.

While the overruns grew, members of Congress were kept in the dark about the ultimate cost. When they requested information, the air force claimed that the data were not yet available or that the stage of the contract did not allow their release. In 1968, Fitzgerald was invited to testify before Senator William Proxmire's Subcommittee on Economy in Government. Knowing that Congress had not received accurate reports on the development of the contract, Fitzgerald decided not to withhold information, even though it would cut all ties to his superiors. Proxmire, a long-term foe of government waste, had been investigating the C-5A project and suspected that it had not proceeded according to the original estimates. Fitzgerald's offense in testifying was best summed up in his now classic statement: "When I was asked by Senator Proxmire to confirm his estimate of C-5A cost increase, I committed truth."[43]

The cost overruns exposed by Ernest Fitzgerald remain a volatile issue. Scandals involving exaggerated prices and government-industry collusion have continued to surface. Employees who witness such breach of procedures have continued to speak out in the tradition of Ernest Fitzgerald. Like him, they found their superiors little disposed to punish companies that have abused government contracts. Only the testimony of ethical resisters and the resultant congressional and public outrage have succeeded in forcing investigations of ludicrously priced weapons systems and spare parts. The idea that coffeepots and toilet seats could cost hundreds of dollars each, or that military procurement consultants could bribe Pentagon officials to release confidential information about future contract requirements, has been sufficient to trigger investigations by the Justice Department, to win media attention, and to astonish the public, resulting in indictments and punitive sanctions against offending corporate defense contractors and colluding government officials.[44]

Ernest Fitzgerald in the Pentagon and Frank Camps in the Ford Motor Company were prototypes of the new ethical resisters. Like the whistleblowers who were to follow, these men decided to resist the pressures to acquiesce to clear violations of government regulations. Camps felt such practices would directly harm thousands of consumers and destroy Ford's reputation as a company built upon management integrity. Fitzgerald had given up his own firm and had accepted the Pentagon position to help cut government costs while providing the best national defense. He would not be party to the pervasive norms that dominated the military-industrial complex and countenanced massive waste of taxpayers' money. These situations were to be repeated many times in both government and industry. Employees risked their jobs by refusing to accept management definitions of appropriate behavior, insisting on legal compliance, and seeking a public outlet for their concerns.

The Dangers of Technology

Whistleblowing in the 1960s and 1970s also emerged out of a larger disillusionment with corporate and government management of a highly technological society. As revelations of widespread practices endangering health and safety and contaminating the environment were widely circulated in the media, reformers, journalists, and national political leaders became increasingly wary of those entrusted to control technological developments. They feared that failure to control technology directly threatened both the quality of life and life itself. These critics undertook to educate the public to the potential disasters from nuclear power plants, chemical dumping, and unsafe products, and they documented the public harm resulting from uncontrolled production. They publicized rising rates of cancer and other illnesses, such as asbestosis and brown lung, that were attributed to corporate and governmental failure to protect workers from dangerous levels of exposure.

Several new "miracle" products developed by advances in high technology also furthered distrust. The public—upon learning, for example, that a presumably safe and effective tranquilizer, Thalidomide, had resulted in the birth of hundreds of deformed babies in Europe—questioned the procedures employed to avoid such disasters.[45] Later revelations of problems from DES and other medications continued to erode confidence in government and industry's ability to assure the public of the safety of its products. Similarly, Rachel Carson's *Silent Spring,* published in 1962, created great controversy. Carson, a science writer, detailed the long-term toxic consequences of indiscriminate spraying to control insects, arguing that by allowing and encouraging widespread use of DDT and other popular pesticides, the Department of Agriculture was contributing to the poisoning of the food chain and increasing the incidence of carcinoma. Although the USDA immediately denied her allegations, Carson's charges were picked up by environmental groups and the media. Once again, questions were raised about the ability of federal agencies to control the effects of technology.[46]

THE BATTLE OVER NUCLEAR POWER

As the public became ever more doubtful about new and potent drugs, unsafe cars, and carcinogenic substances emitted into air, ground, and water, it also came to doubt whether industry and government had either the competence or the will to prevent illnesses and disasters whose effects may not surface for decades.[47] Nowhere has concern about public safety and the risks of industrial progress been as great as in the burgeoning nuclear field, which has produced more ethical resisters than any other sector of the economy. Given its significance, we will examine the controversial industry in some detail. The initial stages of nuclear power were developed in secrecy for military purposes, and the public was first made dramatically aware of its potency in 1945 when the United States bombed Hiroshima and Nagasaki. After a serious debate about the wisdom of military control of atomic energy, the Atomic Energy Commission was established in 1946 under civilian administration, but atomic research continued to be linked to the construction of bombs. Most of the opposition to these developments came from small antiwar groups and from distinguished scientists who, having worked on the bomb, cautioned about the consequences of radiation and of atomic war.[48] Ordinary Americans were not yet attuned to the dangers. Only years later, for example, did some U.S. servicemen, who had been stationed at test sites, even learn that they had been exposed to dangerous levels of radiation when they had unknowingly been used as experimental subjects. By that time many of them were suffering from terminal cancer.[49]

In 1954, Congress revised the Atomic Energy Act to allow private companies to own nuclear power, and construction of the first nuclear power plant in Shippingport, Pennsylvania, began almost immediately.[50] The government, fearing competition from the Soviet Union which had exploded an atomic bomb several years earlier, actively encouraged the development of this nascent civilian industry. Federal officials believed that national security and supremacy depended on maintaining nuclear superiority in civilian as well as military facets of the field. To assure success for industries embarking on this project, the government actively subsidized research and development. In a period when the safety of nuclear reactors was still unknown, Congress passed a bill that limited the liability of utility companies to sixty million dollars in case of accident, even though estimates for accident costs went as high as seven billion.[51]*

While the government was enthusiastically fostering the nuclear industry, scientists were uncovering increasing evidence about the ill-health effects of strontium 90, a radioactive material found in high proportions in milk and in children's bones as a result of atmospheric testing. Scholars continued to document long-term problems of low-level radiation both for human health and for the environment. The Atomic Energy Commission did everything in its power to suppress these findings and supported industry's insistence that it could provide cheap and safe energy. The debate grew in intensity even as plans were pressed forward for the development of nuclear power plants throughout the country.[52]

A growing number of scientists, many of whom had worked for the AEC or had their research funded by it, became increasingly critical as their findings pointed to a strong relationship between exposure to radiation and the increasing cancer rates. These scientists argued that the people most at risk were residents living near nuclear plants and the workers at the government nuclear bomb factory at Hanford, Washington. On the other side were government scientists and their industry colleagues, who denounced the critics as hysterical and unreliable in the rush to destroy the nuclear industry. Despite the intense pressure to back off, the critics would not be silenced. Scientists whose conclusions differed from the official AEC position found their research funds cut, their scholarly papers censored, and their jobs terminated.[53]

As the debate raged throughout the 1960s, it was unclear whether nuclear power would gain public acceptability. Most troubling to the AEC and the industry was the question of whether it could compete economically with coal. In order to win contracts from utility companies, General Electric, Westinghouse, and the other producers needed various forms of assistance from the AEC. Both the companies and the regulatory agency believed that strict regulation of the plants might increase the expense and threaten economic viability. In his study of the nuclear industry, Mark Hertsgaard summarized the meaning of the emerging position: "If nuclear power was to make it in America, then the AEC had to carry out its regulatory responsibilities in the words of its former

*Total liability would be $560,000,000. The government would pick up the remaining $500,000,000.

chairman, Lewis Strauss, 'with progress and profit in mind, as well as safety and security.' "[54]

By the early 1970s, there was a boom in the nuclear construction industry, and plans to build new plants multiplied rapidly. As plant construction raced forward throughout the country, critics in the scientific community and antinuclear political groups continued to raise serious questions about safety and about the increasing evidence that the AEC was withholding information about health hazards. These criticisms were strongly validated when several nuclear workers revealed safety problems that they had personally witnessed in their plants. The most famous of these was Karen Silkwood, the technician and union activist in the Kerr-McGee plant in Oklahoma, who later became a national symbol of this growing movement. In September 1974, she testified to the AEC about safety violations and possible worker contamination from the carelessly monitored plutonium, a lethal substance needed in the production of breeder reactors for nuclear power plants as well as for nuclear weapons. With prodding from the Oil, Chemical, and Atomic Workers president, Tony Mazzocchi, Silkwood agreed to collect evidence of corporate efforts to tamper with the records demonstrating poorly constructed fuel rods, vital to the operation of nuclear plants. On 13 November 1974, she was killed in a mysterious car accident as she was driving to meet *New York Times* reporter David Burnham to show him the evidence she had assembled to document her allegations.[55]

Silkwood's death and the disappearance of the evidence she may have been carrying did not end the serious issues she had raised. The events illustrate how a knowledgeable insider willing to serve as a witness to a major social problem can generate an alliance among several national groups. The death of Silkwood was publicized throughout the country because members of the women's movement, antinuclear activists, and her union suspected that her car had been deliberately run off the road. The Labor Task Force of the National Organization for Women championed her cause after the Justice Department decided to close its investigation of her death. Mobilizing their membership nationally, NOW leaders succeeded in making the Silkwood case a symbol of violence against women. By actively drawing upon the press and Congress, they were ultimately able to force a reopening of the investigation. A multimillion dollar suit was lodged against Kerr-McGee by the Silkwood family, and a national campaign was organized to collect funds for a team of attorneys to press the case against this powerful corporation.[56]

The women's movement and the antinuclear groups also succeeded in catapulting the Silkwood tragedy into the larger issue of worker contamination in nuclear plants. The ultimate victory in the courts came when Kerr-McGee was found guilty of negligence resulting in plutonium contamination. At the time Silkwood may have been the only nuclear worker killed under mysterious circumstances, but the entire nation recognized that she was not the only plant employee exposed to the dangers of plutonium.[57]*

After several subsequent unpublicized nuclear accidents and the continuing need to shut down plants for repairs, other employees began to speak out.[59] For the first time, professionals with managerial credentials issued a countrywide warning, arguing that the dangers from unsafe plants went well beyond risks to workers and threatened whole communities. In 1976, three years before the disaster at Three Mile Island, three management-level engineers at General Electric made a daring decision. They resigned and offered public testimony about the risks involved in operating the nuclear plants.[60] One of the three, Dale Bridenbaugh, a highly respected engineer in the nuclear field, had worked for GE for twenty-three years. His final position was manager of GE's nuclear complaint department, which made him responsible for worldwide servicing of disabled GE reactors. It became increasingly apparent to Bridenbaugh that safety was being sacrificed to keep the plants operating. When, in nineteen of GE's United States plants, he found deficiencies so serious that an accident could cause lethal damage, he tried to convince his superiors and the utility company executives operating the plants that it was imperative to shut down and make serious and costly modifications. His advice was not received kindly:

> I remember at two o'clock in the morning in a Holiday Inn saying (at a meeting with the utility companies), "Look, it doesn't make a goddamn bit of difference whether you have the authority or not! . . . We've got to quit screwing around with this thing and go to the NRC tomorrow and say, 'We know it's a bad design. We don't know if it will withstand an accident—but we're going to commit ourselves to correcting it just as fast as humanly possible.' " But no. One after another these bastards said, "I can't make that commitment."[61]

---

*The nuclear-weapons-producing plants, in particular, have been criticized by Congress for long-standing neglect of worker and environmental safety. Several have been shut down.[58]

When Bridenbaugh's superiors upheld the position of the utilities, he resigned. He and two other colleagues, management engineers equally concerned about the eroding margin of safety, decided upon an unprecedented joint resignation as part of an effort to publicize the hazards of nuclear plants and the vast potential for future deaths. They were joined by Robert Pollard, an experienced engineer working as a project manager in the Division of Reactor Licensing for the Nuclear Regulatory Commission (the successor to the Atomic Energy Commission), who shared their view that unsafe plants were being allowed to operate without adequate protection.[62]

Although the engineers expected the active opposition they received from the industry's representatives, they were shocked by the reaction of the NRC and the Congressional Joint Committee on Atomic Energy. Representatives of both these groups focused more on attacking the engineers and implying that their motives were suspect than on addressing the substance of the engineers' testimony about the failure of safety systems and the problems of nuclear waste.[63] Despite this hostile reception and their inability to achieve safer standards, these engineers were significant pioneers. In the course of five years, hundreds of other nuclear employees would join them in disclosing serious problems in plants throughout the country.

The testimony of these engineers was particularly credible because they held responsible positions and were actively engaged in critical aspects of a highly complex work process. As professionals they were working with privileged information and possessed the expertise and rank in the bureaucracy to know of unethical or irresponsible decisions. As insiders they observed the crucial decision-making processes that gave them access to the information and the evidence to challenge wrongdoing. By coming forth publicly, they had breached a cardinal rule governing both public and corporate bureaucracies: "Never air your dirty laundry in public."[64] Like police and intelligence agents, corporate and government leaders in the nuclear energy field espoused a policy of secrecy so that a presumably gullible and potentially hysterical public would not be stampeded into an antinuclear stance and batter down the gates protecting the development of nuclear power. Employees like the three GE engineers thus posed a special threat. As knowledgeable insiders with years of service, their allegations could not easily be dismissed.

High corporate executives, aware of the potential threat posed by their professional employees' independence, expend great energy to claim their loyalty. These executives believe that an ability to compromise is essential in a field marked by technological uncertainty and human fallibility. Expedience rather than abstract principle is the hallmark of managerial survival.[65] Such efforts to persuade employees of the pragmatic realities have been largely successful. In recent years, however, a small but important number of professionals have rejected these standards and refused to pretend that the evidence was not cause for grave concern.

After the 1979 accident at Three Mile Island resulted in a partial meltdown, public sensitivity and fear soared. Americans had been caught unaware. For the first time, an entire community of hundreds of thousands of people felt threatened by a single industry. Worldwide press coverage underscored the realization that human error had led to what had previously been thought impossible.[66] While recent national surveys had shown that the public largely favored nuclear power and considered the plants safe, the trauma of Three Mile Island reversed popular opinion.[67] Antinuclear groups, which had been protesting potential hazards for more than a decade, were quick to argue that Three Mile Island was not the only plant with the potential for disaster—a point enhanced for millions of Americans by the coincidental release of *The China Syndrome,* a dramatic film about a near meltdown. The innocence about nuclear power had come to an end.[68] Ethical resisters had been among those who had sounded the original warnings, and later events proved that they had carefully considered their charges and "gone public" only after trying to obtain corrective action from their superiors in the organizations.

While their evidence and willingness to risk their careers did not convince the nuclear advocates in Congress and the Nuclear Regulatory Commission, a major accident had drastically transformed the nature of the debate. In the months ahead, more whistleblowers came forward to describe deficiencies in the plants. Most were employees, but they were occasionally aided by others who discovered problems. In one dramatic instance, a young private detective, Thomas Applegate, was hired by Cincinnati Gas and Electric to investigate timecard fraud among workers at the construction site of the Zimmer nuclear power plant in Ohio. Although he did discover some irregularities in this area, Applegate inadvertently uncovered much more serious construction problems and took them to the utility officials. They refused to hear about the safety issues, and he received little satisfaction when he turned to the NRC, which conducted a cursory investigation and claimed to have found no serious problems at Zimmer.[69]

Applegate refused to be deterred. When no official body would pay attention, he took his information to the Government Accountability Project, an organization that defends whistleblowers and has a special interest in the nuclear industry. By 1982, GAP submitted twenty-six affidavits alleging poor quality control in the construction of the Zimmer plant. The affidavits were based on interviews with seventy-five plant employees who were willing to come forward. After GAP forced several additional investigations by the NRC, the commission found gross violations and imposed substantial fines for safety infractions. The NRC subsequently halted construction and ordered a total reinspection. When faced with massive costs for rework, the utility canceled the plant.[70]

Similar patterns surfaced throughout the country as more employees were willing to risk future jobs in the industry and face overt hostility from fellow workers who feared that plant shutdowns would lead to unemployment. Such widespread and persistent resistance has not been matched in any other industry. Workers complaining about improper welding, clerks recognizing inadequate adherence to quality-control regulations, and engineers confronting poorly designed safety systems all encountered an unwillingness on the part of their superiors to slow down production to attend to potentially hazardous situations. The fear of a deadly accident, the reports of increased cancer, leukemia, and birth defects in areas where there has been exposure to radiation, the support of environmental groups, and the existence of a public licensing procedure all served to motivate these workers who increasingly felt that the public should know the risks to which they are exposed.

In addition, the Energy Reorganization Act of 1978 protected employees who spoke out on safety issues. Congress provided that "no employer . . . may discharge any employee or otherwise discriminate against any employee with respect to his compensation, terms, conditions or privileges of employment because the employee commenced . . . a proceeding for the administration or enforcement of any requirement . . . imposed by the Atomic Energy Acts." This form of overt support encouraged workers to believe that public disclosure was not off limits, but was indeed sanctioned by the highest levels of government.[71]

Political Scandal and the Decline of
Government Credibility

Corporate managers who ignored regulations, and public officials who were lax in their oversight, were only two of the sources of entrenched deviance that provoked ethical resistance. Equally serious was the revelation that high government officials were using the federal bureaucracies to engage in unethical and illegal practices under a cloak of secrecy. These practices emanated from decisions made in the White House by presidents and their closest advisers. The degree of deception was graphically revealed to the public when the secret "Pentagon papers" were published in the *New York Times*, analyzing the history of the Vietnam War. Corruption in the government was also highlighted when the Watergate scandal emerged and details of illicit behavior by President Nixon and his advisers made the national headlines over a period of many months.

THE VIETNAM WAR AND THE PENTAGON PAPERS

In the late 1960s and early 1970s, much of the disillusion with government integrity stemmed from the prolonged and agonizing war in Vietnam, which was to end in a major defeat for a policy supported by four administrations. The rapid escalation during the 1960s, and the commitment of U.S. troops to support the failing non-Communist government of South Vietnam, produced serious unrest and protest at home.[72]

In 1967, the secretary of defense, Robert McNamara, increasingly skeptical about the possibility of winning the war, ordered a major historical review of the history of U.S. involvement in Southeast Asia. Thirty-six anonymous government historians undertook the task of compiling and analyzing the documents found in the files of the secretary of defense and the assistant defense secretary, with additional materials from the State Department. Most of the writers worked in either the Defense or the State department. Some, such as Daniel Ellsberg, were "defense-oriented intellectuals from government-financed research institutes."[73]

The project took a year and a half to complete. All claimed that the study of Pentagon papers was not a final and comprehensive history of the Vietnam War because there had been no access to presidential archives. Nevertheless, it became abundantly clear to many working on the study that the public statements of confidence by key government officials had belied their serious doubts about the viability of the South Vietnamese government and the possibility of winning the war, of which the United States had become a principal architect. The Pentagon papers also revealed systematic plans, at several key points throughout the 1960s, to escalate the conflict by deliberately provoking additional belligerence from the Vietcong and North Vietnam—secret actions that could then be reinterpreted to convince Congress and the public that American expansion was simply a response to enemy attack.[74]

By 1969, Daniel Ellsberg, one of the anonymous authors of the Pentagon papers, had become totally disillusioned with America's role in the war and with the climate of subterfuge that supported the ineffective policies. Two years as a State Department representative in Vietnam had transformed his views of the war, turning him from an ardent advocate of American military intervention into a critic of U.S. support for corrupt and tyrannical regimes. He now concluded that there was systematic dishonesty by political leaders that was destroying American lives and the nation's reputation. He believed that democracy depended on a more informed public, and that major decisions about war and peace should not be left in the hands of a president and a small coterie of advisers. The struggle of Ellsberg and others in the federal bureaucracy against clandestine government created the context for ethical resistance.[75]

Ellsberg spoke to various colleagues who had been involved in writing the Pentagon papers about the advisability of releasing the classified documents, but received no encouragement. They felt obligated to keep the report secret since access to classified documents had been provided by the Johnson administration on the understanding that the findings would not be publicized. While Ellsberg understood the desire to keep such commitments, he became increasingly exasperated that the newly installed Nixon administration seemed intent on pursuing the war. Ellsberg felt that the Democrats in Congress had to take greater responsibility for past policies, so that the new president would not feel that he had to shoulder the entire burden for "the loss of Saigon." Ellsberg's reading of the Pentagon papers had led him to believe that no president in this period would willingly accept the responsibility for presiding over a defeat in a conflict with any Communist nation. The release of the papers could prove, Ellsberg believed, that the responsibility lay with four different administrations.[76]

Once he decided to release the papers, Ellsberg first approached Senator William Fulbright of Arkansas, chairman of the Senate Foreign Relations

Committee and an opponent of the war. Unfortunately for Ellsberg's plan, Fulbright did not agree to release the papers, apparently believing that the public would not bother to read those thousands of pages. He told Ellsberg that the revelations in them would not justify running the risk of being charged with releasing secret government documents. Respecting Fulbright's decision, Ellsberg waited two more years before deciding to take the materials to the *New York Times*. By 1971 he felt compelled to act. In the intervening period, ten thousand more Americans had been killed in combat, hundreds of thousands of Vietnamese on both sides of the conflict had died, and the Nixon administration had launched several secret invasions of Cambodia and Laos. Ellsberg decided that he personally had a central responsibility to expose the hidden documents. He was in a unique position since he had been in Vietnam for an extended period and had read every word of the Pentagon papers, which he believed documented the illegitimacy of the U.S. position in Southeast Asia.[77]

Predictably, there was a national controversy over Ellsberg's actions and the *New York Times*'s decision to publish key portions of a report that had been classified as top secret. The Justice Department immediately instituted legal proceedings against Ellsberg and obtained an injunction against further publication by the *Times*. After a fifteen-day legal battle which was actively covered in the press, the Supreme Court overturned the injunction and, in a six-to-three vote, decided that the entire nation had the right to know of commitments and decisions made by several earlier presidents. Justice Hugo L. Black, who voted with the majority, articulated the essence of the decision in his concurring opinion:

> Only a free and unrestrained press can effectively expose deception in government. And paramount among the responsibilities of a free press is the duty to prevent any part of the Government from deceiving the people and sending them off to distant lands to die of foreign fevers and foreign shot and shell. In my view, far from deserving condemnation for their courageous reporting, The New York Times, The Washington Post and other newspapers should be commended for serving the purpose that the Founding Fathers saw so clearly. In revealing the workings of government that led to the Vietnam war, the newspapers nobly did precisely that which the founders hoped and trusted they would do.[78]

The public was as divided about the war as about Daniel Ellsberg and the growing antiwar movement which quickly made him into a hero, but he had made it clear that he stood ready to accept the risk for his audacious act of whistleblowing. The willingness of the *New York Times* to print the Pentagon papers reinforced public skepticism about the ability of the executive branch to conduct national affairs with integrity. The decision of the Supreme Court, endorsing the public's right to know, lent further credence to Ellsberg's charges of presidential deception.

THE WATERGATE SCANDAL

National confidence in government was further shaken with a major scandal that ultimately implicated even the Oval Office. The burglary at the Democratic National Headquarters in the Watergate Hotel in June 1972 by five conspirators employed by the Committee to Re-elect the President for a time raised serious questions about the viability of the political system. Once again, insiders played particularly key roles in exposing the depth of corruption during that era. Testifying before the Senate Select Committee, the White House counsel to President Nixon, John W. Dean, documented the low ethical standards in the White House. The president, according to Dean, implemented illegal methods to elicit information linking domestic dissidents to foreign powers:

> To one who was in the White House and became somewhat familiar with its interworkings, the Watergate matter was an inevitable outgrowth of a climate of excessive concern over the political impact of demonstrators, excessive concern over leaks, an insatiable appetite for political intelligence, all coupled with a do-it-yourself White House staff, regardless of the law. . . . After I was told of the Presidentially approved plan that called for bugging, burglarizing, mail covers and the like, I was instructed by Haldeman [President Nixon's chief of staff] to see what I could do to get the plan implemented. I thought the plan was totally uncalled for and unjustified. . . .
>
> In early February of 1972, I learned that any means—legal or illegal—were authorized by Mr. Haldeman to deal with demonstrators when the President was traveling or appearing someplace. . . . We never found a scintilla of viable evidence indicating that these demonstrators were part of a master plan; nor that they had any connection with the McGovern campaign.[79]

Public testimony from insiders like Dean, who had been complicit in the illegal acts and was facing criminal indictments, was augmented by the revelations of Deep Throat, a celebrated but anonymous whistle-blower who provided crucial information to two reporters, Bob Woodward and Carl Bernstein of the *Washington Post.* Deep Throat also signaled the investigating committee with suggestions about witnesses to call and questions to ask. The hearings ultimately revealed information about the plot to break in to the Democratic headquarters by the Committee to Re-elect the President, about a White House–approved cover-up in the face of public investigation, and finally about attempts to destroy revealing tapes that would expose the complicity of President Nixon. When it became clear by the summer of 1974 that the highest office in the land had become a staging ground to break the law, the president was forced to resign. Confidence in the government had reached an all-time low.[80]

Years later, an ethical resister in the Federal Aviation Administration, Jim Pope, reflected admiringly on Deep Throat's effectiveness and ability to survive:

> Take a valuable lesson from the most successful of all whistleblowers in this generation—Deep Throat of the Watergate scandal. To this very day, more than ten years later, only a handful of people know the identity of this individual or individuals. Deep Throat's revelations were all covert, provocative, suspenseful, serialized, accurate, and documentable. As far as is known, Deep Throat is the only whistleblower to have successfully accomplished the two major objectives of any whistle blower: (1) to suffer no repercussions for his revelations and (2) to successfully accomplish his mission.[81]

Corporate lawlessness, disenchantment with technology, and government scandal all created the conditions and issues that gave rise to ethical resisters. But the ability of whistleblowers to expose deception also required legitimacy, which could be supplied only by other major institutions including the press, the courts, and Congress.

Conclusion

When, in 1968, Ernest Fitzgerald, one of the first ethical resisters, publicly exposed collusion between the Pentagon and defense contractors, there were few laws to safeguard civil servants or to encourage employees in industry to denounce illegal acts.[82] Ten years later, the Civil Service Act was reformulated to provide for the protection of federal employees who reported fraud, waste, and abuse.[83]

The lack of protective legislation was not the only impediment to ethical resistance in 1968. While a handful of employees in industry and government had come forth earlier, Fitzgerald found few resisters available in Washington or other major cities to guide him through the labyrinth of bureaucratic traps. Public-interest groups were not yet defending whistleblowers, and there were no organizations dedicated to building a network of resisters with connections to sympathetic members of Congress, reporters, and legal experts.

Despite his vulnerability, Fitzgerald refused to be driven out of Washington and, in an unprecedented action, stayed on to fight for his job. While he blazed his own path and fought his case with the help of a few members of Congress and later of the American Civil Liberties Union, he understood that such assistance was unlikely to be sufficient in the future, that for other whistleblowers to succeed they would need greater organizational support and ongoing political contacts. In the two decades of struggle that followed, he helped to build and encourage small, flexible organizations that could offer leadership for those who followed in his footsteps.*

Fitzgerald has remained a symbol of the courageous employee fighting against both corporate and government bureaucracies whose interests are so entrenched that they would rather destroy their critics than reform their methods. His victories in the courts and his eventual reinstatement were publicized widely in the mass media. At the same time, the costs to

---

*Fitzgerald's efforts to institutionalize aid for whistleblowers culminated years later in the founding of an organization expressly dedicated to fighting waste and inefficiency in the military-industrial complex. In late 1981, he urged Dina Rasor, a young public-interest lobbyist, to form the Project on Military Procurement which offered support to new resisters and also enabled employees to channel information anonymously where that seemed most appropriate.[84] In this process Fitzgerald himself became a repository for information about questionable practices throughout the defense industry.

his career and family came to represent the paradox of a society that celebrates individual responsibility while it thrives on bureaucratic organizations that define dissidents as enemies to be destroyed.[85]

While Fitzgerald's role was crucial in legitimizing whistleblowing, he, of course, could not accomplish these changes alone. Other early dissenters were also critical in establishing avenues for future ethical resisters. These pioneers came forward in the 1960s and 1970s, treading into uncharted areas where resistance was unprecedented. They, too, had to establish contacts with congressmen who might assist them and with committees investigating issues about which they could provide unique evidence. They also forged relationships with a few influential journalists. These latter-day muckrakers developed significant stories by encouraging insiders to provide documentation of major national problems.

These events persuaded the leaders of several newly formed public-interest groups that protection of ethical resisters was crucial in their struggle to build institutions that would safeguard a viable democracy. The three cases discussed in the next chapter elucidate the ways in which early whistleblowers and their allies in the Congress, the press, special commissions, and public-interest groups helped to legitimize ethical resistance and to develop mechanisms to assist those who followed them.

Chapter 2

The Legitimation of
Public Disclosure

IN 1959, Senator Estes Kefauver of Tennessee became chairman of the Senate Subcommittee on Antitrust and Monopoly and initiated an inquiry into the pricing practices of the pharmaceutical companies.[1] Among the many witnesses invited to testify were several industry employees, including Dr. A. Dale Console who had worked as director of research for a major pharmaceutical firm.[2] While Congress learned how valuable such an insider witness could be, whistleblowers like Console experienced firsthand the opportunities that congressional investigating committees could provide for publicizing and legitimizing the whistleblowers' concerns. When Ralph Nader called together the first whistleblowers' conference a dozen years later to build a more durable network, Dr. Console was a key participant. So was Senator William Proxmire of Wisconsin who had provided a public forum for Ernest Fitzgerald and become a forceful advocate for resisters willing to expose government and corporate transgressions.[3] Console, Proxmire, and the other participants supported Nader in his conviction that building links among resisters, Congress, and public-interest groups was essential if more employees were to speak up when they witnessed unethical and illegal behavior. The stamp of congressional interest moved the isolated dissenter to center stage. The investigating committees gathered evidence from individuals in order to act on public policy concerns. For the witness like Console, the interest of

Congress provided a public forum, an opportunity for vindication, and the possibility of legislative action to address significant social issues.

As Console represented the forerunner of corporate resisters who turned to Congress for support, James Boyd and Marjorie Carpenter were pioneers in the federal government who enlisted crucial assistance from the press. As staff members in Senator Thomas Dodd's office, they uncovered blatant misuse of campaign funds by the senator from Connecticut who had misappropriated tens of thousands of dollars for his personal use. Their decision in 1964 to take this information to the press raised the most profound challenge to deeply held ideas about loyalty and betrayal. Did they owe the greater loyalty to a powerful senator who had been Boyd's mentor for twelve years, or to the American public whose right it is to be represented by people of integrity? If Boyd and Carpenter spoke up, could they prove that their motivations were grounded in principles of democratic behavior, or would they be tarred by Dodd and his supporters as disreputable stool pigeons? The battle over definitions was central for their own futures and for the possibilities that others in government would be willing to follow their lead if they witnessed blatant fraud and abuse of office.

The situation became even more complex when Boyd and Carpenter had to confront the difficult issue of how to secure documentation for their allegations. How could they defend their decision to remove documents from the senator's office, even if this were the only way to prove their allegations? This issue was particularly sensitive because Congress itself was the target of serious charges of corruption. Boyd and Carpenter's actions served to sensitize many senators and representatives to the ethical issues in their own house as well as to the power of the press to force investigations even when Congress proved highly reluctant to do so.[4]

Frank Serpico, the New York City corruption-fighting policeman, forged a third path to legitimation in 1970.[5] Serpico and his fellow officer David Durk had to invent ways of disclosing systematic bribery on the municipal level. After they tried every avenue within the police department, they were ultimately successful in initiating a major *New York Times* series on police corruption.[6] As a direct result of this exposé, Mayor John Lindsay was forced to appoint a commission, headed by Whitman Knapp, a prominent lawyer, with a mandate to conduct a major investigation into the extent of police lawlessness in New York City.[7] The commission's recommendations resulted in the establishment of permanent mechanisms to reduce misconduct in the rank and file and require accountability from high-ranking police officers.[8] When Serpico's story was widely publicized through a popular book and film, honest police officers throughout the country identified with him as their model of appropriate behavior, his experiences both encouraging and forewarning them.

These early whistleblowing cases were landmarks in the legitimation of public disclosure. The first resisters developed links to the media and to public officials in a position to aid them, helped to build permanent organizations to defend their actions, and also lobbied for legislation that would provide greater protection. But for their efforts to succeed, these pioneer resisters and their allies needed to go further and to change the negative cultural connotations associated with whistleblowing. They sought to build a new vocabulary that could distinguish acts promoting the public good from the popular concept of informing with its connotation of disloyalty and betrayal by self-serving individuals. Their allies portrayed them as the embodiment of the American ideal of individual responsibility whose allegations were invariably confirmed by later investigations, and asserted that the resisters were in the forefront of a nationwide movement committed to making both government and industry accountable for their actions.[9] Their supporters in the media, Congress, and public-interest groups argued that resisters could have best served their own self-interest by turning away and avoiding the dangers of confrontation. But, by speaking up and supplying validated evidence of lawless acts, these early whistleblowers redefined the meaning of loyalty and established their identity as courageous defenders of American ethics.[10]

Holding the Government and Corporations Accountable

ARTHUR DALE CONSOLE AND THE PHARMACEUTICAL INDUSTRY

The late Arthur Dale Console studied at Cornell Medical College and later practiced neurosurgery. In search of less strenuous work after a serious illness, he joined the E. R. Squibb and Sons pharmaceutical company in 1949 as associate director of research. He found Squibb an ethical company, still run by its founder and maintaining an orientation in which the physician in charge of research was defined as a "physician's physician." During the ensuing years, according to Dr. Console, much changed in the pharmaceutical industry. Larger companies bought out the smaller ones, and the search for profit became more intense. The transformation affected all members of the company staff, including the director of research, a position Console had by then assumed. As he worked, he experienced an increasing tension between his sense of what was appropriate medical decision making and what was required by his more business-oriented superiors. He was particularly disturbed by having pressured physicians to certify drugs they had not sufficiently tested. He resigned from his position in 1956 after six and a half years in the drug industry, and soon after trained for a new career as a psychiatrist.

In 1960, Console's continuing sense of self-estrangement led him to take the initiative and testify before the Kefauver committee. As the former research director, he was in a particularly good position to detail the ways in which drug companies distorted the truth about their products, engaged in deceptive testing, and dumped drugs declared unsafe in the United States onto foreign markets. He described how testimonials were "used not only to give apparent substance to the advertising and promotion of relatively worthless products, but also to extend the indications of effective drugs beyond the range of their real utility."[11]

Several years later, at one congressional hearing, he was asked why he had left Squibb. He recounted how a physician can capitulate to the pressures of a large corporation and the resultant disillusionment:

I believe that the best answer can be found in my unfinished essay on *The Good Life of a Drug Company Doctor.* Toward the end I said: "These are only some of the things a drug company doctor must learn if he is to be happy in the industry. After all, *it is a business,* and there are many more things he must learn to rationalize. He must learn the many ways to deceive the FDA, and failing in this, how to seduce, manipulate, or threaten the physician assigned to the New Drug Application into approving it even if it is incomplete. He must learn that anything that helps to sell a drug is valid even if it is supported by the crudest testimonial, while anything that decreases sales must be suppressed, distorted and rejected because it is not absolutely conclusive proof. . . . He will find himself squeezed between businessmen who will sell anything and justify it on the basis that doctors ask for it and doctors who demand products they have been taught to want through the advertising and promotion schemes contrived by businessmen. If he can absorb all this, and more, and still maintain any sensibilities he will learn the true meaning of loneliness and alienation."

> During my tenure as medical director I learned the meaning of loneliness and alienation. I reached a point where I could no longer live with myself. I had compromised to the point where my back was against a wall and I had to choose between resigning myself to total capitulation or resigning as medical director. I chose the latter course.[12]

After he left the pharmaceutical industry, Console received a grant from Squibb to train for a career in psychiatry, which placed him outside the authority of all corporate structures. Console's widow, a respected psychiatrist in her own right, has provided additional insight into her husband's background, his commitment to Squibb, and his ultimate decision to blow the whistle soon after entering private practice:

> He was one of two surviving brothers who both carried out their father's ambitions to complete medical school. Arthur did so with great distinction. . . . In spite of two bouts of tuberculosis during this period he went on and completed a neurosurgical residency—the first resident chosen in this separate specialty considered the most prestigious in surgery. Trouble really began when, in attempting to establish a practice, he fell ill a third time, necessitating complete bed rest at home. We had an infant son with club feet requiring frequent surgical intervention and casts, absolutely no income except mine from an also newly established practice and the resulting pressure on me from multiple conflicting responsibilities was overwhelming. It was apparent that he had to find a less physically demanding and an economically sound alternative. It was at this time he accepted the offer to join Squibb as associate medical director. The decision to give up neurosurgery as a career was a bitter and lasting defeat.[13]

Console's attitude toward Squibb was ambivalent from the beginning. His deep disappointment about giving up his chosen field of neurosurgery weakened his identification with work in a pharmaceutical company. At the same time, as his wife explained, the company was moving in a direction that deeply offended his professional ethics:

> The coincidence of Dr. Console's tenure as medical director of Squibb with its changeover from an ethical drug house to a competitive business-oriented company could not have been foreseen, but his sense of having been condemned to second-class medicine then became more

and more intolerable. Because of Dr. Console's increasing and outspoken alienation from the drug industry it was clear that an open break was pending. It was imperative for him to look elsewhere for the future. The choice of psychiatry was made after considerable discussion together.[14]

Console was now freed from economic dependency on the company. He felt liberated by the knowledge that he had an independent career which did not require the good will of executives concerned with running a business. Although the issue of loyalty to his former employers was still thorny, it did not prevent him from disclosing the unethical and illegal acts routinely perpetrated by the pharmaceutical industry. His wife recalled that he managed this conflict by removing himself from relationships with any former colleagues, but he never succeeded in totally resolving his ambivalent feelings:

> When the opportunity arose to testify in the Kefauver hearings, my husband had already distanced himself from almost all his former colleagues. . . . The real problem was one of conflict from some sense of loyalty to Squibb, which had been very generous to him, and the pressure of his need to speak out. I did not share this intensity and had some misgivings but felt that he had to follow his own conviction. His moments of "speaking out" appeared then to be an opportunity to vindicate himself in his own eyes before the world.[15]

Console chose to reveal his own complicity in a massive effort by the drug industry to profit from unethical testing and marketing procedures. Public disclosure helped to alleviate his guilt for not resisting pressures he considered unethical and medically unsound. But guilt alone did not provide sufficient motivation. He had hoped to write a book about his experiences but feared that a libel suit might engage him in lengthy and expensive litigation. When the Kefauver committee established hearings on problems in the drug industry, it provided him with a forum for his testimony which assured him immunity from legal harassment.

Console presented the insight of the insider who had worked for years in a position that gave him a unique vantage point. He made it clear that he was not specifically going after his former employers and had, in fact, destroyed his files after leaving Squibb. Rather, his statements drew upon his extensive knowledge of the entire industry. While he recognized an obligation to Squibb for the funds they provided him to retrain for a new field, he felt he owed his greater loyalty to the millions of people in this country and abroad who were both paying excessive prices for medication and were insufficiently protected from unsafe products. He argued strongly that it was the responsibility of individual citizens and every employee to protect the public interest, that they could not rely on large organizations:

> We could make no greater mistake than to be lulled into a sense of false security by believing that some disembodied force called the government will act like a beneficent big brother and make certain that the special interests will not predominate. If the general welfare is to be protected, it will be protected by the actions of people, not the government.". . .[16]

Console's public disclosure of practices in the pharmaceutical industry addressed three major issues that had to be resolved in order to legitimate the activities of early resisters. First, there was the question of loyalty to his employers. He argued persuasively that his first loyalty lay with unsuspecting consumers who believed they could trust the drug companies. Knowing that this trust was betrayed by marketing procedures that reflected the decisions of those who were committed to profit rather than service, Console felt it to be his responsibility to make this information public.

Second, he had to prove that his actions were not self-serving. The Kefauver committee played a key role by recognizing his contribution and defining him as a man of courage who had willingly exposed his own involvement in questionable practices and risked disruption to his professional and personal life. Had he remained silent, no one in his small community in New Jersey would have guessed that the successful former industry research director had hated his work and engaged in actions he considered unethical. In speaking out, he made no excuse for his actions and took the responsibility squarely on his own shoulders. His admirers in Congress could enthusiastically praise him for his emotional fortitude in facing his own culpability and placing the spotlight on the actions of an industry that always claimed to act in the public interest.

Finally, to win legitimation, Console, like other early whistleblowers, had to demonstrate that the issues he pointed to were not trivial. Both committee members and other analysts quickly recognized that he had exposed deficiencies in a major American industry that could seriously undermine public health and safety. A series of dangerous and irresponsible acts by the pharmaceutical companies has since been confirmed by many other witnesses and subsequent scholarly research.[17] Recent commentators have emphasized the significance of Console's early testimony and his alerting Congress and the public to corporate policies that endanger thousands of consumers.[18]

The three major issues Console faced continued to challenge other whistleblowers who brought to public attention serious allegations against powerful individuals and organizations.

PUTTING THE SENATE ON TRIAL: JAMES BOYD, MARJORIE CARPENTER, AND SENATOR THOMAS DODD

A few years later, a small group of resisters on the staff of a U.S. senator faced an even more serious crisis of personal loyalty than had Console. In acting, they knew they would be subject to intense criticism for denouncing the senator and for breaking the sacrosanct norms of loyalty that dominate Washington politics. The importance of their allegations, the nature of their support, and their ultimate success in forcing the Senate to confront corruption in its own ranks was a significant landmark in the intense battle to legitimate whistleblowing.

James Boyd's association with the future senator from Connecticut occurred by chance in 1953 when the twenty-four-year-old Boyd first met the newly elected congressman, Thomas Dodd. Boyd was delighted to volunteer his services to this "man of vision"; and his devotion was rewarded several years later, in 1958, when Dodd was elected to the Senate and Boyd became his chief aide. The freshman senator quickly won a reputation as an articulate reformer who was willing to take on the pharmaceutical companies and even the doctors themselves for making drugs too readily available to people of all ages. He opposed the lax gun laws and also worked on issues of juvenile delinquency. Like many cold war liberals of that time, he went after those whom he thought too friendly to the Soviets and used his position on the Senate Internal Security Committee to interrogate well-known activists. Dodd's rise in national politics culminated in 1964 when President Johnson seriously considered him for the vice presidency.

In the midst of this growing national recognition, Boyd saw the underside of the senator's performance. The man who had long boasted about his humble origins now had two fine homes and a stable and enjoyed the favors showered on Congress by corporate benefactors. Boyd developed a gnawing doubt about Dodd's integrity.

During the 1964 re-election campaign, Boyd worked tirelessly on Dodd's behalf. Yet, with several other staff members close to the senator, he began to piece together a picture of Dodd's compromising activities. Boyd and his colleagues realized that individuals who had lent Dodd money that remained unpaid later received jobs from him. Drug and electrical firms involved in litigation with the government had provided Dodd with the use of private planes, hotel rooms, and other gifts. Large sums of money allegedly donated for campaign purposes went unrecorded.[19]

The exhilaration of Dodd's landslide victory in 1964 did not dispel the disquiet felt by Boyd, Marjorie Carpenter, then the senator's secretary, and several other staff members. While Carpenter in particular wanted to move against the senator, Boyd remained reluctant, his twelve-year association with Dodd still too strong a bond to sever. Marjorie Carpenter described to us the basis of her resolve and Boyd's more cautious response:

> I was more enthusiastic about doing something than Jim. It was understandable. I was younger, less sophisticated, more naive. Maybe I was more outraged for that reason. I also worked closer to Dodd than anyone else. I knew him better than the others did. I saw a terrible misuse of power and an arrogant attitude. And when you observe arrogance with illegal behavior, it is easy to become outraged. There was never any question in my mind that I would withstand the stress of coming forward. I am a mixture of naiveté and toughness, and Jim knew me well enough to know that about me. Jim, on the other hand, knew more about the pitfalls than I did.[20]

Senator Dodd sensed that Boyd and Carpenter were suspicious of him and had begun to gather incriminating evidence, and unceremoniously fired both of them. The break had come. The intense attachment Boyd had developed to his mentor of twelve years was destroyed by his dismissal and by the rumors Dodd circulated. Dodd told other senators and newspaper reporters that he had discovered a distasteful and indiscreet sexual relationship between Carpenter and Boyd which made their dismissal essential. Boyd felt that his loyalty had been misplaced and his trust abused:

I didn't come to the decision to really go at it, tooth and nail, until I saw him trying to keep me from getting a job. I didn't want to go back with him. I was trying to get away from him for some time, but he tried to use the power to keep me from getting a job, and then, in a roundabout way, boasting to me what he was doing, toying with me as if I were some kind of a creature, instead of a partner as we had started out.[21]

Boyd and Carpenter agreed to pursue their suspicions and expose Dodd's activities publicly—a task requiring the assistance of others still employed by the senator. Michael O'Hare, a top assistant to the senator, and Terry Golden, a secretary, had been part of the earliest discussions and decided to join Boyd and Carpenter.

Immediately, the potential whistleblowers had to decide what to do with their allegations. They believed that past history had shown that the Senate had little inclination to investigate the alleged malfeasance of its own members, and had never brought charges against any senator for financial improprieties. The four thought about the possibility of taking their material to the FBI but were dissuaded by the knowledge that the bureau would never investigate the senator without authorization from the attorney general's office. The Justice Department would alert Dodd to the charges against him, and he could easily destroy any incriminating evidence.

The press was the only alternative. Hoping that publicity might force a Senate investigation, Boyd and Carpenter approached Drew Pearson and Jack Anderson, two long-standing investigative reporters. Fascinated by their information, Anderson felt that this could be the biggest corruption story in all his years of reporting. He urged them to obtain the evidence that would prove their suspicions. They all agreed that it would be necessary to remove Dodd's files from his office and photocopy them—an action whose legal and ethical implications the group agonized over. Boyd understood its gravity but argued there would be no way to assure public accountability unless official records were available for public scrutiny.[22]* The decision became even more difficult when O'Hare and

*In his review of Boyd's account, the columnist William Shannon endorsed the decision to release the documents. "Boyd has been severely and, in my judgment, unfairly criticized for secretly copying thousands of documents in Dodd's files and turning them over to the press. In his book he argues convincingly for the rightness of his course. A private citizen aware of wrongdoing by another private person can complain to the police

Golden decided at the very last moment not to join in this phase of the action, feeling that it was inappropriate for them, as current employees of the senator, to act against him in this way.

Boyd and Carpenter were forced to go on alone or drop the entire plan. Boyd believes that their friendship was crucial in the final decision:

> It is important to have a companion in something like this. You are not alone. You have mutual support. When our two partners temporarily withdrew, had either one of us been alone it would have been the end of it. But together we were somehow a group and so we decided to do something we had never intended to do. We had always expected that Terry and Michael would take the documents out. That would have been legal since they had access to them as part of their job. When they opted out, we had to act alone.[24]

Boyd and Carpenter entered Dodd's offices, took out thousands of pages of materials, photocopied them, and returned the documents to their proper place. The documents indicated that their suspicions were well founded. Boyd and Carpenter now had proof that Dodd had used over $200,000 of campaign funds for his own personal expenses—contributions that had not been reported, and on which no taxes had ever been paid. Even more troubling was the finding that some of the money had come from companies under investigation by Senate committees on which Dodd served. Despite his public posture, the records revealed that Dodd had deliberately downplayed or actually squashed the efforts of his staff to regulate more carefully the arms manufacturers, the drug industry, and insurance companies. The senator had set a price on his principles.[25]

Drew Pearson's first articles on 24 January 1966 set people buzzing throughout Washington. Securing an official response was more difficult. By immediately charging that the theft of the documents and Pearson's articles created an untenable situation in which no senator or congressman could feel safe about the security of his files, Dodd astutely managed to shift the discussion to the issue of document security. Carpenter succinctly captured the intense congressional anxiety about staff loyalty

---

or the District Attorney. If there is corruption in a Government agency, a federal employee can, as a last resort, carry his story to one or another of the investigating committees of Congress. But to whom can a Senate employee turn if he wants to accuse a senator?"[23]

which made Dodd's appeal effective: "On Capitol Hill members rise and fall quickly. Everybody has to face elections. They are very security conscious and almost paranoid about their staffs. While an outsider might not understand the reaction, an insider would sense that what we did was the ultimate blasphemy of their carefully constructed system."[26]

This early case clearly revealed how vulnerable whistleblowers were to an attack on their motivations and credibility. To their critics, they were not only undermining an individual but were also guilty of treason to an institution that had carefully guarded rules of behavior. All four staff members quickly lost their jobs and their Capitol Hill friends and thus were isolated as they awaited reaction to the press exposé.

The Senate moved carefully, and the leadership appointed John Stennis, the Democratic senator from Mississippi who revered the body and would do nothing to cause its disgrace. Stennis began hearings and called the four whistleblowers to testify in executive session. For months nothing happened. It appeared that the charges against Dodd would not get a full hearing. Despite Pearson and Anderson's influence, not one major newspaper or television station felt the allegations warranted an investigation by their staff. Other agencies that might have intervened—such as the Justice Department, the Internal Revenue Service, or state authorities in Connecticut—all displayed decided reluctance to deal with issues of Senate ethics and corruption.

It was only Pearson and Anderson's persistent prodding that led several senators to call for a thorough public airing. In addition, the case against Dodd suddenly gained momentum when the *Washington Post* revealed that he had taken $100,000 for personal use and had paid no income tax. This information had come from a spokesman for the senator who argued that the money was a tax-free gift from testimonial dinners, that such gifts were part of the American way of life, and that all senators engaged in such activities. The statement, which was picked up by cartoonists all over the country, was quickly repudiated by the White House as well as by members of Congress.[27]

After a lengthy delay, the Senate Ethics committee reopened the hearings. Under Stennis's careful direction, the committee limited the focus of the investigation and completed the hearings in five days. It ignored charges that might implicate any other senators, and scrutinized only those activities that reflected on Dodd himself. Even under these constricted circumstances, substantial evidence of impropriety was presented, particularly about Dodd's relationship with a West German lobbyist, his double billing of the government for travel, and his personal use of funds clearly donated to retire campaign expenses. Dodd responded by attacking the legitimacy of the Senate hearings and calling for the resignation of the committee's vice chairman. Stennis and the other senators were shaken by both Dodd's outburst and his inability to answer the most straightforward questions. In an unprecedented action, the Ethics Committee voted unanimously to censure Dodd on several counts of financial impropriety.

During the subsequent full Senate debate, Dodd and his supporters predictably claimed that he was being pilloried for activities that had long been a common part of Senate practice. Dodd gave a masterful performance until several colleagues questioned him closely about the large sums that had been collected for campaign expenses and used for major personal purchases. It became clear that, with the exception of the major industries under investigation, virtually all who had contributed to Dodd had done so with the belief that the funds were expressly for campaign purposes. A dejected Senator Dodd left the Senate chambers on 23 June 1967 as his colleagues voted him the first senator in the history of the United States to be censured for financial misconduct.[28] While Thomas Dodd completed his Senate term, both his stature and his influence were sharply reduced.

The Ethics Committee report that had recommended Dodd's censure also rebuked the four whistleblowers who had uncovered the evidence against him:

> While the Committee recognizes the duty of every Senator, or officer or employee of the Senate, to report wrongdoing to responsible authorities, the Committee believes that the unauthorized removal of papers from a Senator's office by employees and former employees is reprehensible and constitutes a breach of the relationship of trust between a Senator and his staff, is an invasion of what must be considered privileged communications between a Senator and his correspondents, and is a threat to the orderly conduct of business of a public office.[29]

The self-protective and self-serving congressional norms that demanded loyalty above all else had been dented, but uneasiness about staff betrayal remained strong.

After the Dodd hearings, it would be a full decade before the Senate passed a code of ethics governing the behavior of its members—and only after Watergate and in a package that awarded Congress a substantial pay raise. Nonetheless, the Dodd case was one important factor in requiring full disclosure of campaign and personal finances. Congress may have repudiated whistleblowers in their own chambers, but it could not forever escape the implications of gross abuse of public office.[30]

While the motivations of Boyd and Carpenter always remained suspect in Washington circles, elsewhere they fared far better. When Jim Boyd published his book on the case in 1968, it received excellent reviews for its admirably balanced analysis of the Dodd affair.* Boyd argued persuasively that the fall of Thomas Dodd had a significance far beyond the ruined career of any one individual. In Boyd's view, Senator Dodd had the potential for greatness, but unfortunately his Senate experience played to exacerbate his weakness rather than to reinforce his strength. Corporations, with their massive resources, were able to erode the independence of too many government officials. Dodd had begun as a stalwart reformer, intent on investigating abuses in the pharmaceutical, insurance, and firearms industries, but after a few years he became a captive of their largesse. Boyd concluded his book with a sense of the tragedy of Dodd's career as the senator became the servant of corporations rather than of his own constituents:

> He was not without precedent when he accepted both personal financial gifts and campaign contributions from officials of the arms industry, which naturally sought to delay controls and to alter any restrictive legislation to its advantage. Dodd's crusade against mail-order firearms sputtered spasmodically and dragged on ineffectually for years, while gifts and contributions poured in from arms-industry officials.

Boyd also captured the lust for standing and recognition that exists in American society. He saw Thomas Dodd not only as guilty of major transgressions but also as a victim of the desire to make a name for oneself and reserve a place at the table of the mighty and the wealthy:

*"A New York Times reporter covering the Dodd story once said that it was Dodd's hard luck to have had as an administrative assistant a man with a conscience and total recall. The Senator's bad luck didn't end there. Boyd's book also reveals writing skill, humor, and an unreciprocated exercise of fairness. At the height of the censure debate— when most men in his position would have been blind with anger over swamp water attacks from the likes of Russell Long (Democrat-Louisiana) and Dodd—Boyd would halt and correct overheated companions if they inflated Dodd's crimes. This detachment raises what would have been an interesting report on a dishonest senator into a thoughtful and literate account of a contemporary tragedy—a tragedy 'not without its moral on public life in a free society.' "[31]

And there was the need for money, for the symbols of success, for some guarantee of security and status at the end. After all the struggle, all the sacrifice, all the victories, there had to be a commensurate reward. But the monetary rewards of government service are modest . . . For Dodd, like many another, there was in defeat no family estate to retire to, no inherited fortune to give solace, no corporate portfolio to assume. . . . A Senator knows that he may not always be the millionaire's darling, holidaying at the estates of near-strangers. Why, he asks himself, should he be poor, while his deferential hosts are rich?[32]

Boyd, like Console and other early whistleblowers, did not believe that major institutions would reform themselves: the pressures were too great, and the temptations omnipresent. Despite all the calls for a code of ethics in the Senate, Boyd believed that "whether the Senate would go beyond the mere offering of a public sacrifice and reform the system itself would depend, in the end, on the unrelenting insistence of the American people that the temple must be cleansed."[33]*

Breaking Ranks: Frank Serpico and the New York City Police Force

The bold public disclosures by Dr. A. Dale Console in 1960 and James Boyd and Marjorie Carpenter in 1966 were matched by Frank Serpico in 1970, when he and two fellow police officers took their allegations of corruption to the *New York Times.* For Serpico this was the end of the line. Although for several years he had attempted to evoke a response from high-ranking police department and public officials, no one had been willing to intervene. When he reported the widespread corruption of an entire precinct by gamblers in the Bronx, he forced an investigation, but only a few "flunky cops" were prosecuted. The higher-ups in the station house and at division headquarters remained untouched. Serpico was threatened and isolated as the honest cop who would not remain silent. In a final attempt to formalize his charges and effect change, he committed the unpardonable offense: he broke ranks and took his evidence to outside agencies. With the corroborating testimony of Inspector Paul

*The new disclosure laws seriously affected the fate of another senator a few years later. Senator Herman Talmadge (Democrat-Georgia) was censured in 1979.[34]

Delise and the continuing encouragement of officer David Durk, who had used all his contacts in New York City for several years to no avail, Serpico decided to risk all on one final gamble. This time the results merited the risk. The *New York Times* series detailed the illegal actions that permeated the force, and the story forced a reluctant Mayor Lindsay to establish the Knapp Commission to investigate police corruption.[35]

The findings of the lengthy investigation supported all of Serpico's allegations.[36] The commission's report, rejecting the "rotten apple" theory of police corruption, concluded that the violations were rampant throughout the department. Bribes by gamblers and narcotics dealers influenced the behavior of many police. The rank and file's dereliction of duty was aided and abetted by their superiors who were "on the take" themselves or willing to ignore evidence of their subordinates' involvement in corrupt behavior. Some officers, the commission asserted, were "grass eaters," who accepted the bribes when offered them. Others, dubbed "meat eaters," actively solicited bribes from gambling and narcotics dealers.

The corruption in the system was able to thrive not only because of the abuses of high-ranking officials, but also because the police demanded absolute loyalty from their peers. Honest officers learned to turn away if they were to survive on the force. They could avoid becoming involved, but they were forbidden to interfere with a partner's corrupt activities. "Never hurt another cop" was a byword of the force. In one social science study of police, officers were asked whether they would perjure themselves to protect their partners—a question to which many respondents were so hostile that they refused to cooperate further with the researcher. Of those who did reply, the majority affirmed that they would rather perjure themselves than expose a fellow officer.[37]

In the face of such strict norms, how was Serpico able to come forward? How would he deal with the paramount issue of loyalty? How could he convince others that his acts were those of a man of courage and not of a traitor who had turned in those bound to protect him at the least sign of danger? How could he breach the informal code that guided police in their relations with one another and countenanced illegal acts? Serpico violated the cardinal rule governing relationships among police. He broke group solidarity. He exposed his comrades to attack and increased the hostility of the public toward all police. In return he lost the protection of the group. He could no longer count on support from the officers with whom he worked.

Serpico was able to move ahead because he was already disenchanted and estranged. Unlike other police, he had never "shopped" or taken any small bribes which could have demoralized him. He never experienced the erosion of his personal values. He never became "bent."[38] Equally important, he remained psychologically and socially distant from his peers. His primary loyalty remained to his early sense of what a police officer could be and to the formal regulations of his department.

Serpico's independence was supported by the unusual twist his personal life had taken. An intense interest in opera and dance, an ability with language, a boredom with the world view and life style of most policemen pulled him away from his fellow officers. Off duty he lived in a different world in Greenwich Village, whose environment did not constantly reinforce the belief that the police were misunderstood and could best find solace and acceptance among their own kind. On the contrary, Serpico developed another network of friends from whom he could draw sustenance. Indeed, his new friends feared the police and the constant harassment for their countercultural life style. Immediately sensing this attitude, Serpico told no one about his police work. His loyalty to these friends helped him resist the heavy pressure that he conform to the behavior required by the informal code of the police.

Serpico did indeed pay a heavy price for exposing corrupt officers. Although he was vindicated by the prestigious Knapp Commission and lauded in the media, he was ostracized by colleagues. When he was subsequently shot in a drug raid, serious questions arose. Had he been deliberately set up by his partners, or had he been careless in approaching a drug dealer who had recently been robbed by a gunman claiming to be a police officer? Whatever the facts of the case, the near-fatal shooting won Serpico additional public sympathy and support. A widely acclaimed book (Peter Maas's Serpico, 1973) and movie (1973) used these events to cast Serpico, standing virtually alone against armed superiors and peers, as the quintessential American hero.[39] He retained his loyalty to the people who needed his protection, and rejected the enticements of corrupt officers who had forgotten their oath to uphold the law.

Injured and disillusioned after being shot, Serpico retired on a disability pension and left the country to live abroad for several years. Even without his presence, his name became nationally identified with integrity and courage. The legend of Serpico went beyond popular imagery. His actions and the response of the Knapp Commission helped set a standard for police behavior across the nation and created an environment in which honest officers felt they could speak up. Bob Ellis, another principled member of New York's "finest," recounted his decision to confront a fellow officer with the information that he would not accept any offers of money. They almost came to blows. Serpico and the Knapp Commission were very much on Ellis's mind: "We resolved it somehow or other without fighting. At the time this was going on, there were already rumblings from the Knapp Commission which were coming down. Changes were being made. It was becoming fashionable not to take money." Although Ellis settled his dispute with his colleague, he knew that working with this fellow officer would not be viable: "Then I got lucky. They created two super precincts in the midtown area. I was offered a position in one of these precincts to go into plainclothes. It was the perfect resolution for me."[40]

Ellis's problems were not over. Despite the changes already occurring in the department, he soon learned that several of his new fellow officers were taking substantial bribes to protect local racketeers. The situation worsened dramatically when a gambler fatally shot two patrolmen. Ellis learned that the killer had been stopped by several detectives shortly before the murders. Despite the fact that he was carrying a weapon, they allowed him to walk off scot-free in return for a substantial bribe. Ellis was horrified. How could experienced officers allow a racketeer to hold on to his loaded gun? Unable to live with this knowledge, Ellis decided to approach his commanding officer, who took the information to the Internal Affairs Unit. The investigators interrogated Ellis and told him that they could not pursue the case unless he were willing to wear a "wire" (a hidden recorder) to gather direct evidence from his partners. Although he felt a powerful sense of loyalty to his dead comrades, he knew that he would never be trusted again on the police force. It was an emotionally grueling time. While Serpico's earlier experiences had helped Ellis decide on his direction, they could not fully ease the guilt he felt about breaking ranks. Both he and his wife believe that his subsequent heart attacks were a direct result of the intense stress he experienced. Later threats of physical retaliation against him and his family exacerbated his emotional upheaval but steeled his determination to see his ordeal through to a successful conclusion in which several offending officers were indicted.

While knowledge of Serpico and the Knapp Commission provided Ellis with some psychological support, the commission had a much more direct impact on other cases. As the Knapp Commission delved into Serpico's charges of corruption, it sought out officers who might assist the undercover investigation. One of the most significant connections came when Nicholas Scoppetta, a commission attorney, persuaded detective Bob Leuci to cooperate.[41] Leuci, at thirty-one, had spent several years doing undercover work in narcotics and had been an important member of the department's elite Special Investigating Unit. Unlike Serpico and Ellis, he had succumbed to the temptations to augment his salary. Not only had he given his informants illegal drugs in order to elicit information, but he also had personally accepted bribes from major drug dealers. Scoppetta did not know that, in questioning Leuci, he had tapped into an elaborate network of SIU corruption, but sensed that the presumably "clean" detective acted nervous and hostile.

Scoppetta had approached Leuci at a crucial moment. Leuci had recently been rotated out of the SIU and was having difficulty living with his secret past. Without his partners to sustain him, he felt guilty that he had broken all the rules and was seeking a way out. The Knapp Commission offered him the opportunity to help ferret out corruption and return to a law-abiding career. Leuci made it clear to Scoppetta that he had no intention of going after his former partners in the SIU. He believed he could steer the investigation away from them and toward crooked lawyers and judges who deserved to be behind bars.

To this day, Leuci cannot fully explain his turnabout.[42] His wife, Gina, fearing that he would eventually have to sacrifice his own partners and would not be able to live with himself after hurting the only people truly concerned with his well-being, pleaded with him not to become involved with the Knapp Commission's investigation. Did he want to save his own skin, as many have claimed, or did he want to return to a more honest time in his life?[43] However complex Leuci's motivations, it is clear that Scoppetta was a crucial catalyst in helping him deal with the loyalty question. Leuci had found someone else to identify with, someone to help him find his way back on track:

> Scoppetta was something special. He came from an even tougher environment than I did. Like me he was a first-generation Italian. So we had a lot in common. I think I reminded him of his younger brother. So we became very close, very quickly. I trusted him totally. I undertook the investigation because of the incredible support I got

from Scoppetta, incredible support. It was the same kind of support
that I had received from my partners when I was working in the
streets. You have a sense that somebody really cares about you.[44]

The Knapp Commission and later the federal investigators offered
Leuci an alternative to the network he had developed in the police force.
The officials were his new group of friends, and he identified with them.
They gave him physical protection and emotional sustenance. In turn, he
helped them gather invaluable evidence against drug dealers, unethical
lawyers, and ultimately corrupt policemen. Despite his earlier protesta-
tions, Leuci could not control the direction of the undercover investigation. By wearing a hidden recorder, he helped expose fifty-two members
of the SIU, actions that led to the suicide of two of his former partners
and the emotional breakdown of a third. Many on the police force remained convinced that Leuci was a self-serving traitor, but the federal
prosecutors labeled him an invaluable and courageous witness. In return
for his cooperation and the risks he had taken, they did not indict him
for his own previous involvement in illegal acts. Leuci's story became the
basis of a popular book and a well-known film.[45] While never resolving
the complex doubts about an undercover officer who had been deeply
implicated in lawless acts, Robert Daley's *Prince of the City* served to
reinforce the prosecutors' definition that Leuci had engaged in heroic
behavior.

Serpico had demonstrated that whistleblowers could play a significant
role even in organizations where secrecy and solidarity supersede all
other values. For him, loyalty to the ideals of the police force was ultimately more potent than allegiance to errant partners or corrupt commanding officers. His actions were dangerous and personally costly.
Nonetheless, he and those who came in his wake were successful in
helping to bring about significant changes in departmental procedures.
As a result of Knapp Commission recommendations, commanding officers were no longer immune and were now held accountable for the
actions of their subordinates. Turning a deaf ear could result in the loss
of a high rank. Other provisions reduced the exposure of police to some
of the most likely sources of corruption. The transformation of the police department received wide public recognition, and Serpico has come
to embody the individual who successfully confronted "the system" and
helped to reform it.[46]

The Development of Public-Interest Groups

The public disclosures of the early whistleblowers established the precedent that corporate employees and government officials would expose lawless acts despite intense loyalty to superiors and peers and in violation of the norms that forbid employees to go outside the organization. This act required more than a strong conscience. Ethical resisters needed others to stand with them on the job. In addition, acts of resistance depended on the availability of an alternative authority that would review, process, and publicize the information. When Console testified about the drug industry, Congress provided the outlet and the stamp of legitimacy. For Carpenter and Boyd, influential journalists disclosed their findings and demanded an investigation. In the case of Frank Serpico, an appointed commission confirmed his allegations and helped institute reforms.

The public-interest group provided another major form of support. These organizations, staffed and energized by youthful activists, developed strategies to promote issues of public health and safety. Defining the whistleblowers as more than employees with integrity, public-interest groups saw them as living witnesses to the existence of serious problems and as testaments to the idea that individual citizens could take action to promote organizational accountability.

One of the most significant leaders in garnering public attention and support for ethical resisters was Ralph Nader. His 1965 book on automobile safety, *Unsafe at Any Speed*, written when he was a young lawyer, had exposed the deficiencies of the Chevrolet Corvair.[47] General Motors quickly retaliated by contracting with a private detective agency to investigate Nader's private life. The corporation hoped to uncover damaging material to discredit his appearance before the Senate subcommittee holding hearings on a National Traffic and Motor Vehicle Safety and Highway Safety Act, and thereby divert attention from his serious charges. When the GM investigation was revealed, the company's president was forced to apologize publicly, and Ralph Nader was catapulted to national attention. Within a few years, he had established "Nader's Raiders," groups of college students who worked summers investigating special issues, such as the deficiencies of the Federal Trade Commission in its protection of consumers. Other reports were issued on air pollution and automobile safety. He also founded the Center for the Study of Responsive Law, the Center for Auto Safety, and the Public Interest Research Groups, all employing young lawyers, scientists, economists, other professionals, and scores of volunteers. Nader recruited students and graduates coming out of the civil rights and peace movements who were eager to find opportunities for public service.[48]

He used proceeds from the settlement of his suit against General Motors to establish a web of organizations designed to expose inadequate consumer protection and to promote corporate and government accountability. Nader provided ethical resisters with continual publicity about the need and value of exposing corrupt and unsafe conditions. In the organizations he founded, resisters encountered a network of socially committed young professionals with well-developed ties to the press and to Congress. The many books Nader and his colleagues wrote, edited, and compiled often featured stories about whistleblowers, thus giving them increased legitimacy and publicity.[49]

A turning point came in early January 1971 when Nader and his associates organized, in Washington, D.C., the Conference on Professional Responsibility to provide a public forum for men and women who had exposed such dangers as the overly optimistic radiation standards set by the Atomic Energy Commission, the production and marketing of unsafe drugs and dangerous automobiles, and the illegal surveillance of civilians by military personnel.[50] In trumpeting these issues, the conference actually set forth a litany of some of the nation's most serious ills. It also provided an opportunity for distinguished leaders in business, government, and the academy to urge employees to continue to disclose dangerous and costly malfeasance despite the risks inherent in such courageous behavior. Nader emphasized that insiders are always the first to know of problems that will ultimately victimize the public. Indeed, Nader's own exposé of the Corvair's deficiencies had been prompted by the data provided by a General Motors engineer.

The conference was yet another important step in legitimizing the role of ethical resisters. While urging caution and setting forth detailed criteria for those contemplating public disclosure, all the speakers emphasized the importance of employees exposing organizational policies that could injure and defraud an unsuspecting public. The conference leaders called for greater legal protection for ethical resisters and more extensive congressional investigations into their allegations. The speakers promulgated a set of beliefs that celebrated whistleblowers and the importance of individual responsibility, arguing that this character trait was essential for the survival of a truly democratic society. The 1971 conference was a central event in the effort to reduce the isolation of individual resisters. It stressed that their private concerns were significant public issues. Speakers assured resisters, who often acted alone, that there were many hundreds of them and their efforts were part of a larger, if somewhat amorphous, social movement to promote accountability.

The establishment of the Nader-inspired organizations was soon followed by other public-interest groups, some of which were even more specifically designed to assist ethical resisters. One of the most successful was the Government Accountability Project, organized in the early 1970s by a group of young attorneys to defend and investigate problems of national security resisters, such as Daniel Ellsberg. By the mid-1970s, their mission had expanded to include a larger set of issues concerning waste and mismanagement in government bureaucracies and other large organizations.[51] In 1977, GAP (then called the Project on Official Illegality) followed the Nader model and called a second national conference on whistleblowing, bringing together federal employees, legislators, lawyers, journalists, union representatives, and others to explore ways to protect the rights of government employees who disclose abuse. This meeting provided a widespread network in Washington and gave whistleblowers an institutional home.

While reiterating many of the themes of the earlier meeting,[52] the conference went beyond praise of heroic individuals to consider the consequences of confronting large organizations and proposed new mechanisms of support for whistleblowers. The participants analyzed the continued lack of real protection for government workers who speak out, and emphasized that the price of ethical dedication too often entailed loss of job, destruction of family security, and the bitterness that derives from knowing that corrupt superiors continue to pursue successful careers. Ralph Nader spoke forcefully about the need to establish a publicly supported fund to provide legal protection for those who suffered retaliation. Ernest Fitzgerald recounted his nine-year battle to convince the Pentagon that patronage for defense contractors violates the public trust. Other whistleblowers told of their experiences exposing corruption and illegal activities and detailed the reprisals they had suffered.

The GAP-sponsored conference, like its predecessor, clearly labeled the whistleblowers as crucial actors in an ongoing drama whose outcome could not be foreseen. To protect them, laws guaranteeing freedom of speech had to be strengthened. The move toward greater government secrecy and the classification of millions of documents had to be repudiated because it allowed agencies to mask many questionable activities.

Because the struggle for protection of whistleblowers and more accountable government promised to be long and bitter, GAP and other groups knew they had to build organizations that could directly assist whistleblowers in all sectors of the society. As an activist organization, GAP could no longer remain tied to the Institute of Policy Studies, the liberal academic think tank that had spawned it. The IPS encouraged the split because it feared expensive lawsuits by nuclear power plant builders in response to GAP's success in closing down several plants. Once GAP became independent, its leaders decided that it was important not to identify with a partisan political position.[53]

Louis Clark—the executive director of GAP, an attorney, and a former minister—led the organization in defending scores of ethical resisters. Within five years, GAP became well known to government agencies in Washington and highly respected by congressional staff; it also received substantial media attention, which helped to alert new resisters to this resource. GAP was able to win support from a series of foundations which ensured its financial survival.

In the intervening years, GAP has defended a diverse group of whistleblowers, ranging from a federal meat grader who was dismissed for disclosing the use of bribery to misgrade low-quality beef to a scientist who criticized the swine flu inoculation program, accurately predicting that a large-scale program would produce severe illness and death. GAP became particularly expert in defending dozens of resisters in nuclear power plants who testified to serious problems in their construction. As a result, GAP has been denounced by those in the nuclear industry who argue that the organization is nothing more than a thinly disguised group of antinuclear political activists and left-wing radicals. To maintain its credibility, the organization has taken no political position on nuclear power or other controversial issues, but has argued that its goal is to ensure safe construction.[54]

By the 1980s, GAP's independent strategy had proved successful. In the course of a few years, it had become the central organization dedicated to the defense of whistleblowers. The staff members gathered experience that enabled them to offer guidance and to establish a network of resisters who could support each other. They provided legal counsel for those who faced retaliation, and used a productive relationship with Antioch Law School to recruit legal interns and future staff members. This program was the brainchild of a young law student, Tom Devine, who later became GAP's legal director. Further, their very existence reinforced the legitimacy of ethical resistance by those otherwise isolated in a hostile work environment. One resister's wife told us that she had GAP's number on her refrigerator, and that it is comforting to know that she could call staff members any time she felt overwhelmed by her husband's case. Like her family and church, GAP was a haven during a dark time when she and her husband felt vulnerable and alone.

GAP, the Project on Military Procurement, Nader's groups, the Coalition to Stop Government Waste, along with several other groups provide an ongoing forum for ethical resisters.[55] Mostly located in Washington, D.C., these public-interest organizations have contacts with congressional committees and the press who publicize and act on their complaints. They have helped transform actions of isolated and vulnerable individuals into a burgeoning social movement.

Protective Legislation

Legal developments in the 1970s also served to legitimize the role of the whistleblower. When Congress held hearings on irregularities in Medicare, Medicaid, and the General Service Administration in 1977 and 1978, members were shocked by the extent of fraud. Witnesses repeatedly testified to the ongoing use of kickbacks, bid riggings, false billings, and illegally inflated costs. Several major federal agencies seemed to be out of control, costing the taxpayers millions of dollars. In an attempt to respond to these elaborate fraudulent schemes, Congress passed the Inspector General Act that established an inspector general in twelve major federal departments and agencies. The IG integrated previously dispersed auditing and investigating functions to facilitate the uncovering of illegal activities in the government.[56]

The act went to great lengths to establish the independence of the IG's. Like federal judges, they are presidential appointees, who are confirmed by the Senate. They are to report only to the head of an agency (for example, the secretaries of Agriculture, Labor, Interior or the directors of NASA, EPA, or GSA) and semiannually to Congress. To achieve their mission of promoting economy, efficiency, and effectiveness in the administration of federal programs, section 7 of the act establishing the inspector general's office made specific provisions for the inspector general to receive and investigate information from any employee alleging violations of the laws and regulations, or charging mismanagement, waste of funds, abuse of authority, or substantial and specific danger to public health and safety.[57]

These were precisely the kinds of charges that ethical resisters were making, and the law now provided a specific office to hear and investigate employees' concerns about such abuse. In language that sounded highly protective when it was debated and passed, the act specified that "the Inspector General shall not, after receipt of a complaint or information from an employee, disclose the identity of the employee without the consent of the employee." It further guaranteed that no personnel action could be taken against any employees who disclose information to the inspector general.[58]

Further protection seemed to be guaranteed by the Civil Service Reform Act passed in 1978 which established the Merit Systems Protection Board to ensure fairness and high standards for government employees. When this new law used identical language to the Inspector General Act to protect workers who disclose violations, reformers and whistleblowers believed that a new era of protection for ethical resisters had been born. The Office of the Special Counsel of the Merit Systems Protection Board was authorized to assist any employee who faced retaliation for disclosing violations or abuse, and thus gave a further institutional base to the law's explicit statement that whistleblowers are vital to the effectiveness of public service.[59]

As we shall see, the results often fell far short of the expectations. Ethical resisters found that when they took information of illegal or unethical practice to the Inspector General or to the Office of the Special Counsel, their confidentiality was often violated, the investigations were frequently inadequate, or the resisters themselves were defined as malcontents. As a result, disappointingly few cases were resolved in favor of the ethical resister. In studies by the Merit Systems Protection Board in 1980 and 1983, most federal employees reported that they knew of waste and fraud but would not speak up. They either believed that nothing would be done to correct the wrongdoing or were convinced that they risked reprisals. Although the passage of the Civil Service Reform Act and the Inspector General Act did not make ethical resistance a commonplace event for the majority,[60] it did initially help to give a sense of legitimacy to people who felt they could not remain silent despite the risks to their careers. Notwithstanding the failure of these new agencies to protect ethical resisters consistently, their very creation served to signal employees for the first time that responsible workers might come forward when confronted with lawless behavior in the government.

Workers in Private Industry

Historically, the government played no role in regulating the relationship between employer and employee in the private sector. Both Congress and the courts recognized a doctrine known as "employment-at-will" that allowed management to discharge employees for any or no reason. This classic underpinning of private enterprise provided the ultimate flexibility to employers in determining their needs and in hiring and firing whomever they pleased.[61]

Although there are still vast areas of employer discretion, over the last several decades a variety of laws has increased protection for workers by placing special limits on employment-at-will. In the 1930s, the National Labor Relations Act prohibited firing workers for union activity. Thirty years later, the Civil Rights Act prohibited any form of discrimination in the workplace based on race, religion, sex, or age. These two historic laws increased employee protection for specific purposes.[62]

As we pointed out in chapter 1 (see pages 12–15), when the interest in regulating environmental quality, consumer rights, and worker safety emerged in the 1970s, Congress extended protection to workers in the private sector to help assure enforcement of the new regulations. Under the Energy Reorganization Act of 1974, for example, any employee in a nuclear plant who reports violations of the mandated safety regulations to the Nuclear Regulatory Commission has the same protection from retaliation as do federal employees. Similarly, the Clean Air and Water Act covers those who report violations to the Environmental Protection

Agency. All of these laws established agencies that monitor the regulations and give concerned workers a forum for their allegations. Several states passed whistleblower protection laws that go even further. Connecticut, Maine, and Michigan were among the first to guarantee protection to all employees, not just those in regulated industries, who report any violations to a government body or assist in a government investigation. Despite this dynamic and expanding area of guaranteed protection for workers in industry, many who disclosed wrongdoing were dismissed. They had the choice of filing a complaint with the Department of Labor for an administrative hearing on unlawful discharge or bringing suit in the courts. But the legal process is slow and expensive, and it is difficult to obtain remedy for retaliation in the courts. Nonetheless, since the 1970s, legal protection of employees in the private sphere has expanded considerably. Twenty-six states have granted a public policy exception that limits an employer's right to fire at will, further legitimizing the role of the employee who refuses to comply when management insists on engaging in lawless behavior.[63]

Taken together, the creation of the Inspector General and the Merit System Protection Board, the expanded legislation prohibiting retaliation against bona fide whistleblowers, and the growing use of public policy exceptions to limit the employment-at-will doctrine all served to provide a legal infrastructure to protect ethical resisters. As individuals began to come forward and test the possibilities, many found that the protections were still inadequate and filled with loopholes.

Nonetheless, strong and internalized values led some employees to adhere to the guidelines that protect worker safety, public health, and fiscal responsibility. These values were embedded in their professional ethics, their religious beliefs, and their ties to the community. When asked by their superiors to discard these commitments, employees were caught in a crucial conflict between the requirements of the organization and their own definition of appropriate behavior. The resolution of this conflict and the unfolding of their ethical odyssey are the subjects of the following chapters.

Chapter 3

Professionals as Ethical Resisters

PROFESSIONALISM has come under considerable scrutiny and criticism in recent years. Traditionally, the American Medical Association, the American Bar Association, and similar organizations representing the interests of other professions have stressed their commitment to merit and service as the hallmark of their special status. By emphasizing merit as the critical component of the modern professions, leaders differentiate their fields from business or the trades where the work can be learned on the job. The professions require rigorous graduate training based on a body of scientific knowledge and a theoretical orientation. Their organizations monitor entrance into educational institutions and license only the most qualified graduates. Achievement, not patronage, has been the required avenue to success.[1]

In addition, the spokesmen for the professions have claimed that they differ from conventional occupations by their emphasis on disinterested service—an ideal requiring practitioners to serve the greater public good. According to this belief, doctors, lawyers, scientists, engineers, and others are entitled to a reasonable remuneration for their services but can never make their professional decisions solely to support the profit motive. Poor people are not denied necessary medical care, nor do scientists falsify experimental results in the interests of personal gain. In practice, this ideal should have resulted in a strong ethical commitment to serve the needy, regardless of their ability to pay, to do pro bono work, and to stand as guardians of the public interest ensuring that responsible decision making and quality production are never subordinate to demand for greater profit or efficiency.[2]

These central commitments, according to the professionals, have distinguished their fields from all other occupations—managers, workers, storekeepers, or skilled craftsmen. The lengthy training, based on scientific method, argue leaders, provides practitioners with a core of expertise entitling them to the workplace autonomy that is at the heart of their special identity. Toward this goal professionals have sought to make themselves sovereign, keeping regulation and government intervention away from their fields.[3] It is the professional organizations, backed by state laws, that set up educational requirements, establish licensing exams, and investigate misconduct. Such self-regulation has been considered crucial to ensure the informed, independent judgment of trained experts.

The new scholarship has challenged many of the premises promulgated by the professions and no longer accepts them at face value. Re-examination of the work of physicians, lawyers, scientists, and engineers has uncovered elaborate efforts earlier in the century to eliminate women and minorities from professional schools and even to bar from opportunities for advancement those who overcame the educational barriers and quotas. Scholars have also described the bitter battles in which the professions sought to extend their authority well beyond their areas of training. Physicians, for example, have laid claim to expertise in areas ranging from alcoholism to childbirth, even when there was little evidence that they have superior knowledge. They have sought to eliminate or subordinate competing health professionals, such as midwives or osteopaths, even when they cannot ensure that their own treatment is superior.[4] All of this discriminatory behavior occurred in the face of the professions' public assertions about access and advancement based exclusively on merit.[5]

Moreover, insurance companies, government officials, and other analysts have given critical scrutiny to the elaborate forms of specialization and excessively high salaries that have come to characterize many of the professions. These observers have noted a strong pull toward major urban centers where doctors develop highly specialized practices for well-to-do patients, where lawyers join high-priced corporate law firms, and where engineers select lucrative management positions over jobs in manufacturing and product development. The argument that professionals are disinterested and service-oriented has been called into question amid reports of salaries that often rise into the six figures. Critics asked whether the demand for autonomy is necessary to support the highest quality of expert services for the public, as the spokesmen insist, or whether it serves primarily to buttress the professionals' rights to focus on elite clienteles and to charge high fees.[6]

Consistent with this far-ranging critique, scholars have also emphasized that many individual professionals have internalized the best of the professional ideology and remain deeply dedicated to serving the public good. Certain practitioners have always done outstanding pro bono work, served the poor, and insisted on the highest quality of service. But advancement in the profession has not usually depended on such strict adherence to ideal standards. While certain values have been professed in the graduate schools, few committees have insisted on or monitored the breadth and range of service contributions.[7]

Many critics of the professions have assumed that the typical professional is an independent practitioner, working on a fee-for-service basis and determining not only the conditions of work but also its very nature. For some fields, like medicine and law, this may often have been the historic reality. For others, like social work or engineering, the work has traditionally been located in a bureaucratic setting where professional autonomy has always been restricted and has competed with other organizational needs, such as profits for shareholders, limited public budgets, and civil service regulations. Increasingly since the Second World War, the majority of professionals have not practiced independently and have found themselves pressured to subordinate their expert judgment to the demands of corporate and government hierarchies. Conversely, professionals have been keenly aware that their expert knowledge is important, and many have tried to negotiate for greater independence in return for their services. This tension remains a central issue in the operation of contemporary large bureaucracies.[8]

Ethical resisters are among those who have taken the ideology of their professions most seriously. The scientists, lawyers, physicians, engineers, and social workers whom we have studied were all socialized during their professional training to a high set of standards for appropriate behavior. They had developed a strong commitment to upholding professional values that emphasize the significance of making decisions on the basis of their expertise and with primary responsibility to their constituents.

When asked to subordinate these values to meet the requirements of the bureaucracy, many conjured up a "red line," a point they could not cross. For them, additional profit for the company or a promotion for a supervisor or the demands of a designated schedule could never rationalize compromising their judgments about appropriate actions to protect the health and safety of workers, clients, patients, or the public at large. Their definition of professional conduct was integral to their sense of what a good person does who holds a position of trust. They rejected a definition of professional ethics that required only a narrow range of responsibilities to colleagues and clients. Their brand of professionalism was enriched by a broad obligation to others deriving from humane, religious, and communal values. For them, a betrayal of those principles meant an erosion of their definition of self. As idealistic as it may sound, they espoused an uncompromising commitment to use their skills for the well-being of others.

The ethical resisters' ideology of responsible professional behavior developed in graduate school and was tested and reinforced in early employment.* Many looked back nostalgically to school and jobs where they had been rewarded for their competence and their dedication to service. One physician described his background which had led him to believe that medicine was a profession of impeccable standards:

> I grew up with the concept that medicine is a noble profession. I spent some fourteen years, or one-quarter of my present life span, cloistered in an ivory tower. For four years I was a medical student. Eight years were spent in postdoctoral (or residency) training, and the remaining years I was a member of the faculty of the medical college. Throughout these years I was exposed to all the very best that medicine had to offer. . . . Naively I came to believe that the totality of my personal experience was a true and accurate representation of the reality of medical practice.[10]

Similarly, a lawyer spoke longingly of his employment in two major corporations, in each of which he had worked under the direction of men whose integrity he respected highly. They had helped him refine his approach to attorney-client relations; and when he later encountered illegal activities by the management of another corporation, he continued to believe that ethical practice was possible and defined himself as a

*Eliot Freidson argues that the work environment is even more important than the socialization that takes place in the graduate school.[9]

"corporate animal." He hoped one day to regain the opportunity to work in a business that allowed high professional standards. "Perhaps," he added wistfully, "I am hoping to capture what is now long gone."[11]

Others, not quite so fortunate in their first jobs, had changed positions precisely because they had rejected the unethical acts of their employers. One engineer left private industry when he saw safety standards so compromised as to result in the death of several construction workers. He sought a government position where he hoped that the profit motive would not make it difficult to maintain standards. In a reverse situation, a physician resigned from the Federal Drug Administration over ethical disagreements about the use of a dangerous product and went to work in private industry where she expected greater autonomy.

Several people in our study regretfully learned that their professional assessment sometimes had to be tempered or even submerged because opposition was not welcome in organizations largely characterized by hierarchy and the absence of a democratic culture.[12] Their superiors had a tendency to define dissent as insubordination and disobedience as rebellion. From the professionals' perspective, the demand for compliance was in direct contradiction with their beliefs in their independent judgment based on their special expertise and training. Whenever they found themselves in situations where the management of large organizations made decisions that resulted in unsafe products or fraudulent acts by putting bureaucratic imperatives ahead of expert judgment and values, some professionals felt they had the obligation to resist. This obligation was central in confronting a powerful and often centralized authority. Sometimes colleagues who shared their determination joined them; at other times, they stood virtually alone. In either case, they forcefully advocated the ideology they had absorbed in their professional training: the credo of disinterested service and autonomous professional judgment which can never be subordinated to material gains or the illegitimate orders of superiors. Furthermore, they believed that those who acquiesce can rightly be held personally liable by potential victims.

Unfortunately for these professionals, their respective professional associations were not willing to step forward and support their positions. Ethical resisters have not found spirited support from the local branch of the bar association, the engineering organizations, or the boards of medical societies. Whatever the lofty ideals professed in graduation speeches, collective action to support those who have put themselves at risk has been rare, according to the testimony of those ethical resisters we have studied and to scholars in the field.[13]

Some ethical resisters never even considered approaching a professional organization for fear of becoming enmeshed in yet another bureaucracy. Others gave some consideration to seeking such assistance, but decided against it when they noted that some ethics committee members were employed by large corporations that had skirted the law. Others did seek active intervention of their local societies, only to find that their appeal was "put on the back burner." They began to suspect that the very groups presumably committed to maintaining professional ethics had an even larger interest in assuring good relationships with government or corporate officials whose actions the ethical resisters were calling into question.

The cases we discuss in this chapter reveal how professional values have impelled ethical resistance in the fields of nuclear engineering and medicine. Those values are highly significant despite recent criticism of professionalism itself and the failure of the major professional organizations to live up to their own ideals. These cases also show the significance of collegial support and the availability of alternative authorities as central features of resisters' ability to implement the professions' highest ideals.

Demetrios Basdekas and the Nuclear Regulatory Commission

The experience of one engineer reveals the chasm between the requirements of bureaucratic authority and those of professional integrity. For Demetrios Basdekas, expertise and autonomy were the major components of his professional identification, entailing a responsibility for the common good which he fully expected to characterize the climate at the Atomic Energy Commission. Later he came to distinguish dedicated engineers from bureaucrats who were all too willing to compromise for short-term gains. His professional ideology not only motivated his decision toward ethical resistance, but also helped him explain why the risks he had taken were necessary as he faced reprisals for his actions. For him professional ethics require active concern with decisions that will have an impact on the population now and in the foreseeable future.

Demetrios Basdekas told us of his early years in Greece, his migration at the age of twenty-three to the United States, and his engineering education at Texas A and M, where he received both a bachelor's and a master's degree in electrical engineering with a minor in nuclear engineering:

> During my student days at Texas A and M, I had my first opportunity to work in the nuclear sciences. My initial ambition was to be able to control a nuclear reactor remotely in outer space. I thought the whole field of nuclear reactors was quite a challenge, and I made sure that I took all the courses in this area, which included quite a few focusing on control theory. I started the work early so I got practical experience in the problems associated with the design and operation of nuclear reactors. I got my operator's license in 1962.[14]

Basdekas had been delighted when the Atomic Energy Commission (later the Nuclear Regulatory Commission) offered him a job in 1972 in the Division of Systems Safety, and viewed the opportunity as the culmination of all of his professional goals:

> After finishing my studies I had several jobs in both government and industry and I would say that the most challenging one and the most useful one to me was at Los Alamos where I spent about three years. In 1972 I came to the Washington area and joined the Atomic Energy Commission in the Office of Regulation. I began working on applications to license and construct nuclear power plants. That has been a major focus of my work until the present time.[15]

His wife, Rita, on the other hand, was far more ambivalent about his choice of jobs. She feared government bureaucracy and its requirements for conformity and knew that her husband was not the kind of person to go along. This had certainly been his reaction several years earlier when, working in private industry, he found that his colleagues and superiors had "fudged" technical data in order to get a continuance of their grant. Basdekas had felt extremely uncomfortable and had jokingly raised objections to "cheating on procedures":

> After all, to falsify technical data is morally wrong in my view. It is fraud to do such things in order to win a grant. What is the difference

between that and going to the bank and securing a loan under false pretenses? When the issue of fudging data came up, I did raise a facetious point about it, but the joke did not go over very well. My supervisor asked me whether I had noticed that I was the only one laughing. Maybe it was a poor joke. The point I wanted to make was that I had trouble accepting that kind of practice. At a minimum, I hoped that they would not come and ask me to do something like that. Although I was involved in the process, it was out of my hands. I gave them some material, and they changed it before it went out. That hit me as being very important.[16]

Although Basdekas had not changed the group's actions, he had set his own standards and refused to allow his ethics to be eroded. While he had not yet been ready to take a firm stand and openly defy his superiors or confront his co-workers, he was, in effect, rehearsing for future action as he formulated images of boundaries that must never be crossed and values that had to be affirmed.

About a year after joining the Nuclear Regulatory Commission, his enthusiasm for the agency slowly turned to grave concern as he gained greater insight into its procedures for licensing nuclear power plants. He felt that the NRC was under extreme pressure to grant licenses without having sufficient guarantees that control systems would be effective in the event of an accident. He knew that it was imperative that each plant have a fail-safe way to shut down operations in an emergency before radioactive material leaked into the atmosphere:

My first encounter with things that didn't make sense came as part of my asking questions about plant design, especially in reference to control systems. I raised several questions to be sent to the utility companies, but my supervisors refused to approve them. They said, "Don't ask these questions." I said, "What do you mean?" This question was intended to give me some basis to decide whether the system is designed properly. Is it safe or not? The control systems in a nuclear plant are extremely important, and they are giving us grief today, including that at Three Mile Island.[17]

Basdekas was not the first person to find that there was serious undermining of those who attempted to regulate safety systems. Throughout the 1960s, a strong feeling developed among industry leaders that nuclear power could not survive economically if safety regulations were too stringent. Industry's top executives continually requested easier licensing procedures and more leniency on siting plants closer to their customers. Corporate representatives participated in drawing up licensing criteria and continually downplayed the need for basic accident research.[18] The priority for the Atomic Energy Commission was to ensure commercial viability and United States leadership in the field. Safety was relegated to a subordinate position. In the 1960s and early 1970s, for example, the agency spent hundreds of millions of dollars to bolster the economic possibilities, while budgeting about $35,000,000 a year for safety research.[19]

At the same time, the government agency deliberately suppressed emerging findings about potential dangers of nuclear energy. When Brookhaven National Laboratory completed a study about the dangers of a meltdown, the AEC kept the findings secret. Employees charged that their reports were being censored, and top scientists commissioned by the AEC to study health effects of radiation later found themselves stripped of budget and staff when they recommended a substantial reduction in the allowable amount of radiation released on the general population.[20]

By the time Basdekas came to work for the NRC and began raising questions, a long-standing pattern of minimizing safety issues was in place. Industry consistently blamed environmentalists for delays that resulted in spiraling costs, and argued that endless restrictions undermined their progress. Despite systematic studies by the Rand Corporation and others that documented management problems and an immature technology as the most serious causes of rising budgets, officials continued to harp on the costs of environmental regulation. In 1974 and 1975, when eight utilities canceled orders for nuclear reactors and instead returned to the cheaper coal-fired plants, William R. Gould, chairman of the Atomic Industrial Forum, testified before the Joint Congressional Committee on Atomic Energy. He argued that speedier licensing procedures were crucial in order to prompt new orders for reactors:

> When the AEC insists on a design change after a construction permit has been issued, it may well mean replacing a piece of equipment or a system that requires so long a lead time for delivery that it prolongs the construction schedule. Delays mean price increases and erode competitiveness.[21]

Both Presidents Nixon and Ford essentially supported industry's viewpoint, thus further strengthening the effort to de-emphasize safety regulations.

In this atmosphere, it was not surprising that Basdekas found his superiors unreceptive to his concerns. But he would not relent or remain silent. His wife sensed that he was coming to a crossroads that would have unforeseen consequences for their entire family. Her expression during our visit, years later, bore witness to the costs the family had paid for his resolution. She spoke softly of her resentment at the path he had chosen: "Everybody has to do what he thinks is right, but sometimes when you are standing back and watching him do it, it is difficult even though you know that this is the only thing that he can do." Like Rita Basdekas, many spouses were ambivalent about the possibility of resistance, and some actively advised their husbands or wives to exercise great caution before taking actions that might harm the family. When the situation at work deteriorated and tension and worry permeated the household, most spouses recognized that whistleblowing might be the only choice even though they were deeply apprehensive about the consequences. Rita Basdekas defined the quandary: "There is no choice. It is like there is a highway and you have to go right or left. You know that the person cannot live with himself if he goes in one direction, but you know if you turn down that other road, it is going to be awfully hard."[22]

Demetrios Basdekas's growing disenchantment reflected the predicament of many other resisters who did not relish challenging their superiors. Yet they, too, slowly became alienated from procedures that did not make sense, from orders that they refrain from asking certain questions. They rejected the implication that they should operate solely as narrowly trained specialists, concentrating on their specific task while ignoring the design of unsafe airplane brakes, the production of dangerous automobiles, or the abuse of hospital patients. Basdekas, like many others, could not fathom how his superiors could ignore or minimize such profoundly disturbing problems, and these reactions of presumably responsible authorities began to whittle away at his trust in their competence and integrity.[23]

Basdekas and most other ethical resisters joined their organizations with enthusiasm and the conviction that they could significantly aid the achievement of a mission. They were not alienated or even cynical employees but, on the contrary, trusted their superiors. Indeed, such trust was a cornerstone of their definition of a predictable and worthy social order. When this trust was eroded, they sensed they were at a crossroads. In one direction lay obedience to authority and likely career advancement; in the other, the affirmation of their own professional and human values and the dangers of retribution from powerful adversaries. Basdekas cogently explained his inability to take the safer route:

> As I was struggling to get my points across, I was assigned to review the Clinch River breeder reactor plant. Again, I asked questions because they were making claims about their protection system. My questions were approved, and they were sent out, but there were no answers.
>
> Apparently there were no answers to my questions because the justification for the design of the protection systems did not exist. Nonetheless the plant wanted a license. I was expected to go ahead and give my approval to the plant design. I was now under pressure from my own management to come up with the report basically saying that the plant was okay. Go ahead and give them a license. I could not do it.[24]

The Clinch River breeder reactor was intended to represent a major technological breakthrough for nuclear energy. The first nuclear plants had been light-water reactors because they could be built quickly in a highly competitive environment. From the beginning, the AEC wanted a more mature technology and heavily subsidized the research to develop the breeder reactor because it simultaneously produced electricity and plutonium for bombs. If large amounts of plutonium could be produced, then U.S. uranium reserves could be protected, and an inexhaustible supply of low-cost energy was a real possibility.[25]

After extensive investment in research and intense competition among the industry's giants, the AEC awarded the major contract to build the breeder reactor to Westinghouse in 1972. The proposed cost was $700,000,000, and the site would be Clinch River, Tennessee. Almost immediately, delays and rising costs became a serious problem. Within a decade, the Government Accounting Office estimated that the cost had increased to $6,000,000,000, and the plant's reliability was seriously challenged.[26]

But in 1976 the pressure to assist the project and minimize questions was overwhelming. Basdekas was aware of these pressures but felt his professional obligation strongly. He had to validate that the control system would operate in the event of a malfunction. Basdekas declared that he was more than an ordinary civil service employee: he was an engineer who believed his own knowledge and expertise superseded the desire to contain costs for Westinghouse or even to ensure commercial viability for breeder reactor technology. Basdekas soon learned that a sense of responsibility does not necessarily guarantee the power to sustain one's judgments:

> I said to myself: "Look, you are at a crossroads and you have to decide which way to go. You can either roll over and play dead or stand up and say what you think." I hit the wall, the red line. I could not go beyond that line. I was being asked to become a party to an act of fraud on the public where health and safety are concerned.
>
> Management's response was to remove me, to assign a greenhorn to do the job. I was simply told that I was no longer responsible for this part of the work. As a result of this, I and other engineers who were performing in similar situations decided to take our case to the Congress and to the public. That was in the fall of 1976.[27]

Basdekas's rejection of agency policy and the pressure his superiors placed upon him to distort his own belief system puts him in the category of professionals who are not simply content to go along with management decisions despite the heavy cost of resistance. Psychologist Stanley Milgram's classic experiment on obedience to authority conducted in the 1960s documented the depth of his subjects' willingness to comply with orders even when they despised the implications of their actions. In one telling paragraph, Milgram summarized the significance of his findings:

> This is, perhaps, the most fundamental lesson of our study: ordinary people, simply doing their jobs, and without any particular hostility on their part, can become agents in a terrible destructive process. Moreover, even when the destructive effects of their work become patently clear, and they're asked to carry out actions incompatible with fundamental standards of morality, relatively few people have the resources needed to resist authority. A variety of inhibitions against disobeying authority come into play and successfully keep the person in his place.[28]

Basdekas is not an "ordinary" man by Milgram's definition. He did have the personal "resources" necessary to voice his dissent to agency policy and to disobey his superiors when he felt his professional judgment under attack. His training and ideology stood between him and those who would order him to acquiesce to improper standards of plant safety.

Basdekas's disenchantment was exacerbated by the humiliation he felt when his superiors took him off the job and replaced him with an inexperienced engineer who would comply with their orders. This reaction was not unique. Many employees who protested their superiors' policies were punished for their dissent. They could then "back off" and re-enter the fold or persist and seek additional means of protest. In 1976, the NRC had no procedures to allow concerned employees to air their differences. Basdekas faced a choice. He decided to move ahead and publicize his view that nuclear plants had insufficient safeguards in the event of an accident. His professional ideology provided the appropriate vocabulary and symbols to put his private concerns and anger into a larger context.

To take such action, Basdekas had to convince himself that he had a legitimate interest in the potential dangers of poorly constructed nuclear power plants. He felt that his education and experience gave him the expertise and competence to make judgments that contradicted his superiors:

> In the nuclear business you are dealing with effects that can manifest themselves twenty or thirty years from now and have an impact on unborn children. I decided not to go along. I accepted it as a reasonable price for me to pay. I was an engineer who had a good paycheck coming in, but at the same time I felt an essential responsibility that came along with it. The public out there had their trust in me, and without sounding too melodramatic, I took an oath to do good for them.[29]

By any rational calculation of self-interest, Basdekas should have either denied any awareness of the potential danger or backed off when his superiors disagreed with him. After voicing his opinion, he could readily have deferred and allowed them to accept responsibility for their decision, but he refused to accept this role. He enacted his belief in professional responsibility and judgment and sought out United States senators who, he hoped, shared his concerns.[30]

The decision to challenge directly the authority of superiors is the most difficult one for an employee of a large bureaucratic organization to undertake. Milgram points out that the step from dissent to disobedience is long and only a few people are able to accomplish it. Most others are content to voice their concern and then believe that they have done what is possible. They feel reassured that in their hearts they are on the right side. Milgram demonstrates that the moral issues remain untended unless thoughts are converted into action:

> Between thoughts, words, and the critical step of disobeying a malevolent authority lies another ingredient, the capacity for transforming beliefs and values into action. Some subjects were totally convinced of the wrongness of what they were doing but could not bring themselves to make an open break with authority. Some derived satisfaction from their thoughts and felt that—within themselves, at least—they had been on the side of the angels. What they failed to realize is that subjective feelings are largely irrelevant to the moral issue at hand so long as they are not transformed into action. Political control is effected through action. The attitudes of the guards at a concentration camp are of no consequence when in fact they are allowing the slaughter of innocent men to take place before them. . . . Time and time again in the experiment people disvalued what they were doing but could not muster the inner resources to translate their values into action.[31]

Basdekas knew of the three GE engineers who had resigned in protest and of Robert Pollard, a colleague at the NRC, who had joined the GE employees in publicly decrying the hazards of dozens of plants then in operation.[32] (See pages 28–29.) Basdekas was well aware that they had received a hostile reception from the congressmen who had interviewed them, and hoped that Senator Abraham Ribicoff of Connecticut would be more receptive:

> I was apprehensive when I called Senator Ribicoff's office. Nevertheless I was determined to see it through. I talked to one of his staff members, explained why I was calling, and asked for help in bringing this to congressional attention. I felt that I had reached the end of what I had been able to do on my own. I needed help from outside. The committee staff got very busy, and Senator Ribicoff assigned Senator [John] Glenn [of Ohio] to follow this specifically. Glenn was chairman of the subcommittee dealing with nuclear matters.
>
> Basically Congress said we have this allegation and we need answers to certain things. Now it was Congress asking the questions. From that point on, my agency got into high gear and submitted a report. A lot of paperwork went back and forth.
>
> After I was interviewed by the committee staff I reported back to

some of my co-workers who had expressed their own safety concerns. At that point, four joined me. They were willing to speak to the committee and to speak publicly. The committee decided to hold a hearing.[33]

Collegial support was essential. It strengthened the case for a public hearing and validated Basdekas's own testimony. He could not be discounted as an eccentric engineer at odds with his superiors and colleagues or with an overblown image of his own expertise. The group support provided both emotional sustenance and a confirming view of his professional assessment. The fact that four other engineers were willing to confront their superiors, and put themselves on the line, helped to mitigate the terrible sense of isolation and fear of reprisal that often prevents employees from challenging organizational policies.[34]

Stanley Milgram's findings underscore the significance of ethical solidarity provided by the support of peers: "The mutual support provided by men for each other is the strongest bulwark we have against the excesses of authority."[35] Milgram found it the single most significant factor in facilitating resistance to the illegitimate commands of authority figures. Such solidarity, unfortunately, did not extend to the intervention of professional organizations. Basdekas considered approaching his professional association, the Institute For Electrical and Electronic Engineers. Yet he feared that its ethics committee was dominated by engineers employed by the same corporations that were doing business with the NRC. He assumed they would have a conflict of interest that would prevent them from supporting his allegations. Basdekas was certain that neither the IEEE nor any other professional organization had taken a determined stand on ethical controversies involving its members and management. The reluctance to become involved in corporate or government controversies and the fear of potential suits had led to a hands-off approach.

During the last dozen years, Demetrios Basdekas has remained in the NRC, battling to gain greater attention for his concerns about plant safety. He has continued his contacts with Congress, written letters and Op-Ed pieces for major newspapers and has appeared before the NRC commissioners. Like that of most ethical resisters, his career has been seriously curtailed. He repeatedly states that he has done all he can from inside the organization and must soon give up on the fight. Yet he never does. Basdekas has not simply been a lost voice in the bureaucratic maze.

His concerns have meshed with those of thousands of other professionals and workers in the nuclear field. Even the NRC commissioners have praised him for his forthright stand. In a hearing held in 1982, one commissioner made it clear that Basdekas has had an impact: "Let me preface [my questions] by saying that I certainly agree that as far as the control system issue goes, from what I have seen, you have been a leader in trying to get that addressed, and I recognize that it has been very difficult to move that." The chairman, Nunzio Palladino, added his own observations:

> I think you have gotten a long way. I think you have influenced this agency effectively and properly in very significant ways. So I have difficulty under-standing what the frustration is. You have caused some very marked and very important improvements in our operations and I would like to take advantage of your thinking in a professional way. I find it very difficult to debate in the *New York Times* [where Basdekas had published an Op-Ed article criticizing the NRC].[36]

One staff member had earlier summarized Basdekas's impact succinctly. After the accident at Three Mile Island, he said: "I think in the largest sense, Demetrios has for a long time pointed out a problem which we share today a whole lot more than we shared several years ago. And to that extent he deserves credit for being a prophet."[37]

Doctors Stand Together: Mary McAnaw, Betsy Brothers, and the Veterans Administration

The combination of professional ideology, breach of trust by manage-ment, and ethical solidarity that drove Demetrios Basdekas to challenge his superiors at the NRC is repeated in the experience of other practition-ers. In another notable case, a group of health care professionals at a Veterans Administration hospital, fearing that immediate damage could be done to vulnerable patients, united to protest a dangerous drug study. Unlike Basdekas, these professionals did not have to look into the future and imagine the fate of unborn generations. Their responsibility lay with incapacitated veterans who trusted the medical staff with their care.

Professional ethics drove these employees to seek a speedy remedy. At their center was a forty-two-year-old surgeon, a mother of six children.

Dr. Mary McAnaw, chief of surgery at the Veterans Administration Hospital in Leavenworth, Kansas, had a traditional Catholic education. She describes herself as a "tomboy" in her teens, who was determined to do what her male relatives and friends did. She had thought of a nursing career but decided that she would not do very well taking orders from physicians. She attended the University of Cincinnati Medical School as one of four women in a class of ninety-six. While McAnaw did not feel any overt discrimination against her in medical school, she always believed that she had to work harder than the men to get ahead. After graduation, she spent two difficult but satisfying years in Ethiopia with the Peace Corps. She returned to the United States, accepted a residency at the VA hospital, and married Dr. Mike Brigg, an anesthesiologist.[38]

At the end of the Second World War, the Veterans Administration had sought to expand its facilities and overcome its reputation for corruption and poor service. The leadership of the VA developed affiliations with medical schools throughout the country, and VA hospitals became centers for research and the training of residents. To maintain this much-needed tie, the VA agreed to have medical school committees approve all physician appointments, and emphasized the doctors' control over the quality of medical care even in a federally funded bureaucracy.[39]

For McAnaw this program provided an excellent opportunity for specialization. In the 1960s, she recalled, there were few surgical residencies for women. She liked training under the chief surgeon, who was tough and talented in keeping the administration from criticizing or interfering with his unit. She learned to dislike administrative intervention and to keep medical diagnosis in the province of the doctors. After giving birth to the first of six children, she entered private practice on a part-time basis. Within a few months, she returned to the Veterans Administration system which seemed like a reasonable place for a full-time career that would still allow time for family responsibilities. When the post of chief of surgery became available, she accepted it and became the first woman to hold this position. As a board-certified surgeon, she had the credentials for the job and could help the hospital maintain its residency program.

Unlike Demetrios Basdekas, Mary McAnaw did not have a romanticized notion of the mission of the VA hospital. Working there was not a lifelong ambition but rather a convenient appointment allowing her to pursue her career and meet her family's needs. From her vantage point, she was able to see the deficiencies as well as the talents of the administration. She characterized several former chiefs of staff as "windbags" and believed that the hospital administrator was "out of her depth." McAnaw felt that this nurse had been appointed not for her qualifications, but rather because the VA needed to name a woman. McAnaw's critical attitude was not lost on the management, which later defined her as a difficult person and as someone who had "problems with authority."[40]

Mary McAnaw never saw herself as a compliant team player, but rather as a highly competent, combative physician. By her own account, she irritated her administrative superiors by her insistence on improving the facilities in her unit and particularly by her readiness to tackle problem situations in other parts of the hospital. She often articulated the concerns of less assertive colleagues to the upper levels of the hospital administration. Staff members asked her to speak up, in part because they recognized her high set of principles, but also because they defined her as expendable. If she lost her job, they reasoned, her husband could support her. The others, particularly the foreign doctors, enjoyed no such security and were much less willing to take any risks.[41] Their traditional attitude that women's work was not essential to the well-being of the family totally ignored the fact that McAnaw was neither psychologically nor financially prepared to be unemployed.

McAnaw's seesaw relationship with the hospital administration and the chief of staff took a decidedly downward turn in 1980. Dr. Arthur Shaw, a staff psychologist, learned that one of his patients in the VA hospital was a subject in a study testing Anafranil, an antidepressant drug. Shaw believed that some of the patients were inappropriately chosen for the research and, given their medical condition, could suffer harm from the drug's side effects. Like many professionals, Shaw was keenly aware that in the last decade there had been a major transformation in the protection of research subjects.[42] Government regulation now required informed consent by subjects and a carefully monitored protocol. Researchers who had often deceived their subjects in the name of science were now required to brief them on any dangers they faced by cooperating with an experiment.* Shaw, a Ph.D. in psychology, knew that his complaint, no

---

*The Tuskegee syphilis experiment, conducted on poor rural black men who were led to believe they were receiving treatment for a serious illness, represents one of the most troubling accounts of the abuse of patients by physicians in medical experimentation.[43]

matter how well grounded, would carry little weight with the new chief of staff, a physician who respected only those with an M.D. degree, and decided to consult McAnaw, who offered to accompany him when he discussed the study with the administration.

McAnaw's predicament was markedly different from most professionals who confront illegal or unethical behavior within their areas of direct responsibility. Since the study, though potentially dangerous to the subjects, was not affecting her department of surgery, she did not have to become involved but could claim lack of jurisdiction. Indeed, her husband, Mike Brigg, also a staff physician, advised her against challenging superiors who favored the research and were impressed by the $20,000 grant it brought to the hospital. He spoke plainly, and his words echo other spouses we have described. He feared for her career if she insisted on confronting bureaucratic authority, telling her:

Look, be quiet. Don't say anything. They will kick you out. Those making decisions in the VA don't like to hear contrary decisions. VA administrators won't tolerate a different opinion and certainly no criticism. For that they put a stigma on you and you are out. We have an old proverb. "If you scratch the devil, scratch it with the fur, not against it." But, Mary, you are doing it against the fur, and this they don't like.[44]

Having grown up in Europe and suffered under both Nazi and Communist dictatorships, Mike Brigg's caution was grounded in firsthand knowledge of oppressive political systems. He felt that his wife was insufficiently astute about the realities of the bureaucracy's functioning and its potential to inflict severe reprisals. He reminded McAnaw that a top hospital administrator had even been outraged when an adviser to then President Carter had dared to question a pending administration policy. Clearly, Brigg observed, the VA officials would brook no opposition. Should McAnaw persist in protesting the drug study, her superiors would label her as the bearer of bad tidings, the person whose information now required action. They would be forced to embark upon an investigation, which would be embarrassing to another staff member and might raise questions about the adequacy of their own supervision. Such an outcome would surely weaken their position in the eyes of the central VA hierarchy in Washington. What his wife defined as a clear situation of danger to patients, her superiors would see as a potential threat to their own positions. As McAnaw and many other resisters learned the hard way, this proved to be a shrewd analysis of how bureaucracy operates.[45]

Mary McAnaw understood her husband's analysis. Yet she would not retreat; she felt compelled to protest the Anafranil study and other problems in the hospital. Her words are reminiscent of many other resisters in her emphasis on individual responsibility and the requirement that "evil" has to be actively opposed. Voicing objections was simply not sufficient. Implicit in her statement lies a clear sense that her professional ethics required a sensitivity to the costs of an abusive system. She believed that the veterans were entitled to first-rate medical treatment which should not be compromised because of their dependent status. Just as they were not to undergo surgery in unsanitary conditions, so they should not be exposed to potentially harmful drug experimentation. McAnaw was objecting to more than an isolated act of a colleague or superior. She was challenging institutional arrangements that tolerate and even sanction poor medical care. The responsibility was no longer located in another department; it had become *her* responsibility:

> First of all, there wasn't anyone else willing to do it. There was no one else around. Secondly, some of the things they did were so unfair that my conscience simply bothered me and I couldn't allow these things to go unnoticed. I just couldn't do that. I know it may sound like a hackneyed phrase today, but I believe it: *"The only thing necessary for evil to prevail is for good men to do nothing."* That sentence kept recurring to me. I felt if I didn't do anything, who will?
>
> I think I also felt that this was essentially a foreign hospital in the United States. I was one of the few Americans in this primarily foreign-doctor hospital. I thought that as an American I should at least try to be fair.[46]

For McAnaw there were serious tensions between her professional role and her place in the bureaucracy. As a medical student she had been taught that the physician's expert judgment takes priority over other considerations. Autonomy is the key to good medical practice, and much of the medical training was geared to preparing future doctors for private practice where they would control the work and the working conditions. But McAnaw, having spent most of her professional life in the VA, knew it to be one of the most bureaucratic settings in which doctors can practice.

Characterized by hierarchical organization, the VA demands respect for authority; employees are judged by their ability to be good team players. At the time that these events unfolded, the VA system was providing care to more than 2,500,000 veterans. The staff included over 10,000 physicians, as well as 22,500 medical residents and almost 20,000 medical students. In total the VA employed approximately 250,000 workers, who comprised 8 percent of the federal government's full-time employees.[47] The local administration of each hospital is backed by the national VA system and an elaborate set of policies that regulate and prescribe the limits of professional flexibility. The one area where a doctor's views are theoretically pre-eminent is in medical diagnosis and treatment, but even here the boundaries are not always clear.

McAnaw's sense of her rights and obligations as a physician had already put her in conflict with the administration several times. When she complained of inadequate facilities—and even bats in the operating room—her superiors acted to remedy some of the problems. Nonetheless, they regarded her as a poor team player, who did not respect the problems they encountered in doing their jobs. But she felt that she was upholding the mandate for adequate care for her patients. Her decision to speak up in the Anafranil study grew out of the same reasoning. She hoped to use her status as a physician to force the hospital to define the study as a serious issue of patients' rights and medical ethics instead of seeing it as a question of funding, organizational improvement, and the administration's right to determine policy.

When she did not succeed in getting the VA to agree that this was a medical and professional issue where the doctor's view should prevail, she, like many resisters, buttressed her professional commitment with a more general philosophy that good people, and certainly conscientious professionals, are obliged to stand up for their beliefs. Thus, in her view, she transformed the battle from a local disagreement to a global struggle of good versus evil.

McAnaw's actions paralleled others who rebelled against unjust authority. To protect herself from allegations of irrational behavior, she had to "divest" herself from her allegiance to bureaucratic superiors. From her perspective, the legitimacy of the administration's authority had been ruptured, and her superiors released her and her colleagues from the requirements of behaving like loyal subordinates and following orders. Her professional values were central in justifying this break. She believed that she, and not her superiors, was devoted to providing the best patient care. Her medical training, her early work experience, and her position as head of surgery allowed her to challenge those above her in the hierarchy who abused their position by endangering the health of the patients. She "reframed" her definition of loyalty by allegiance to a belief system that posited responsibility, compassion, and expertise as more important than bureaucratic conformity.[48]

For McAnaw, like Basdekas, a strong conviction that action was required offset the specter of retaliation and the anxiety about disturbing accustomed patterns of social relationships with superiors. Inaction would be too costly, for it would force her to redefine herself as a person who was unable or unwilling to safeguard the safety of others. Her years in bureaucratic organizations had not dissipated the strength of her commitments.

Like Basdekas, group support also propelled McAnaw forward. Her colleagues, who were looking for leadership, believed that she had the competence to assess a problem, the integrity to know what reaction was required, and the personal qualities to endure a tough fight. A former student and part-time staff physician in the surgical service, Dr. Betsy Brothers, turned into a particularly ardent advocate. When Mary McAnaw failed to obtain an administrative investigation into the drug study, she confided in Brothers in order to verify her opinion on the gravity of the situation. Brothers, in turn, consulted with her father, an experienced physician in private practice. After examining the protocol of the study, they agreed that it would be difficult to find twenty appropriate patients in that particular hospital population, and that many of the subjects should not have been included.[49] This confirmation was important for McAnaw who was making judgments outside her own department of surgery.

Brothers also played a central role in taking the case beyond the confines of the hospital. She wrote lengthy confidential letters to the Office of the Inspector General of the Veterans Administration and later to several congressmen, in which she detailed the problematic conditions at the hospital, including lack of staff and inadequate facilities.[50] She questioned the effort to make McAnaw the scapegoat for poor staff morale and conflict between the health care professionals and the administration. In this correspondence, Brothers pointed to the question of medical judgment as central to the effectiveness of the surgery unit and referred to the excellent training she had received from Mary McAnaw in her surgical residency:

> She is a meticulous surgical operator, and her logic and judgement in matters relating to daily patient care can seldom be debated. She is a strong proponent of the concept of the physician as "captain of the ship," being morally and legally responsible for the well-being of each of his/her patients.
>
> It has been obvious to me for some time now that Dr. McAnaw's views regarding the priority of patient care are in conflict with at least some ideas/policies held by administrative personnel in this Medical Center. I have been aware of this conflict since at least 1977, but it seems to have intensified recently.[51]

Betsy Brothers went on to point to poor physician retention in the hospital, high turnover of chiefs of staff, and the probationary status of the residency program after its last reaccreditation as signs that serious management problems needed examination. This correspondence escalated into a well-publicized struggle for the dissident group who supported McAnaw. It initiated several years of investigation and litigation in which each side had to defend its version of the events to the press, the Congress, and the courts.*

During her drawn-out battle with Washington officials, McAnaw's colleagues offered her consistent affirmation of her competence and integrity. As they themselves became the targets of reprisals, they shared in the anguish and humor of the lengthy proceedings and established an elaborate network of communications with the media and local congressmen. As Arthur Shaw succinctly put it: "We kept each other from feeling helpless and hopeless—either one of which is terrible. It's having some kind of action possibility that is important. We cross-fertilized ideas with one another. That makes a hell of a difference."[52] McAnaw's colleagues felt that as a group they had played a major part in challenging the

---

*At various points during the investigation, members of the Kansas congressional and senatorial delegations were contacted. Even former President Reagan was informed of events as Betsy Brothers attempted to widen the scope of possible outside intervention. The *Kansas City Times,* and particularly its Washington correspondent, Richard A. Serrano, reported on the developing controversy.

administration, which probably would have succeeded in forcing any single individual to relent.

The accounts of the Veterans Administration resisters confirmed the importance of group solidarity in confronting an unresponsive bureaucracy and supporting the maintenance of high ethical standards—although, of course, there were tensions among them and some were willing to take greater risks than others. As long as they had a vision of what the future might be like with a more responsible administration, they could keep going. At the time of the interview, Shaw was the only one of the resisters still working in the hospital. He described the great sense of caring that developed among the dissidents, and the sense of loss when the group disbanded: "Being alone, I care less. I have simply been less effective in what is going on in the hospital as a whole than I was before. We fueled one another and when you are alone with it, that doesn't count."[53]

In addition, McAnaw and Brothers had the strong support of their husbands. Although McAnaw's husband had initially counseled caution, once the battle began he urged her to fight it to a successful conclusion. Doug Brothers, a physicist in a small college, understood from the beginning the necessity of fighting an arbitrary administration. He became a significant advocate for the group—editing his wife's letters, accompanying her in her interviews with VA officials, and reinforcing her sense that professional ethics require strong action. Others in the group also felt that he was sensitive to their plight. Unlike most spouses, Doug Brothers harbored no illusions about the possibility of avoiding a battle with an abusive administration. He did not believe that all would be well if only his wife could learn to be more tolerant of bureaucratic decision makers. Doug Brothers is a prime example of a spouse who could completely identify with his wife on a professional level, accept her emotional turmoil as the fight proceeded, and help sustain her and her colleagues during the periods when frustration overshadowed professional commitment.

While Brothers and McAnaw could both rely on their local colleagues and family, their adversaries found potent allies in government agencies. The Washington VA office consistently sided with the hospital administration in declaring McAnaw a difficult personality and a central cause of the dissension. To resolve the crisis they ordered her transferred to another VA facility. The acting chief medical director of the VA expressed the official condescension for McAnaw in a letter to Kansas senator

Robert Dole in which the director described the review that found McAnaw herself to be a crucial part of the problem. He referred to her long-standing "disruptive behavior" and her poor administrative ability. He went on to assert that her impoverished managerial skills could not help but have serious consequences for patients and concluded that new leadership was necessary in the surgical department at Leavenworth.[54]

McAnaw refused to go without a fight and took her allegations of administration incompetence and punitive transfer to the courts. The decision went against her. The trial judge ruled that she had adequate opportunity to present her case against the Veterans Administration by using administrative grievance procedures within the organization. In addition, the judge found that she had not proved her allegations of organizational retaliation.[55]

While McAnaw was finally unsuccessful in warding off the transfer, she did feel vindicated when the Food and Drug Administration unequivocally condemned the Anafranil study and barred its principal researcher from any further studies requiring FDA approval. After a lengthy investigation, the FDA found that Dr. Walter C. Bruschi, the chief investigator, had seriously violated the protocol in several ways, having used patients who did not fit the required diagnosis and changed the diagnosis of some other subjects. In a strong critique, Dr. Bruschi was barred from conducting "clinical investigation involving investigational new drugs."*

Mary McAnaw was ultimately forced to leave the hospital because she could not mount a successful defense of her position outside the VA

---

*"Agreement with Respect to Use of Investigational New Drugs," signed by Walter C. Bruschi, M.D., and Peter H. Rheinstein, M.D., and Jerome A. Halporin, acting director Office of Drugs of the United States Food and Drug Administration, 6 June 1983. The agreement reads as follows:

"a. Dr. Bruschi has participated as an investigator in three clinical studies with the investigational new drugs Ludiomil and Anafranil at the Veterans Administration Medical Center in Leavenworth, Kansas.

"b. Dr. Bruschi will not conduct clinical investigations involving investigational new drugs nor will he receive investigational new drugs.

"c. With respect to receipt of investigational new drugs, Dr. Bruschi waives his right to the regulatory hearing specified in 21 C.F.R. Part 16 and 21 C.F.R. & 312.1(c).

"d. Should Dr. Bruschi desire to receive investigational new drugs at some time in the future, he will follow applicable FDA regulations, by proceeding under 21 C.F.R. & 312.1(c)(6).

"e. The Office of Drugs will inform the sponsor of investigational new drug studies conducted by Dr. Bruschi of this agreement and the steps that they should take accordingly."

system. She thought she was acting appropriately as a doctor in confronting the administration on improper drug testing and other issues of patient rights. Yet when the VA bureaucracy moved against her, no court would hear her case and no medical organization came forward to defend her despite the publicity afforded her in the local press. Perhaps even more ironic was the resisters' failure to seriously consider approaching available medical societies. According to Brothers, they feared becoming enmeshed in the bureaucracy of the Joint Commission on the Accreditation of Hospitals and doubted they would receive a strong positive response[56]— although, in the course of their struggle against the VA, McAnaw and Brothers did contact numerous attorneys, legislators, and newspaper reporters. While the medical associations might have mounted a determined investigation, they had done little in the past to persuade members of their willingness to intervene in ethical controversies involving large bureaucratic organizations. The resisters also notified the American Legion and the Veterans of Foreign Wars, but found them to be adversaries rather than supporters. Representatives of those organizations went out of their way to defend the hospital administration, and Brothers believes they helped increase the perception that the ethical resisters were the troublemakers.[57]

Eventually, Betsy Brothers fared far better. She had been offered a regular full-time position in surgery by McAnaw during the early stages of the confrontation. Once the VA administrators suspected that she was the author of a confidential letter to the Inspector General's office, they refused to appoint her. Brothers filed a lawsuit in 1982. Since, as a temporary, part-time employee, she did not qualify for an administrative review, the court ruled that it had jurisdiction. In 1987 a jury found that she had been inappropriately denied the job. In a major victory, she was successful in her suit against the two administrators who had been her antagonists. She was awarded back pay from the VA and substantial monetary damages from the two administrators. The outcome has been referred to as an unprecedented victory in which a whistleblower working in a federal bureaucracy has won punitive damages. Dr. Brothers and whistleblowers throughout the country are elated by her victory, which is currently under appeal by the hospital administration.*

*The jury verdict was handed down on 13 January 1987 in the U.S. District Court for the District of Kansas. Case no. 82-4079. Under the verdict the jury awarded Dr. Brothers damages of $90,937 for violations of her rights under the First Amendment. In addition,

A Doctor Stands Alone: Grace Pierce and the Ortho Pharmaceutical Corporation

McAnaw's and Brothers's commitment to the welfare of patients was not unique among professionals. Many resisters explained their confrontation with their superiors as a direct result of their responsibility to patients, clients, or even to the public at large. While McAnaw had substantial support in her battle to uphold her professional judgments, in some instances professionals had to stand virtually alone.

Grace Pierce, a research physician in private industry, is a prime example of a resister who faced abandonment by her co-workers and retaliation by her superiors. Pierce joined the Ortho Pharmaceutical Corporation, a division of Johnson & Johnson, in 1971 after holding positions in the Food and Drug Administration, in another drug firm, and in private practice. In 1975 she was assigned to direct a research team attempting to develop Loperamide, a drug for the relief of acute and chronic diarrhea. The liquid Loperamide formulation originated with Janssen, a Johnson & Johnson company in Belgium, and had a high saccharin content to hide its bitter taste. Pierce and all the Ortho team members agreed that there was a need to reformulate the drug to diminish the saccharin concentration, particularly with the ongoing controversy over its carcinogenic potential. When management pressured them to accept the high saccharin formulation, her colleagues ultimately acceded. Pierce refused. As the only physician on the team, she would not agree to discount her medical judgment and begin clinical trials with a questionable formulation.[58]

After her refusal, Pierce stated that her immediate superior questioned her judgment, loyalty, and competence and later accused her of misusing company funds on a research trip and of taking an unauthorized vacation. Although she rejected and refuted the accusations, the attack was a clear signal of her diminished prospects:

> When the situation came up and I couldn't get the other people to go along with me, I asked my superior whether we could get three objective consultants outside the company. If they say it's okay, I'll do it. Or

she was awarded punitive damages of $100,000. The defendants—Dr. K. Paul Poulose, chief of staff at the hospital, and Margaret C. Michelson, former director of the hospital— were ordered to pay punitive damages of $50,000 each.

if you will permit me to go to the FDA and put the situation to them openly and they say okay, I'll do it. I think I offered alternatives for a reasonable compromise. He refused.

Use of saccharin remains a question yet. Nobody knows where this problem of carcinogens is heading. It probably won't be resolved soon, if ever. I was on the spot. I had to get with it or get out. I hated that. I was cornered. There was no compromise. Nobody from higher up came and said, "Why don't we do that or do this?" They were just riding roughshod all over me. I always like to feel I'm a person, not a cog in a machine.

Pierce expressed a willingness to compromise if others with professional credentials suggested a reasonable path. From her perspective, experts could debate various options, but no administrator had the right to over-rule her professional judgment in order to maximize corporate profits. She was determined to stand fast even without any of her colleagues' support. She was contemptuous of their timidity: "One of my colleagues said, 'Grace, you're nuts. Why not write a lengthy memo for the files, make sure you're on record? They're responsible.' " Uttering words that could be the credo of professionals who become ethical resisters, she went on: "If I do the research, I'm responsible. I feel responsibility as a physician first. My responsibility to the corporation is second. I think my colleagues' attitude is commonplace. People salve their conscience. They keep the benefits of the job. This memo gives them an escape hatch."[59]

Pierce resigned and joined a medical practice on a part-time basis. Although these colleagues were delighted to have her work with them, neither they nor any local or statewide medical society assisted her in her subsequent legal battle despite its clear-cut significance for the integrity of medical practice in large organizations. Later the vice president of Personal Products, another subsidiary of Johnson & Johnson, invited her to join his research staff although she alerted him that she might sue Ortho. Within six months she had become director of research. Her new work situation changed dramatically when she actually filed her suit for "damage to her professional reputation, dissipation of her career, loss of salary, as well as seniority and retirement benefits." Despite their excellent relationship, the vice president's attitude cooled, and, not unexpectedly, he summoned her at the end of one work day:

I was fired. He said it was unconscionable that anyone working for Personal Products would sue a sister company. I said I didn't think so. He had been aware of the legal thing with Ortho. He was dejected and hurt by the whole thing. The next morning he seemed very sad about seeing me go. . . . I haven't seen him since.[60]

Pierce carried her suit to the New Jersey Supreme Court, which broke constitutional ground by affirming a professional's right to challenge superiors where professional ethics are at stake. This was a major victory for resisters who had argued just this point. The court found that an "employer's right to discharge an employee at will carries a correlative duty not to discharge an employee who declines to perform an act that would require a violation of a clear mandate of public policy." This was of great importance to professionals when the court further clarified that in "certain instances, a professional code of ethics may contain an expression of public policy."[61]

In Pierce's case, however, five of the six judges for the New Jersey Supreme Court ruled that her judgment and Ortho's were simply at variance because there was no consensus in the profession about the dangers of saccharin. Professional ethics were not the issue, according to the court, which sustained Ortho's actions. The majority ruled that Pierce had not specified a particular provision of the American Medical Association's code of ethics in her arguments. In addition, it expressed the fear that chaos would prevail if any research physician could simply refuse to work on an assigned project.

In a strongly worded dissent, one judge supported Pierce's position and rejected the majority's argument. The dissent emphasized the significance of professional autonomy and thus Pierce's right to refuse to perform the experiments even before the FDA approved of the experiment. The protection of such refusal, the judge continued, fell under the general proviso of the AMA code that a doctor must refuse to proceed with experimentation that might cause harm to subjects. The dissent argued that such ethical refusal posed no substantial threat to an organization, which could, if it so desired, simply reassign personnel rather than close down the entire procedure.

To this day, Pierce believes she acted appropriately and did not compromise her professional judgment or ethical values. She also knows that her case has helped establish a crucial "public policy exception" to the right of employers to fire employees at will. Currently twenty-six states have established laws that protect private sector employees from dismissal if their protests impinge on an area that protects a vital public interest. These laws represent one of the most significant steps taken to shield employees from retaliation and to encourage knowledgeable insiders to come forward. Professionals are in a unique position to benefit from this recent legislation.[62]

Conclusion

The decision not to comply with the demand for obedience puts workers in a vulnerable position. Whether in the federal bureaucracy, state or city governments, major national corporations, or smaller industries, resistance to illegal and unethical acts has forced employees into direct confrontation with those who hold the power either to reward or to punish them. Whether they expect it or not, resisters are immediately enmeshed in a battle with political consequences and unforeseen career and personal dangers. Both superiors and co-workers warn them repeatedly that they will pay dearly if they persist in their dissent. No protest can remain a simple disagreement between employees and their supervisors. Since pursuit of unethical and illegal practices frequently uncovers serious systemic problems, efforts to bring about reform are invariably rebuffed by a network of people who benefit from the ongoing arrangements or from those who fear the consequences of "upsetting the apple cart."

Resisters do not define themselves as rigid or unaccommodating troublemakers. They deeply resent their detractors' accusations that their issues are trivial, reflecting some personal eccentricity, and therefore unworthy of serious attention. By taking a principled stand against a policy they defined as poorly conceived, the resisters believe that they and not their superiors are the true defenders of the company's or agency's long-term interests. They have accepted positions in their organizations because they believe in its goals. They maintain that the achievement of these goals, whether regulating nuclear plants or producing safe drugs, can best be served by their conscientious performance. They cannot remain silent when they see the goals subverted. In their minds, the only way to stop unethical behavior is for concerned individuals to protest within the organization or, as a last resort, to speak out publicly to appropriate authorities.

Chapter 4

The Power of
Belief Systems for
Ethical Resisters

ONLY THOSE EMPLOYEES who have a highly developed alternative belief system can withstand the intense pressure to conform to the requirements of management. As we have seen in chapter 3, professional socialization inculcates such values. In other cases, strong religious commitments reinforce the resolve to live up to the professions' highest standards. The beliefs of religious resisters are unshakable and provide powerful motivation to act out their ideas of individual responsibility. Other whistleblowers, usually workers, are motivated by concern for the well-being of neighbors and friends. As residents of their communities, they feel compelled to act against hazards that might injure those whom they see on a day-to-day basis. One worker, who protested illegal dumping of untreated sewage in the local river, explained his inability to stand idly by, watching children at play in areas he knew to be contaminated. For this man, and others like him, neither the promise of reward nor the threat of retaliation by his superiors was sufficient to override his deeply held values about the meaning of community.

In this chapter we shall present the experiences of an engineer, a lawyer, and a physician who drew upon profound religious beliefs in standing up to what they considered illegal and dangerous practices. We will then examine the case of nuclear workers who confronted a major corporation when they came to fear for the safety of their community.

Religious professionals initially chose jobs that did not seem to conflict with their strongly held beliefs. When they did encounter ethical breaches in their organizations, they concluded reluctantly that their superiors had failed them. Once the resisters had defined the conflict in moral terms, no organizational demands and priorities could persuade them to abandon or even modify their strong commitment to actions they had long deemed appropriate for an ethical, religious person. They defined compromise as an unacceptable betrayal of their principles, an approach whose essence was articulated by one religious resister: "It's very simple when you get right down to it. You either do what's right or you do what's wrong. It's black and white. It's very cut and dry."[1]

The religiously committed resisters had applied spiritual teachings to lawless behavior and concluded that God and their religion demanded that they stand in battle for the moral cause. Despite the condemnation and retaliation of superiors and co-workers, they felt they would ultimately be vindicated. The most devout among them were even willing to await that judgment at the hands of a Higher Being. They were conversant with a tradition of martyrdom in the Judeo-Christian tradition that celebrates the incorruptible believers who suffered for their commitment. The wife of one resister related how the power of faith sustained her husband through difficult times: "I think it comes from his trust in God—knowing he's done his best, he will be exonerated. It may be next year, the year after, or may not be until he dies . . . if it's only by God, he will be exonerated. . . . I would like it to be now, but it may not be. It's just his faith that gives him his peace and his trust."[2]

While these ideas might seem anachronistic to the modern, secular temperament, they are in the prophetic tradition. Like the prophets of the Old Testament, religiously committed resisters undertook the task of exposing and condemning widespread corruption, heedless of the popular belief that these practices are so deeply embedded in modern society that it is foolhardy to try to change them. Thus, like other religious resisters, three men in public service—Bert Berube, a Catholic; Mark Price, a Mormon; and Zalman Magid, a Jew—put themselves, their families, and their careers at risk to force their organizations to adopt a higher standard of ethical behavior.

Religious Belief

BERT BERUBE AND THE GENERAL SERVICES ADMINISTRATION

Bert Berube did not hesitate when asked what background factors were most significant in explaining his ethical behavior, pointing immediately to his religious beliefs. He grew up in Massachusetts, attended Catholic school, and received his engineering degree from Norwich University in Vermont. He pursued an engineering career in private industry from 1957 to 1963, but became disillusioned after he successfully completed a management training program and worked for a large company for several years. His Catholic faith had set a standard for behavior that guided his evaluation of industry's actions: "It was not a conscious thing at that time. But without fully knowing it, I had a set of ethics set by my faith. It was there internally all the time."[3]

Berube was not enamored of the ethical climate in the company and was particularly disturbed after a bridge collapsed during construction, killing twelve people. He felt that the accident could have been avoided if the company had followed its own policy and authorized an independent check of the design:

> I'm a structural engineer, and we were doing designs of buildings and bridges. It's expected that there will be an independent check when someone designs a bridge. If he makes a mistake and the bridge falls, it is going to kill a lot of people. In many instances at the company, the bosses decided to save money by skipping the check. One bridge was designed by one of our most competent people, but there had not been a check. At lunchtime the families of the workers customarily brought a lunch pail, and they all ate lunch together at the work site. Well, the bridge fell during lunch hour, and twelve people got killed. The designer just blamed himself, of course, and it was devastating to see how distraught he was. That, tied in with other unethical situations, left me very unimpressed with private industry.[4]

Berube was delighted to join the General Services Administration in 1963 and expected far better ethical behavior in the government: "It was totally new and different. I felt complete freedom to do things the way I thought they should be done, and my career went very well."[5]

In the next decade, he and his wife, Pat, began a family, and his career blossomed. He moved up in rank, salary, and responsibility. Most important for him, he had the freedom to do quality engineering. He felt he had made the right career choice. In the mid-1970s, after a number of successful years working as an engineer, he was promoted to a high-ranking position that made him responsible for monitoring government regulations requiring competitive bidding for all major purchases. From this new vantage point, he learned that decisions about money allocations had a clear political bias. Funds were provided not necessarily on the basis of need but to solidify deals among congressmen; competitive bidding on contracts, which was required by law, was seldom implemented. According to Berube's calculation, this cost the taxpayer tens of millions of dollars. He decided not to go along even though many of his colleagues felt he was "naive": "I was naive relative to the corruption that does exist. I was very naive in that respect. I just presumed that everything was always safe; that people who wanted to do the wrong thing were punished, and that was the end of it. That was very naive looking back on it now."[6]

Nonetheless, Berube pressed for the implementation of new directives on competitive bidding issued by the Office of Management and Budget. His superiors rejected his initiatives, as he explained:

> A regulation, A-109, specified that there would be competitive bidding in all major systems procurement. GSA was not following that mandate. I had been given the job where it was my responsibility to see to it that the law was followed. My job description stated that I was accountable for seeing that it was done.
>
> In actuality, neither my superiors nor Congress wanted that to take place. In other words the law, or the presidential directive, was there as a farce. These laws and directives are there on the books to make it look nice to the public. Those who are supposed to be accountable are told that if they want to keep their jobs, the law is not to be followed. That's where I got into some real problems. I had been given a job to do, and I insisted on doing it.[7]

In 1977, irritated by his continuing protests, his superiors used a standard government ploy. They demoted and transferred him: "They took me out of management with its decision-making responsibilities and put me back into the area where the decision had already been made and I was to produce the product." Despite this punishment, Berube never felt he had any choice but to implement the regulations. He understood the pressures on congressmen to produce jobs for their districts and the incentives for agency heads to seek larger budgets. But all of this was subordinated to his moral decisions:

> It was a very personal thing. My conscience told me that it was wrong. You either believe in your morals or you don't have them. You have a certain faith or you act on self-interest. It's hard to criticize people for acting on self-interest because there's no question that they benefit from it. The thing is, I don't think the world as a whole benefits from it.[8]

Berube suffered from the costly illusion that his religious beliefs were applicable to his role in the organization. He had never made the appropriate adjustment as defined by a corporate vice president whom Robert Jackall had encountered in his research on managers: "What is right in the corporation is not what is right in a man's home or in his church. *What is right in the corporation is what the guy above you wants from you* [italics in original]. That's what morality is in the corporation."[9] This definition of reality applies to government bureaucracies as well as to corporations.

About a year later, in 1978, the Senate Subcommittee on Government Waste held hearings to investigate GSA acquisitions practices and found widespread corruption. Substantial evidence was presented pointing to lack of competitive bidding, negotiated contracts with favored businesses, acceptance of contractors' inflated prices without adequate investigation by the agency. The GSA developed an unenviable reputation as a center of government waste. A major scandal involving extensive corruption in the Boston area had just come to light, and an employee had gone to the press with his allegations.[10] The GSA was under pressure to reform. In Washington, Berube was called to testify and told the committee in some detail how deeply entrenched corruption was in the agency.[11] His concerns were given careful attention by U.S. senators, who demanded that the GSA refocus its efforts to protect taxpayers' dollars.* As a result, a significant reorganization of personnel occurred. One official retired im-

---

*"The Senate Subcommittee on Government Waste held hearings to investigate GSA's procurement practices and compliance with A-109. The subcommittee supported Mr. Berube, found that GSA was not in compliance with A-109 and requested that Mr. Berube's demotion be reversed (June 1978)."[12]

mediately, and another senior administrator was fired. The newly appointed administrator, Jay Solomon, openly acknowledged that Berube had been wrongfully demoted. Solomon supported Berube and several other whistleblowers in the GSA who had risked their careers to expose unethical and illegal behavior.[13] Bert Berube's tenacity had been rewarded and he was promoted to director of acquisition policy and put in charge of purchasing policy at GSA. Despite this seeming victory, the GSA rejected his continuing efforts to increase competitive bidding and reduce waste. He remained frustrated in his attempts to uproot entrenched practices.

With the election of Ronald Reagan in 1980, Berube hoped that the new administration would be more receptive to efficient management of the agency, using methods closer to those employed by private enterprise. Berube argued that all GSA services, whether janitorial, secretarial, or construction, should be allocated on a competitive basis, including those services provided by its own personnel. This practice, Berube noted, had already been implemented in other agencies and had saved the government millions of dollars.[14]

Initially, the Reagan administration was enthusiastic about Berube's ideas, many of which matched its conservative, private enterprise ideology. Indeed, in late 1981 Berube was promoted to director of the GSA National Capital Region, a division employing seven thousand workers. He was now in charge of a budget of over one billion dollars. In addition, he was one of three employees who received a $7,500 bonus "for courageous whistleblowers on agency mismanagement."[15] The GSA's administrator spoke of them in glowing terms. Berube was riding high. After the national acclaim and new responsibilities, he was still unable to eliminate serious problems in the agency. When he exposed the continuing defects in the GSA as well as new ones created by mandated budget cuts, his short-lived honeymoon on his new job ended. After several futile efforts to influence policy, he summarized his criticisms in May 1983 in a memo to his superior, the deputy administrator of the agency. Unlike his past concerns, he was now most troubled by the safety defects that he believed endangered federal employees:

> Several weeks ago you requested that I identify what I believed to be G.S.A.'s most critical problems. . . . Nowhere can the effect of these across-the-board reductions in resources be seen more dramatically than in the public buildings program. Substantial repair and alterations work, neces-

sary to maintain building standards, has been deferred or reduced in scope by 75% or more of what is specified by regulation. If put to the test of local codes and industry standards, many of our occupied buildings would be condemned. . . . Buildings have been allowed to deteriorate to a point where some of our G.S.A. buildings are unsafe for human occupancy, are inadequate to meet the mission needs of the occupying agencies, do not meet OSHA requirements, and would be condemned if owned by private industry and put under the test of local codes and laws.[16]

Berube was particularly adamant where issues of safety were involved. He believed that funds allocated for these purposes had been inappropriately spent elsewhere. He did not stand totally alone in his criticisms. Another whistleblower who had also been publicly acclaimed and was now an important regional director of the GSA, Howard Davia, supported Berube: "Bert's right. You can drive a car without changing the oil, but in the long run, you'll pay a great price."[17] Collegial support did not increase Berube's acceptance. Though he did not know it at the time, his memo spelled the end of his federal career. He was first transferred, then demoted, and ultimately fired—a retaliation process often instituted in the federal government against employees who will not back down.

According to GSA officials, Berube was a "loose cannon" who was quick to come up with criticisms but not realistic in offering solutions. Gerald Carmen, GSA administrator during the early Reagan years, said of him: "I don't disagree with many of the problems he points out. . . . Where people can show me a need, I'll advocate the resources." The problem with Berube, Carmen argued, is that he seems oblivious to the fact that "resources are finite."[18]

Obviously Berube disagrees with this assessment. In reflecting on the risks he had taken, he remained certain that he had made his decisions in accordance with his conscience. As a deeply religious man whose morality and ethics could not be influenced by a bureaucratic hierarchy or any other external pressure, Berube had not even considered consulting with members of his family about whether he should resist the abuses he observed.

It's not something you discuss with your wife. That never entered my mind. Your conscience is something you deal with yourself. It is not a committee action. It's whether you believe it is right or wrong. It comes back to a question of faith. I am the one who is going to be held accountable for what I do in my life. My wife is not going to be held accountable for it nor are my children. You've got to decide whether you are going to do something because it is right or wrong.

Berube would not go along with orders simply because others told him that he was naive, or that he faced great dangers if he persisted in his criticisms. He felt he had to act alone with only his conscience as a guide. He knew, for example, that friends in his boat club felt that he was "not being too smart" to risk his well-paid job for issues of principle. His decisions were private and not subject to the influence of friends. More important, he did not even turn to his church for support or for reaffirmation: "My church doesn't even know about these problems. They don't become involved in that type of thing, so there wouldn't be an opportunity for them to find out unless I went to them and there would be no reason for that."[19] While this situation partially reflected Berube's tendency to operate as a loner, it also expresses a common attitude about the church.

The absence of any institutional religious defense placed all of the burden on the resister's family. Although Pat Berube knew that her husband might lose his job, she was not prepared when it happened. Nonetheless, she relied on her humor and her belief in God to provide her with the necessary strength in those difficult days:

At first it was a shock. I believed more in the system, and it had betrayed me. He's a good man and he doesn't deserve this. But we'll make it and continue to do everything until it is resolved. He's got to look himself in the mirror and so do I.

After the initial shock, I was bitter for a while. And then after the bitterness came the kind of softening and the acceptance—acceptance, I'm still working on that one. And trust in the Lord that we're doing the right thing, that He will take care of the rest. And I think He will, I really do. And it's taken time. I just sometimes wish He'd hurry a little and give me patience right now.[20]

Pat Berube is not alone among the wives and husbands who found the strength to support their partners' ethical resistance. Indeed, we found it remarkable that in our sample only a few marriages failed despite intense economic and psychological pressures. Religious beliefs provided the necessary cement in several families. Often the identification with the struggle was so strong that the spouses took on the battle as their own. Even when spouses were not closely consulted or realistically cautioned about the dangers inherent in confronting authority, they stayed with the resisters, providing them with emotional sustenance, desperately needed income, advice in fighting their cases, care for children and household, and ties to friends and family when obsession with the case threatened to obliterate all other relationships.

For the Berubes, religious commitment not only served as the foundation of their ethical posture but also supported them when they faced the punishing consequences of Bert's public stand. Louis Clark, executive director of the Government Accountability Project, whose organization has defended Berube and many other whistleblowers, attests to his extraordinary personal strength. Unlike many resisters who face personal crises as they confront the retaliatory process, Bert Berube has always been able to maintain an inner calm, both for himself and for other whistleblowers whom he has counseled. He always reminds them, "You are the same person the day you were fired as you were the day before." While persuaded that his religious beliefs offered no alternative, he does not ignore the heavy costs to him and his family:

I would do it over again simply because I would have no choice. But I certainly would be doing it with a hell of a lot of reluctance because I would know the consequences. The consequences are just staggering as to what it does to your life. They tried to deny me unemployment and spent, I think, at least $200,000 to $300,000 trying to prevent me from getting $5,000 in unemployment. Their objective was to deny me all funds so that I could not continue to fight, irrespective of what the cost was to the government. The consequences in regard to my wife and family were just devastating.[21]

The absolute clarity he felt in regard to his moral choices did not reduce the suffering, but it did prevent "second-guessing" and softened internal doubt:

I don't like it, but I don't see what I could have done to change it. If I did change it, I would become one of the individuals who operates on the basis of self-interest and my life would radically change. It would not be for the good. Let's put it this way. There is no one in the world that could ever sustain anything like this without having thought that he was doing right. There is no way in the world that he could get through it. A major factor for me has been my religious faith.[22]

For Pat Berube, religion has also been central in the process of finding meaning in their suffering. It was important for her to believe that some good could come out of their trials. Her avid devotion helped lift the cloud of despair and bitterness that threatened to descend upon their household:

If I'm not praying and leaving it in God's hand, then I try to mull it over in my mind. I just continuously worry . . . What if? What if? What if he is not reinstated? What if he dies and we don't have any insurance? I want to control everything but I can't. But if I abdicate the authority to my Higher Power, then I don't have to worry about it. I'm at peace and I'm happy and I can go on with my life and I'm not going around with my chin hanging down like I'm wearing sackcloth and ashes.[23]

MARK PRICE AND THE DEPARTMENT OF EDUCATION

One of the most controversial of all whistleblower cases involved Mark Price, a young Mormon attorney who was deeply influenced by his strong religious background and by his faith that his church would back him in times of trouble. That belief may have led him into a trap from which he is only now beginning to emérge: "I come from a very religious family. My grandfather was a bishop in the Mormon Church, as was my father. I've gone to church all my life. As a result of what I have been taught in my church, I have some very strong beliefs about government and what it should and should not do."[24]

Price initially worked for the Utah state legislature. Although a Democrat, he was later recruited by Republican Senator Orrin Hatch of Utah to work for the Senate Labor Committee. Price learned a great deal from both jobs; and while his own strong political views sometimes collided with those of his colleagues, he spoke enthusiastically of those whose work he had observed in Washington: "The people who are there are very dedicated, patriotic Americans. They all have different views, yet they are all fine Americans from left to right." Price also had strong ideas about the value of public service:

When I arrived in Washington, I got the feeling, well, that this is sacred ground. I would go for frequent walks in the parks around the Capitol Building and I would look up and see the white dome of the Capitol that shows you that Congress is still in session. And that was like a beacon of light to me. I was frequently kidded about my naiveté, but I had been trained in my religious upbringing and also my school training that this is what America is: a place where people reason, where they debate, where they consider things on the merits.[25]

After ten months on Senator Hatch's staff, Price lost his position in an administrative reshuffle that resulted from budget cuts.[26] He decided to seek additional experience working in the executive branch and applied for a position in the Department of Education. In June 1983, after being interviewed several times for the highly competitive post, he was appointed attorney-advisor to the Education Appeal Board.

The board had been established to adjudicate appeals of Department of Education audits that had found states guilty of improperly spending federal education grants. Millions of dollars were at stake. A recent report by the inspector general of the Department of Education had criticized the board's inefficiency—a report highlighting the numerous delays that led to the slow adjudication of appeals by the states.[27] In particular, the inspector general asserted that board members were poorly utilized. The report laid responsibility with the chairman, who cited the burden of an excessively heavy case load and the difficulties of working with only one staff attorney. When Mark Price accepted the position as that staff attorney, it was expected that he would help speed up the process.

Price's initial relationship with the chairman seemed amiable. Price enjoyed the work and felt that he was now embarked on a highly successful Washington career. He soon felt some uneasiness, however, about religious jokes that he felt were directed at his Mormon faith, and resented his superiors' change of his work hours which prevented him from attending an early morning Mormon study session. Price later filed a religious discrimination suit with the Equal Employment Opportunity Commission and won the right to resume his initial nine-to-five-thirty hours.* This early dispute over his religion came back to haunt Price, for it led the

*The memorandum of agreement stipulated that the hours of 9:00 A.M. to 5:30 P.M. remain in effect, that Price will be transferred to the Civil Rights Reviewing Authority immediately, and that nothing in the agreement is to be construed as a finding of discrimination.[28]

chairman to argue that the Mormon attorney was both unreliable and unstable.[29]

At about the same time, a far more serious issue arose when Price came to believe that the chairman was engaged in serious fraud and abuse. Price's suspicions were first aroused when he was approached by Department of Education auditors who wanted to meet with him to discuss the outcome of various cases under appeal. According to Price, when he told them it was illegal for one party in the case to meet *ex parte* with the adjudicators of the Hearing Board, they responded that they always had had access to the chairman of the board and his counsel. Price spoke with the chairman and found little sympathy for his concerns. Price later alleged an even more serious breach of procedures, claiming that the chairman came to his office where all files were stored, and removed and destroyed documents that were potentially helpful to the states' position. According to Price, he has clear evidence to prove his assertions:

> One of the things that Mormons believe in is keeping a daily journal and I have a daily journal of the kind of things which I saw transpiring while I was employed with the Education Appeals Board. I can give specific dates. On October 18, October 19, October 20, 1983 I saw at least half a dozen specific pieces of evidence destroyed.[30]

Price knew that any destruction of the documents could have serious consequences. It would allow the Hearing Board to issue decisions based on the argument that the documents submitted to them by the states were not sufficient to prove a state's case. No one would ever know that the available record might have been deliberately distorted.

Appalled by the apparently biased handling of the review process, Price believed that the appeals functioned more as a source of political favors and punishments than as a form of due process:

> It appeared that many of the audit findings which were made against states were timed to assist those that the Reagan administration wanted to assist. For example, during a hotly contested Senate race in California between the incumbent Governor Jerry Brown and Michael Wilson, the auditors issued, to my recollection, about $6,000,000 worth of adverse audit findings against the State of California, alleging responsi-

bility attributable to Jerry Brown. Clearly, this was intended to harm Brown in the election.[31]

Fearing for his future, Price's family in Utah urged him to drop the matter and find a new position. He rejected their advice because he believed that the truth would somehow prevail. He pressed on and decided to take his complaints up the line to higher authorities: "I clung to the idea that at some level there would be an individual that would halt the kind of things that I had seen going on and insist that things be done in the way Congress had decided by statute." Unlike Berube and others who separated their work problems from their church involvement, Price also sought guidance from his bishop in the Mormon Church. The bishop's involvement gave religious backing to what otherwise could be interpreted as a subjective moral stance: "I went and spoke with the bishop, a man whom I greatly, greatly admire, Bishop Gayle Brimhall. He advised me, 'Mark, tell the truth. You should tell the truth.' "[32] Price accepted this advice, which was consonant with his ethical and professional judgment.

The joining of his religious and professional values served to strengthen his resolve and make him less susceptible to organizational pressure:

> Here I am in the Education Appeal Board as the chief counsel and my knowledge of the kind of misconduct that is occurring forces a choice on me. Do I report this and thereby stop it? Or do I acquiesce and implicitly support this? My choice was clear. This is not the way things are supposed to be. Here was a situation that was wrong and it had to be corrected.

In his initial meeting with the chairman's superior, Price states that the office secretary corroborated his allegations. Price knew that she was terrified of losing her job and her ability to support her family: "And so three days later, I went with the office secretary to my superior's immediate supervisor and reported to him what was going on. We reported destruction of evidence, the conducting of illegal meetings, and the forging of documents."[33]

When this official rejected Price's appeal, he went up the chain of command and even tried to reach the secretary of education, Terrell Bell, also a Mormon. On 20 December 1983, he spoke to Secretary Bell's personal counsel and chief of staff who, according to Price, refused to examine any of the documents that he had brought to the meeting. Price believed that this would later allow the counsel to claim that he had never seen proof of Price's "crackpot" complaints. The Counsel may also have believed that since this would undoubtedly find its way to Secretary Bell's desk, it was inappropriate for him to intervene at this early stage.[34]

Price told us that when he returned to Utah a few days later to spend Christmas with his family, he received a call from Secretary Bell's brother-in-law Perry G. Fitzgerald, who invited him to his house. He knew Fitzgerald, a fellow Mormon, from Washington where they had spent some time together and developed a friendly relationship. Fitzgerald had been the one to recommend Price to the chairman of the Education Appeal Board for the Department of Education job. Now in the midst of Price's struggle with the department, Fitzgerald told him, as Price recalled it, that he had a message from Washington:

> "Ted [Secretary Bell] will write you a real good letter of recommendation if you drop this." I told him that I was sorry but I could not do it. He responded, "If you ever want to take Secretary Bell up on his offer, let me give you his unlisted phone number." People can say this never took place, but how else would I have the secretary's unlisted number?[35]

Fitzgerald later denied that any such conversation had taken place, maintaining that Price was very unstable.[36]

When Price rejected overtures to drop charges in return for a personal settlement, he reported that the department escalated its efforts to persuade him. He was first offered a position in another area of the Department of Education, which he agreed to accept but refused to abandon his fight to expose fraudulent practices. When Price finally decided that no internal department action would be taken to correct the violations against the states, he informed the State of Illinois Board of Education and the Board of Education of the City of Chicago of unfair practices influencing their appeals. Given his sense of professional and religious values, he felt obliged to take this course against his superiors:

> The total professional responsibility that governs my profession, disciplinary rule 7-102A and 7-102B, requires me to go to a client when I

am aware that the client has perpetrated fraud. If the client does not rectify the fraud, I go through appropriate channels to the top of the tribunal, which in this case was Terrell Bell. If there is still no rectification, disciplinary rules require me to go to the aggrieved party and report the fraud.[37]

Robert Jackall studied a comparable case of a corporate auditor who discovered financial irregularities in his organization, and whose strong sense of moral obligation did not permit him to remain silent; ultimately he was dismissed by the chief executive officer responsible for the illegal actions. When asked to assess the case, managers in Jackall's research severely criticized the auditor and listed a variety of factors that should preclude an employee from challenging his superiors. In light of the experience of both Berube and Price, it is clear that the managerial strictures apply to government as well as to corporate bureaucracy:

(1) You never go around your boss. (2) You tell your boss what he wants to hear, even when your boss claims that he wants dissenting views. (3) If your boss wants something dropped, you drop it. (4) You are sensitive to your boss's wishes so that you anticipate what he wants; you don't force him, in other words, to act as boss. (5) Your job is not to report something that your boss does not want reported, but rather to cover it up. You do what your job requires, and you keep your mouth shut.[38]

Furthermore, the managers claimed that the auditor had had every opportunity (as did Berube and Price) to disclaim knowledge of the events. Of course, resignation was always an option. In addition, change was unlikely to emerge from a strong protest. The amount of money (or the issues) was "small potatoes," and they argued that no organization operates without some illegal actions. Finally, in absolute opposition to Berube's and Price's perspective, the managers insisted that acting on the basis of a moral code is inappropriate. It makes others feel uncomfortable. Anyone who achieves a high position is tainted. To push such an issue "eroded the fundamental trust and understanding that make cooperative work possible."[39]

The events that followed in Price's case demonstrate the potency of these beliefs. Convinced that Price was a credible witness and that his documentation supported their earlier suspicions, the Illinois State Board joined the Chicago Board of Education and filed suit in the U.S. Court for the District of Columbia. Secretary of Education Bell and three officials of the Department of Education were named as defendants.[40] When Price's superiors received notice of the suit, they immediately knew that he had to be the principal witness for Illinois. According to Price, they forbade him to speak with the attorney for Illinois, to the press, or even to his own personal attorney: "An attorney in the office of the general counsel of the Department of Education told me over the phone, 'If you do not cooperate fully, and I mean fully, in the case against Illinois, you will be terminated.' "[41]

Refusing to back down, Price rejected their advice that he claim that he had suffered "amnesia," a defense other resisters had been pressed to invoke. He responded to a subpoena from the Illinois attorneys to attend a hearing and was summarily fired. The Illinois State Superintendent of Education wrote the United States attorney general, William French Smith, vehemently protesting the dismissal and calling for an investigation by the FBI:

> The timing of Mr. Price's termination and the apparent effort on the part of officers and employees of the Department of Education to harass him as he attempts to pursue legal and appropriate means to challenge his termination give rise to the appearance that such action has been taken against Mr. Price in an effort to prevent or discourage his testimony in case 84–0337. If this is the case, a rather clear-cut case of obstruction of justice . . . has occurred.[42]

Despite strenuous efforts to silence Price, he continued to work with the State of Illinois on its case. Eugene Daly, one of the lawyers for Illinois, continues to believe that Price was a credible witness who exposed serious violations of due process. Daly also asserts that in all his years of legal practice, he has never seen a case handled so poorly by the government.[43]*

Had Mark Price's employment with the Department of Education ended with the ongoing suit by the State of Illinois, the outcome of his disclosure would have been largely positive. To his great misfortune,

---

*A settlement agreement between the Illinois State Board of Education and the Secretary of Education was reached in April 1986. The settlement makes no finding about any charges of impropriety, but sets aside all previous judgments against Illinois and provides newly appointed panels to hear the Illinois appeals.[44]

however, events since his dismissal on 22 February, 1984 have been far more complicated and shrouded in mystery. Just after Price signed the documents filed by the State of Illinois, testifying to their veracity, several of his supporters who had written letters of reference for him received copies of a letter calling him "a sick young man and a threat to all." The letter condemned Price's professional competence, his mental health, his sexual morality, and his religion. The letter was typed on the chairman's office typewriter and bore his signature. An inspector general's report later called the signature a forgery and asserted that Price's fingerprints were on one copy. Price denied any involvement in the incident and claimed that the fingerprint check was done after he had been shown a copy of the letter by the inspector general investigating the case. He further argued that he could not have typed the letter because he had been barred from the chairman's office when the letter was produced. The issue remains unresolved.[45]* Supporters of Price continue to believe he was set up by an increasingly desperate group of department officials who feared exposure if the case came to court. Other observers, including some strong defenders of whistleblowers, see this as the first of a series of suspicious acts that point to self-destructive behavior on Price's part and call his credibility into question.

A second episode in the spring of 1984 had far more disastrous consequences for Price. As the controversy continued over the derogatory letter, a break-in occurred in the office of the inspector general, and documents related to Price's case were stolen. Several weeks later, Price states, he received a letter from Gary Hanna, the Department of Education's deputy undersecretary for internal governmental affairs, in which the official claimed to have department documents that would be useful to Price and that could be obtained for appropriate financial consideration.[46] The authenticity of this letter is also in dispute. Hanna denies ever having sent the letter, which suggested a meeting on Saturday afternoon so that Price could examine the documents. When he arrived, Price found the documents almost useless and refused to pay for them. According to Price the official then offered them to him at no cost. Price photocopied several papers and threw the others away, writing the incident off as a misadventure.

But it was not to be so simple. Price was subsequently arrested for illegal entry into the building and for the destruction of government documents,

---

*The disputed letter is signed from the chairman to Helen Paloukas, 10 January 1984.

some of which had been traced to the earlier burglary in the IG's office. Price bitterly charged that he had been framed in order to destroy his credibility as a witness against the department in the Illinois case. Again, both sides went to great efforts to defend their interpretations. Price had an investigator confirm that the letter offering the documents was indeed written by the undersecretary.[47] But even some supporters of Price began to question his judgment in entering the building alone on a quiet Saturday afternoon.

At first the proceedings went in Price's favor. A federal judge threw out the charges of stealing government documents, arguing that there was not a "scintilla of evidence" against Price.[48] But the situation rapidly turned when, on 14 October 1984, a grand jury indicted Price and charged him with stealing government documents, destroying government property, and obstructing justice. An examination by a court-appointed psychiatrist was ordered. The psychiatrist used Price's Mormon beliefs about revelation to question his grasp on reality and his ability to stand trial. In an unusual turnabout, the prosecution took a tack normally employed by defense attorneys and asked for an indefinite commitment to a mental facility so that Price could be thoroughly tested. The judge rejected the recommendation and found Price able to participate in his own defense.[49] Worried about finances and still concerned that he could be indefinitely committed, Price took the advice of his court-appointed counsel to plea-bargain. He agreed to plead guilty to a misdemeanor and accept a $100 fine and a three-year probation. He later realized that it was a poor strategy. At the time, however, he felt he had no choice, especially when he learned that his public defender had interviewed no witnesses and had never defended anyone in a trial.[50] Price and his lawyer did not part on good terms. Despite their falling out, the attorney later recalled that as they left the courtroom Price's former superior confronted Price in front of several onlookers with a shrill condemnation: "You think your life is working out now Price. But wait until I say to everyone that you have AIDS, you [obscenity]."[51]

The next night the chairman called the local police to report that someone had pushed a seven-foot board through a downstairs window in his house. He accused Price because some neighborhood boys had described a car near the scene that fit the description of Price's red hatchback. The chairman charged that Price had acted to get even for his testimony in court that day, although court records indicate that the chairman had not actually testified. Price denied the charges and claimed his car had been sitting with a broken axle for several months in a parking lot. Despite his denial, he could not prove his exact whereabouts that afternoon. When another public defender advised him to plead guilty to a petty mischief charge, Price acquiesced. It proved a costly decision. His probation on the earlier offense was revoked, and he was ordered to Petersberg, Virginia, for a prison term. Another ordeal began for Price and his fiancée, Linda Donley, whom he subsequently married while in prison.[52]

In the interim, the chairman did not remain unscathed by the controversy and the flurry of charges and countercharges. He lost his prestigious position with Washington's generous perquisites of spacious office, large desk, and power-driven swivel chair and was transferred to far less gracious surroundings. High officials in the Department of Education asserted that this change in fortune for a man with impeccable education credentials and a long history of government service had nothing to do with Mark Price's allegations. The transfer, they insisted, had long been planned.[53]

Even in the midst of his costly confrontation with his superiors, Price reasserted his faith:

> I didn't back off because I was telling the truth. I don't believe God is going to let people destroy an individual who is telling the truth. I don't believe my church would let an individual who is not a Mormon destroy me for telling the truth. What's more powerful—my superior and his power to cause harm or the truth? One thing is certain: the truth is the most powerful weapon we have in the world. It frees slaves, it enlightens the scientific community, and therefore preserves life. So in a battle between my superior and the truth, I firmly believe the truth is going to win. I just wish I knew how expensive it would be in the meantime. That's something I am not taking too well.[54]

However sustaining his fervent belief, it was not matched by active support from his church. He was dismayed when his beloved bishop, who had encouraged him "to tell the truth," left the office while attempting to help him in his difficulties with a fellow Mormon, the secretary of education:

> My former bishop, Brimhall, had attempted to arrange a personal meeting between me and the secretary of education during the week of March 10, 1984. The doctrine of my church requires that when

people in the church have difficulties with each other, we don't sue, we talk it out. [But] Bishop Brimhall was removed from his position and replaced by another individual. My only source of real support was now gone.

Whatever the reason for Brimhall's departure, the loss of a crucial church official and the attitude of detachment that Price perceived in the new bishop were severe blows. From his perspective, the church that had been so influential in forming his views and requiring certain actions suddenly became impartial as he faced the most decisive battle of his life. At that moment Price had to make a distinction between the church and his religious beliefs. In 1985 he told us:

I am a less active member of the church now, but it has not affected my beliefs. I don't engage in all the activities that a good Mormon should engage in regularly. I have great difficulty in understanding the position of my current bishop who seems to believe that this is not a matter for the church to concern itself with even though their members are involved all over the place. I regret my bitterness over this. I suppose when all the court battles are over and the courts have decided who is right, then all of a sudden my current bishop will know who he was behind all along.[55]

To his good fortune, Price changed his church district when his fiancée moved to Virginia, and reconnected with another sympathetic bishop, who visited him during his incarceration and offered him much-needed support. This bishop, who also holds a high position in the federal government, assured Price that in future litigation he would do everything he could to prevent any ad-hominem attacks. The case would be argued only on its merits. The bishop counseled Price that his suffering had a meaning. According to Price, the bishop observed that "life may not look good now, but things happen for a person's growth as a charitable caring church member."[56]

In many ways, Mark Price seemed to be an ideal American. He grew up in a religious tradition, learned to trust civil authority, and saw his family and church's values fully confirmed by his professional education and initial jobs. As an attorney within a bureaucratic organization, he believed that his professional ethics set forth distinct steps to follow when he thought that he uncovered gross abuse. Any doubts or fear he harbored in confronting authority were overshadowed by his understanding of the advice of his religious mentor who had advised him "to tell the truth." Despite threats to his career and the lure of other attractive positions, he refused to turn away. While others might consider his actions "stubborn," "naive," or "misguided," and some of his decisions certainly did seem to exacerbate his problems, he adhered to his vision of the good society and his belief in the necessity of individual responsibility. Yet, aside from the two personally supportive bishops, he felt that the church leaders did little to help him. Perhaps they were constrained by the presence of a Mormon at the head of the Department of Education or by the controversies over the authenticity of several key documents. Whatever the precise reasons, throughout the most difficult stages, Price, like other religious resisters, was left to fight a private battle. He correctly gauged the overwhelming odds he would face if an agency of the government was determined to discredit him. Even more than other resisters, Price's reputation has been severely battered. He was released from prison; and, after a period of unemployment, he and his wife are reconstructing their lives with their infant daughter. In January 1988, Price felt vindicated when he and his former superior reached a settlement whereby the latter dropped a $5,000,000 libel suit and agreed to pay any legal fees Price had incurred in defending himself in this litigation.[57] Furthermore, shortly afterward, all charges related to the breaking of the chairman's window were dropped:[58] "I guess," Price told us, "I was sent to prison for nothing."

ZALMAN MAGID AND THE SAN DIEGO COUNTY MENTAL HEALTH CENTER

Whether Catholic, Mormon, Protestant, or Jewish, several of the resisters we interviewed felt that their religions provided meaning through which they could interpret the events around them and guide them to respond appropriately. All were committed to a wider community of caring. None had the active support of his or her church.

Dr. Zalman Magid had been a staff psychiatrist at the San Diego County Mental Health Center for six years when during 1985 several colleagues who had become increasingly uneasy with the quality of patient care and with the increase in patient deaths approached him with a plan for collaborative action. (For a full discussion of this case, see pages

188–97.) He agreed to join in the effort to persuade the administration to change its policies and to supervise the staff more closely. Despite all of their appeals, no action was taken. As the only physician in the group, Dr. Magid was chosen to write a letter to the Board of Medical Quality Assurance, in which he raised questions about patient care, particularly challenging the competence of one staff physician. After the state undertook an investigation, the hospital administrators pressured Magid to withdraw his letter:

> I was told that I should write to the Board of Medical Quality Assurance and tell them that I had written the letter in a fit of poor judgment and insanity, and that I should also send a copy of my retraction to the San Diego County Medical Society. I decided not to do this because I felt that I had done the right thing.[59]

Like Mark Price, Zalman Magid refused to take refuge behind the false claims that he had acted irrationally or could no longer recall the basis for his allegations. In addition to the central support he received from his colleagues, his decision to expose dangerous practices drew heavily on his strong religious beliefs. While he deeply admired the ethical solidarity of his colleagues, he also emphasized the sustaining quality of Orthodox Judaism:

> I was not alone in resisting: There were three or four others with whom I would share ideas and we would provide mutual support. However, when it came down to the nitty gritty, their support alone was not sufficient. It was, in the final analysis, my religious beliefs that sustained me through the most difficult periods.
>
> My position as a physician with the Oath of Hippocrates plus the requirements of Torah-true Judaism left me no choice but to take an ethical and moral stand. There is a saying in the Talmud that "he who saves one life saves the whole world." Because of this I felt that it was extremely important for me to act. If I did not act, there was a good likelihood that other people would die. According to Jewish law, if one knows that a death is likely to occur and one does nothing to prevent it or warn others, then according to the Torah, one is morally responsible for the ensuing death.[60]

Religion provided the central meaning by which he could explain to himself and to others his potentially risky actions. He was not acting precipitately, but instead was drawing upon a tradition of over five thousand years. Like Berube and Price, Magid maintained that there was a Higher Authority than that of the bureaucracy. Whatever immediate punishment his superiors might inflict, they could not force him to relinquish his belief that other standards existed and would ultimately prevail.

When he persisted in his communications with the Board of Medical Quality Assurance about serious issues of patient care, his superiors reassigned him to a position with no medical duties, requiring him to do simple clerical functions. In this humiliating situation, prayer prevented him from feeling abandoned:

I believe in the efficacy of prayer. During the entire time that I was participating in the attempt to improve patient care in the hospital, and during the ten months that I was persecuted by the administration, I prayed hard for help, both for things to improve and for the courage to continue against what turned out to be tremendous, overwhelming odds against me.[61]

While Magid found prayer to be deeply sustaining and satisfying, he was less successful in his effort to reach out to the larger Jewish community. He reports that individual members of his congregation provided words of encouragement: "You're doing the right thing"; "We can understand your position. We know others who have been in the same boat." Some suggested approaching Jewish organizations dedicated to battling anti-Semitism. But at that time Magid found Jewish community leaders unmoved. They knew of the reprisals against him, yet took no initiative in offering assistance. "There are some people," Dr. Magid suggested, "who don't like to make waves."[62] They do not want to get the Jewish community involved in controversy. They fear splitting their congregation or confronting Jewish civic leaders who may hold high positions that could be jeopardized by a scandal at a public agency.

Rabbi Jeffrey Wohlgelerntner, an Orthodox rabbi from San Diego who leads the congregation of which Magid is currently a member, explained why he would have supported Magid had he been his rabbi at that time.

From the Halachic [Jewish legal] point of view, [the doctor] did the appropriate thing in "blowing the whistle." Because it says in Leviticus 19:16 ". . . Do not stand idly by the blood of your neighbor," meaning that any Jew, and certainly a Jewish physician, has the moral responsibility to prevent another person from having their blood spilt, either through accident or death. These issues of patient morbidity and mortality were what prompted [the doctor] to blow the whistle.

Also in Leviticus 19:14, it says ". . . Do not put a stumbling block before a blind [that is, helpless] man." This means not only that a Jew should not actively place an obstacle before someone who might get hurt or die, but a Jew is obligated to *remove* such an obstacle.[63]

But effective as religious teaching has been in motivating and even encouraging individual responsibility, churches and synagogues have provided little leadership in the day-to-day battle of the ethical resisters. Religious organizations have rarely offered collective or communal support in resolving conflicts, or attempted to serve as mediators before a major confrontation moved into the courts or impersonal grievance procedures for resolution. The resisters had been socialized to believe that they alone had to make the decision to act on appropriate beliefs. They did not believe that help would be forthcoming from the standard-bearers of religious morality. As a result, ethical resisters seldom turned to their churches for direct guidance or collective action. When they did, they were often disappointed.

There is thus a discrepancy between a church's beliefs and its deeds. While religious institutions in American society have historically served to maintain moral standards in the community, in the modern period religion has become increasingly individualized and privatized. Membership in congregations waxes and wanes. Many church members attend services sporadically and change churches without much regard for denominational beliefs.[64] In response, churches have increasingly come to emphasize personal morality over public responsibility. They concentrate on offering their congregants opportunities for the development of self-realization in the context of loving and caring associations. They function in an environment where individuals pick and choose from the body of theology, doctrine, practices, rituals, and beliefs in order to find personal satisfaction rather than fulfill a collective obligation.

Some churches do include social action programs through which they manifest their concern for the less fortunate. Their areas of interest range from sheltering the homeless and feeding the hungry to supporting struggles for civil rights. But rarely does a church move beyond highly prescribed areas of social activism to delve into those issues where political controversy would force the church to take a stand. Sheltering the homeless is an act of charity, but it stops short of pressing for redistribution of income, creation of jobs, or even raising the minimum wage. To take these positions might evoke serious conflict among members whose own economic interests might be threatened by even modest social change. Similarly, churches do not often criticize the failure of ethical conduct in business and public affairs. There has been little religious institutional leadership on the profound issues of corporate irresponsibility or government corruption. Although clergy may deliver sermons exhorting parishioners to assume a moral stance, there has been far less organized effort to exert pressure on industrial and government leaders to abide by their own professed standards. For example, neither Watergate nor the Iran-contra affair evoked an outcry from the religious community. Since churches seldom have internal structures to enforce their values on modern bureaucratic organizations, church members must apply their religious tenets individually in their daily work lives.

Rarely does a church take a public stand on bureaucratic corruption as might the Catholic Church for the "right to life" or would Jewish organizations in instances of anti-Semitism. An ethical conflict in the workplace is not a likely candidate for religious intervention. It would position the church in opposition to powerful public agencies and their leaders. Such a stand would risk a cleavage among its members and might result in a substantial loss of support.

The experiences of Bert Berube at the General Services Administration, Mark Price at the Department of Education, and Zalman Magid at a county mental health facility in San Diego, California, differ in many respects. But in all three cases strong religious beliefs motivated their decision to act when they confronted unethical or illegal activity in their agencies. None of the men would back down in the face of threats to their reputations and careers. They believed they had to do the right thing, even if they were to suffer unfairly in their quests to uproot malfeasance.

Not all religious people, of course, become ethical resisters. Three distinctive qualities propelled Berube, Price, Magid, and others to act on their religious principles. First, they refused to tolerate different standards for private and public morality. For them, what is taught in church or synagogue on the Sabbath must be applied to all situations. The professional ethics of each man served as a vibrant link between religion and the everyday realities of the job. Each knew what was appropriate for an engineer, an attorney, or a physician to do under a set of provocative circumstances. Religion solidified their determination. It also provided essential sustenance which enabled them to continue their protest. As we have noted in several cases, initial acts of resistance could readily be washed away by management's retaliatory methods. Staying power made the difference between forcing public recognition of serious problems or allowing management to represent ethical resistance as the aberrant behavior of a troubled but now repentant employee.

Second, religious resisters believed that individuals are fully responsible for their actions in their organizational roles. Those who make decisions that result in harm to others cannot claim exemption by hiding behind a bureaucratic facade. While religious beliefs often worked in concert with professional ethics, loyalty to an organization and its needs never took precedence over a moral claim.

Third, resisters maintained that their consciences required them to offer active opposition to corrupt behavior. The expression of lofty ideals or even the voicing of dissent was not sufficient. Acts of disobedience against illegitimate authority were required if resistance was to be genuine and effective. The temptation to retreat had to be rejected. Zalman Magid, for example, reported that several physicians, who cosigned an initial letter about patient care with him, backed off when superiors demanded a retraction. Under these pressures, religion enabled Magid, like other religious resisters, to reject the temptation to jump to safe ground.

Bert Berube, Mark Price, and Zalman Magid refused to back down by rationalizing that they did not know enough to act, nor did they harbor the belief that they could continue their pursuit of success while injustice prevailed around them. The religious resisters often had a very personal view of God and fully believed that He would play a role in the final dénouement of their cases. Occasionally these beliefs were reinforced by their participation in religious services and retreats. Though members of these groups offered affirmation of their faith and served as sympathetic friends, religious institutions, as we have pointed out, offered little public support. In only one exceptional case did a Lutheran congregation raise

$14,000 to support the legal defense of a whistleblower who had suffered intense retaliation; and even then, the church was located more than a thousand miles from the small town where many would have been fearful of crossing the local power structure involved in the dispute. Thus, however potent religion was as a private resource, as an institution it neither reinforced moral behavior nor forcefully condemned unethical practices.

These examples and those of other resisters raise profound questions about the effectiveness of institutions that guard ethical behavior in American society. We believe it is incorrect to assert that individual citizens are unwilling to take responsibility for the public good or that workers only seek personal aggrandizement. The failure resides not so much with individual conscience as with major institutions assigned to serve as moral guides and protectors. Less preaching and more direct action could provide crucial protection for those who serve as witnesses for the faith's most treasured beliefs. Such commitment could also encourage other believers to stand up for justice if they felt that they would be supported rather than abandoned. In the absence of such backing, only a few of the more fervent dare come forward.

In Defense of Community: Dobie Hatley and the Comanche Peak Nuclear Power Plant

Blue-collar and clerical workers in large organizations whose practices may entail serious violations of environmental health and safety standards may be inspired to speak out against such practices out of a deep sense of community. The workers we studied were likely to remain in the communities where they had grown up, and thus strongly identified with potential victims who could be relatives, friends, or neighbors. While professionals or managers tended to refer to an ethical code, the workers spoke more frequently of their roots in a particular region or even neighborhood, and of their fear of a work-related accident harming those close to them. At times, they specifically referred to an obligation to the land that had been passed down by parents and ancestors. They often contrasted their sense of responsibility for the community with that of high-placed corporate executives who move frequently to accommodate their careers and have neither roots nor long-term commitments to the people with whom they work.[65]

The response of the larger community to such principled protest was often divided. Where the residents believed that property or health was immediately threatened by toxic wastes, illegal dumping, or other practices that caused environmental damage directly affecting them and their families, they supported those who disclosed problems. But when jobs were involved and the danger seemed less imminent, the response was more divided and ambivalent. If the ethical resisters disclosed practices that could result in a plant closing, for example, then heated opposition often developed from itinerant workers as well as from permanent residents, who viewed the chances of an environmental disaster as remote.[66] Managers knew how to exploit such feelings and effectively turned co-workers, local businessmen, and newspaper editors against the dissenters by calling them a direct threat to economic prosperity and lumping them together with "outside agitators" who only want to stir up trouble.

This response engendered intense fear and a sense of isolation among the resisters. As long-term residents, they deeply valued the friendship of neighbors, storekeepers, and town officials, and their sense of well-being and personal security derived from the good will of their community. When this disappeared and warm encounters were replaced by ugly stares and threats of bodily harm, the resisters suffered a double loss. Dismissed from their jobs with the resultant dislocation, they also felt cut adrift from the community that had long nourished them. Ironically, then, like resisters who drew strength from professional ethics and religious beliefs, these workers also found that the very source of their values—their community—now provided little support and became, moreover, a source of imminent danger. Several of the whistleblowers moved out of their homes. A few relocated thirty or forty miles away, where they would not have to face hostile adversaries still working at the plant. Unlikely allies from within the local area or national arena became their most ardent supporters throughout their ordeal and enabled them to carry on their struggle for recognition and vindication.

In some cases, local activist groups came to the resisters' defense. These organizations—whether dedicated to environmental causes, to an antinuclear agenda, or to consumer protection—welcomed the testimony of workers who as "insiders" could support their cause with detailed and verifiable evidence. In return, these groups provided ongoing affirmation to the resisters that their cause was just. The activists intervened in seeking publicity in the local media, in obtaining legal counsel for those who were fired or blacklisted, and in providing a sense of ethical solidarity with the workers. As public-interest groups they did not worry, as might churches or professional organizations, about dividing their membership or compromising their neutrality or violating their nonprofit status. Since community political pressure groups exist to lobby for special causes, advocacy for whistleblowers is consistent with their *raison d'être.*

While all of this assistance was welcome, these small, often recently formed groups lacked the financial base and political clout to assure the resisters of an adequate shield against management. They were most effective if they could capture the attention of national groups with access to skilled attorneys and to the media. The nuclear power field has been the most fertile in creating such an alliance.

Throughout the United States, scores of nuclear workers have testified about unsafe plant construction before various state and federal government agencies—public disclosure that has led to the delay in the licensing of some plants or to the permanent shutdown of others. These clerical and construction workers-turned-witnesses put aside their immediate self-interest: that is, in coming forward they almost invariably lost their highly paid jobs and foreclosed the possibility of being rehired anywhere in the nuclear industry. Many, fearing for their personal safety and for that of the community, felt that the danger of a nuclear plant accident was simply too great a risk to ignore. They sought the intervention of regulatory agencies and, when this proved insufficient, called in other government departments and also took their cases to court. Among these protesters was a group of nuclear workers at the Comanche Peak plant in Glen Rose, Texas, who went to the Nuclear Regulatory Commission when they sensed that the violation of safety codes in the construction of the plant endangered their land.[67]

Dobie Hatley and her husband, T. E., came from modest economic backgrounds. In the early years of their marriage, they had had serious financial problems, but they had managed to purchase a small farm in Glen Rose and raise their three children. An outgoing and ambitious woman, Hatley became active in local community and political affairs, eventually becoming a juvenile officer working with troubled youth in the county. The opportunity for a job with the Brown and Root Corporation, contractors building a nuclear power plant at nearby Comanche Peak, offered Hatley a major increase in income. She went to work there in 1979 and loved it. The hours were long and there was a lot of overtime, but the job was interesting; there was much to learn and she did well. She worked in various phases of document control, the crucial arm of any nuclear power plant charged with ensuring that actual construction follows initial and revised plans. Hatley received several promotions, supervised a number of other workers, and was jokingly referred to as "Miss Brown and Root," the woman who could get anything she wanted out at the plant. With paychecks sometimes approaching $1,000 per week, it was easy to feel very good about Comanche Peak. Her enthusiasm did not blind her to the problems of working at the plant. She knew that there was no job security, and that people were dismissed for the smallest infractions of the rules: "One worker was fired for eating a banana as he was filling out a time sheet. They decided to make an example of him. Everyone lived in fear of being fired or laid off. There was constant pressure to appear busy."[68]

Dobie Hatley realized that workers often felt that they had no control over their lives. The pressure on the job was so great that men often drank before going to work and kept ice chests full of beer in their pickup trucks so they could drink immediately after their work shifts.* Some children never saw their fathers sober, an observation confirmed for us by several employees. For example, Bob Messerly was a welder at Comanche Peak for five years. The money was excellent but the job conditions took a heavy toll on him and his family:

> When I got fired, it was like somebody took the Rock of Gibraltar off my chest. I don't like working under those types of conditions. I changed when I left there. I became more relaxed. Hell, I couldn't have sat down and talked to you four years ago. I'd have been too damn nervous. I'd have to go out and drink six beers to go to work and as soon as I got off work, I'd start drinking. I was damn near an alcoholic. I had never in my life drank to go to work.[70]

Despite these problems, Hatley did not give up her faith in Comanche Peak. Although she knew that many people were opposed to having a major nuclear power plant in their backyards, she had been involved in

*Problems of substance abuse have been reported at other plants.[69]

Operation Information, an organization that had investigated nuclear power, and she had decided that nuclear power was safe. She would not have continued to work at Comanche Peak, she said, if she thought an accident could destroy the countryside she and her family loved. She had worked too hard to acquire and hold on to a small piece of that land in Glen Rose. Her children had grown up there, and her memories of raising a family were embedded in their farm.

This view about safe nuclear energy began to wane in light of certain management decisions that had a direct impact on Hatley and her work group. When management failed to meet the required production schedule, it intensified the pressure to get the work done. Hatley still maintained that a good job could be done, even as one dismissed employee, Chuck Atchison, began to testify publicly at various licensing hearings about irregularities in the construction.[71] Yet by May 1983, Dobie Hatley also began to experience severe doubts about the plant's safety.

The Nuclear Regulatory Commission regulations required accurate, complete documentation on the design and construction of the plant. Hatley's job was to supervise document control centers throughout the plant which provided the working documents to the field personnel. These satellite locations that she supervised were responsible for millions of pieces of paper. She found, however, that Brown and Root did not make provisions to keep all the plans current or accurate. The inaccuracies became extremely important because there was no way to determine what actually was in the ground. Thus, in the event of a problem or an accident, it would be impossible to analyze exactly why it had occurred.* Hatley understood the necessity of documenting the thousands of changes that go into any plant construction. In a homespun analogy, she related the complex plant construction to problems confronting the average property owner in her community: "If you have a set of pipes in your house and you have a problem, you must know how those pipes are laid out if you

---

*This lack of documentation was in violation of 10 CFR part 50, appendix B, the federal regulations that require all construction changes and identified problems to be committed to writing in permanent documentation. Hatley's concerns of 1983–84 have been found correct by the 15 February 1988 report of Victor Gilinsky and in the 11 February 1988 report of Texas Utilities to the NRC, where the supervisor of generic licensing reports that "inappropriate deficiency documentation" is "no longer in use," and that "the design control program has been strengthened through the implementation of revised procedures."[72]

want to deal with that problem. This is even more serious when you are dealing with a nuclear plant. It was keeping accurate plans that prevented a major tragedy at Three Mile Island." With the specter of Three Mile Island before her, Hatley was not content to stand by. Her superior was sympathetic but, as she learned, powerless to force an appropriate correction: "When I saw that we were not going to get the documentation corrected, I complained to my bosses that they had to stop this. My immediate boss realized what was happening, but he could not convince the higher-ups."[73]

The NRC scheduled an audit for July 1983, and the company had to decide what to do about the irregularities in their records. The managers persuaded Hatley to help rewrite the documentation, assuring her that collaboration in an illegal act, no matter how repugnant, would allow time for an appropriate remedy, which they promised to effect:

> My boss called me in and told me that we had to get the books to match. If we did it right, it probably would have taken a year. So what were we going to do? We had to pass the audit and the only way to do that was to rewrite the documentation. We destroyed the records and wrote new ones to match what we needed. That's falsification of documentation. The supervisor promised us that after the audit we were going to make all of this right. We just did not have the time now because the audit committee was coming. We passed with flying colors.[74]

Hatley knew that what she had done was illegal and potentially dangerous for the entire region. She pressed for the corrections, but did not get clear answers. She became further dismayed when she found herself in the midst of another crisis about some of the steel used in the construction. Her immediate supervisor was so distraught that he walked off the job. Hatley was now enmeshed in a major cover-up:

> According to the NRC regulation, steel construction required steel with a pedigree on it. This meant that you had to know where the steel was milled and what its chisel strength was. The wrong steel was used, and it started to buckle and flake. . . . For all we know, it could have been some of the Mexican steel that had radiation in it. I kept going in and saying this is not right. My boss knew that and he knew about

the paper cover-up. We were all under a lot of pressure, and he felt it very keenly. So he walked out for a week, and his boss replaced him.[75]

Several months later, in October 1983, a second independent audit was scheduled to focus on documentation. Hatley was again instructed to change the documents, with assurances that everything would be cleared up after the audit. The falsification again resulted in a successful audit, but her supervisors took no corrective action.

Hatley's confidence was now badly shaken. She felt that the company would have to undertake a major engineering effort to ensure that the pipes had been installed properly and matched the blueprints. She began to share the conclusions of several Comanche Peak whistleblowers who had joined the local environmentalists in charging that the plant was potentially dangerous to the entire countryside.

Her superiors were aware that her attitudes were changing, and some of her superiors ordered her not to speak about plant business away from the site. Hatley laughingly replied that she spent all her waking hours at the plant, but from that point on she felt her days were numbered. She knew too much and was therefore defined as a potential troublemaker. Within a few weeks, she was unceremoniously dismissed despite several years of loyal service.[76] Hatley, who continued to believe in the importance of nuclear power, decided that the plant was too great a threat to the community. This was not an abstract principle, she said. Real people, whom she knew and cared about, would suffer terribly in the event of an accident. She could no longer remain silent and believe that everything would turn out fine if she just kept her faith in management. She sought out a citizens group which directed her to the Government Accountability Project. Through her lawyer, she approached the Nuclear Regulatory Commission and revealed all the irregularities she had participated in.

Why did the former "Miss Brown and Root," a grandmother in her late forties, take on a major multinational corporation? Like other resisters, her trust in her superiors was shattered when they made no effort to correct the serious flaws in quality control. Furthermore, their enmeshing her in illegal activities increased her feelings of vulnerability. Most significant, her long residence in the area and her profound ties to the community heightened her identification with local citizens and their vulnerability to injury and death in the event of a nuclear accident. Hatley's dismissal severed all allegiance to the plant management. The breach of trust, her sense of legal jeopardy, her identification with the well-being of the community, and her outrage at the shabby treatment she received all coalesced and propelled her to take on a major fight. It would have been easier and safer to walk away quietly, but she no longer found that acceptable.

In becoming a central figure in the public controversy about the plant's safety, she did not stand alone. She was at the hub of a group of five women who protested construction records and procedures. As a result of her public testimony, Hatley also began to see the less supportive side of her neighbors and one-time friends. The local newspaper railed against her; she received threatening phone calls; beer cans and other debris were tossed onto her lawn. Other incidents led her to believe that it would be wise to switch cars with her sons frequently and even to sleep in a different house each night until things calmed down. The company with the million-dollar payroll had developed many allies.

Sue Neumeyer, who worked in quality control at the plant, also began to be increasingly concerned about the violations of regulations at the construction site. After voicing her concerns and challenging falsified documents, Neumeyer left the site before she could be fired. She, too, contacted the NRC.[77] Several death threats by phone and an unexplained beating of a woman co-worker who had spoken publicly against the plant led Neumeyer to believe that this act of resistance put her and her daughter at great risk. She was afraid to be in her own home, terrified that someone from the plant might harm them. Why did she not simply turn her back on the problem instead of jeopardizing her personal security and upsetting her teenage daughter's orderly life? She expressed her motivations succinctly:

I'm a Texan. Like I said, this is my state. My mother's side, I'm fourth-generation Texan. On my father's side, I'm second-generation. This is my state. I am not going until I see that there is nothing that can be done. My roots are here. I'm not going to leave. If they start that plant up, then I'll have no choice but to leave, but in the meantime I'm going to fight it.[78]

Like Dobie Hatley, Neumeyer continued to believe in nuclear power. She felt that the plants could be built safely and was bitter about managers whose decisions might ruin Texas. As itinerant employees moving regularly from site to site, the managers had created a national problem because they cared little about the community and principally focused on profits and their own careers. It was so important, she said passionately, that the whistleblowers win the case in Texas, to demonstrate that their rights could be protected in a confrontation with a giant corporation. She realized, however, that she and her colleagues were fighting a lonely battle. Most people she spoke to were fed up with stories of cancer and danger to their lives, and accepted the view that the whistleblowers' actions would result only in higher utility rates. Neumeyer had no illusion that the majority of her neighbors supported her struggle.[79]

Neumeyer's concern about the safety of the plant and her love of her home were echoed by Stan Miles, a welder and craftsman at the Comanche Peak plant. With his jeans and cowboy boots and Texas drawl, Miles personified the land in which he was raised:

I was born in this state and this state means a lot more to me than just a place to live. If you will look at my work record, I've never gone out of the state to work. I don't like to leave this land. I like the people here. It's changed a lot, though, since I was a boy. For instance, I was born in west Texas, real west Texas, west of the Pecos. You didn't have car trouble without the next person stopping, and if he had to drive eighty miles out of his way, he did, and you didn't have to pay him anything. I have read in several historical novels what this country looked like in 1860. I had several old friends, for instance, an old teacher who lived in my hometown since 1909, who told me about the vineyards they had in that country back then.

That's gone—all gone, and for the sake of a dollar bill. They took something that was priceless and ruined it for something made of paper. Because if you poison the water, you poison the land. How can the dollar bill replace that? This state means something to me. I was born here, my ancestors came here in 1821, my grandmother was a Comanche Indian, and they've been here for ten thousand years.[80]

Despite their resolve, both Sue Neumeyer and Stan Miles ultimately had to leave their beloved Texas to seek work. Their challenge to the plant left them no alternative when they found themselves blacklisted from other jobs. While Miles was able to return, Neumeyer still feels she has no choice but to work in another state.[81]

Like the ethical resisters who acted on professional and religious beliefs, the whistleblowers who were deeply committed to their communities found little institutional support from local groups. Friends and neighbors often shunned them, while local politicians frequently defined them as troublemakers. Ironically, the resisters, who saw themselves as pro-nuclear and had earlier opposed the antinuclear organizations in the region, now found their most sustained support among the safe-energy activists. In the Dallas/Fort Worth region, Citizens' Association for Sound Energy leaders supplied Hatley and the others with information and support when they testified at the licensing hearings, and provided contacts with public-interest groups that might offer legal assistance. In some instances, CASE did much more. Where necessary, its leaders raised small amounts of money to tide over an unemployed family and provided emotional assistance to resisters who felt they had nowhere to turn.[82]

Yet these organizations were essentially small and fragile and frequently marginal in the community. More established civic organizations, such as the Rotary Club, the Chamber of Commerce, or the League of Women Voters, were silent. Many of their members were local business people who may have sided with the nuclear plant managers. Like the religious resisters, those who acted out of loyalty to the community had learned well the lesson of love for their land but were unable to draw on many local resources for new jobs or for assistance in fighting a mammoth corporation.

In 1985, the Nuclear Regulatory Commission issued a report of an investigation launched in March 1984, soon after Hatley blew the whistle. The report confirmed that Comanche Peak's design and construction had serious problems. In 1988, Comanche Peak still had not received an operating license because the problems pointed out by Hatley, Neumeyer, Miles, Atchison, and over eighty other workers had led to the discovery of a decade of failed compliance.[83] (See pages 228–30.)

Chapter 5

Retaliation: Management's Effort to Destroy the Ethical Resister

DEMETRIOS BASDEKAS, Bert Berube, Mary McAnaw, Dobie Hatley, and other ethical resisters were considered a danger by the organizations for which they worked. By protesting internally and then going to the Congress or the press, these employees revealed that their principles commanded their loyalty far more strongly than did management. From their superiors' perspective, the resisters had not uncovered serious breaches of policy but had rather involved themselves in actions against the very bureaucratic hierarchy that had hired them and provided good salaries and the accoutrements of a respected position. The resisters' lack of gratitude and the resultant threat to the organizations' line of command required a firm response. In seeking to regain the initiative by totally rejecting the allegations and undermining the resisters' credibility, managers used the formidable power available to them.

Since they had expected management to be more responsive to their initial complaints, few resisters were prepared for their fate. Most understood that there might be some retribution, but few realized how damaging and extensive it would be. As the wife of one resister employed in private industry described: "I had no idea that they were not through with my husband when he was fired. It never would have occurred to me that there would have been the effort that was made to absolutely squash his career. I could not, did not, imagine the vindictiveness."[1]

Another resister, appointed to a prestigious position in 1981 as an attorney in the Interior Department, charged that he had uncovered his superiors' failure to collect millions of dollars in reclamation fees from coal companies. After numerous efforts to force them to implement the law, he approached the department's inspector general and later informed members of Congress of the violations. Vincent Laubach was totally unprepared for the avalanche of abuse that came down upon him, ultimately resulting in dismissal. Clearly, his superiors regarded him no longer as an attorney of impeccable integrity but rather as a disloyal troublemaker who had taken department business to outside sources, embarrassing the department's leadership and possibly derailing future career opportunities for those charged with violations. Astounded by their acts of vengeance against him, Laubach could not understand how they could have treated him so badly. "What kind of people were they? How could they live with themselves?" he asked.[2]

As Laubach and others painfully learned, the punishment mounted against ethical resisters is no casual matter. While it may seem to take the form of personal revenge by superiors, retaliation is, in fact, part of a rational and planned process initiated by an organization to destroy the resister's credibility as a witness.[3] To achieve this aim, management often invokes such harsh measures as blacklisting, dismissal, transfer, and personal harassment, which far exceed the ostensible provocation.*

There are several reasons for these excessive punishments. First, management insists that employees do not have a right to judge their superiors or challenge organizational policies publicly. Attempts to overturn decisions made by those at the top are defined as acts of insubordination and are considered a threat to the orderly procedures required to operate in a businesslike fashion. Management fears that capitulation would open

---

*Dr. Anthony Morris tracked the fate of others in the federal government by clipping all relevant articles in the *Federal Times* (weekly newspaper for federal government employees) between May 1984 and November 1985. He supplemented the data with reports of whistleblowing from the *Washington Post, Science,* and *Time* magazines. He collected articles on the tribulations of thirty whistleblowers and determined that twenty-two were judged to have had unfavorable outcomes. He concluded from his material that "for every unscathed survivor, there are dozens of wrecked lives."[4]

the floodgates to challenges by other workers. Because the ethical resisters are often respected by their fellow employees and have earned credible reputations, their superiors believe that, as potentially dangerous role models, they must be stopped. In retaliating against the resisters, then, an administration consciously tries to belittle them and thus to signal to others that confronting authority has high risks and can result in harm to one's career and family.*

Management knows it faces a severe threat from knowledgeable insiders who can publicize errant behavior or criminal actions by taking the evidence to outside agencies. Central to management's dilemma is the need to repair the rupture of "mutual pretense" which helps managers sustain the belief that all is under control on matters under their jurisdiction.[6] Rather than allow outsiders to question the workings of a department or an agency, most managers quickly attack a resister's credibility, particularly if the charges are serious, in the hope of diverting unwanted questions.

A prime example occurred in the early 1980s when officials at the Environmental Protection Agency mounted a campaign to discredit and dismiss Hugh Kaufman after he exposed the agency's failure to deal with increasing amounts of chemical waste, despite the Reagan administration's guarantee that the EPA was committed to finding and cleaning up dump sites.[7] Kaufman presented evidence to the press and congressional committees of the agency's failure to attend to this important issue. He would not remain silent about the close relationship that existed between the EPA and the leaders of the industries they were sworn to regulate. His active protest resulted in a secret campaign to track his whereabouts and find evidence to fire him. The EPA's inspector general became implicated in this scheme.† Silencing Kaufman became official policy

---

*In another study, Karen and Donald Soeken surveyed ninety whistleblowers of whom 60 percent were federal government employees and 40 percent worked in private industry. The Soekens found that one out of five people in the sample was out of work. Even among federal employees protected by civil service, half were no longer with the same agency. They also experienced harassment and isolation. These whistleblowers reported extensive retaliation and exhibited physical and emotional deterioration.[5]

†Richard M. Campbell, assistant inspector general for investigations, Office of the Inspector General, Environmental Protection Agency, told us of the efforts to gather evidence to fire Hugh Kaufman. "Ms. Lavelle, EPA assistant administrator, advised me and Mr. Novick [the inspector general] that she wished to fire Mr. Kaufman and hoped that we could accommodate her request for an investigation."[8] Campbell was appalled by the misuse of the IG office and later resigned. Kaufman gained national prominence and became a symbol of an employee who refused to be cowed by an oppressive bureaucracy.

even if it meant invading his privacy in the futile hope of uncovering some personal indiscretion.[9]

The Irony of Retaliation

While the method of retaliation backfired in the Kaufman case, management was seldom so inept. But the harsh punishments managers usually chose often had unforeseen consequences and, instead of quieting protest, exacerbated the conflict and intensified the resisters' loss of trust in the integrity of their superiors. The more abuse the resisters faced, the more confirmed they became that active opposition was the only path to ending the chain of lawless acts. Propelled by various forms of retaliation, resisters sought out new allies and alternative authority structures. Occasionally these were co-workers who shared the resisters' outrage; more often they turned to media reporters, government officials, lawyers, and members of public-interest groups. Where successful, resisters developed a network of supporters who believed that victory even against a powerful organization was possible. Each subsequent act of retaliation intensified the resisters' commitment to seek vindication. Retaliation itself thus became an integral and indispensable spur to ethical resistance.[10]

We have found that punishment, while personally costly to the resisters, serves a vital social function. Ethical resisters do not allow serious problems to remain quiescent.[11] Retaliation intensifies their commitment to press forward. Once harassed and humiliated, they will not acquiesce to managers' efforts to co-opt or intimidate them. Their initial protest is transformed into a mission to prove to the world that they are right and that they have been unfairly treated. Their strong sense of justice is reinforced by a personal need to be vindicated. While the cases presented in this chapter document the personal, familial, and career harm inflicted on dissenters, they also highlight the determination that thrives among those who know that they "have done no wrong."*

---

*Many whistleblowers have become social activists in their effort to prove the merit of their initial protest. As a result, they not only fight their own cases but also serve as constant consultants to others who have come forward. William Bush (see pages 207–9) is a prime example, as are Bert Berube (see page 105) and Billie Garde (see pages 217–19).

Blacklisting

The blacklist is one of management's most potent weapons.* Where successful, it prevents dismissed workers from gaining employment in a comparable organization, excludes them from access to potentially sensitive information, and maintains a feeling of solidarity among managers who agree to forewarn each other of potential troublemakers. A blacklist can be overt, as when particular employees are actually noted on a sheet recording the names of undesirables. It can also be more subtle, relying on negative references which damage the employee's possibility for future employment.

The victims of a blacklist, who initially are often unaware of the conspiracy to isolate and deny them work, may spend long weeks and months in the futile hope that if they persist, their next application will result in suitable employment. As they unravel the pattern of their exclusion, the resisters' frustration often turns to rage and then to depression, and they develop fantasies of destroying those who have deprived them of their achievements and dreams.[13] They are under severe financial pressure, usually having spent both their unemployment insurance and their savings. These resisters, who can no longer provide for their families, exhibit all the symptoms of grief as they mourn a lost job and the future that once seemed so promising.[14]

The plight of blacklisted ethical resisters is not lost on co-workers or colleagues and is a vivid reminder of the power of the organization. Fellow employees are urged not to associate with the outcast employee. A graphic example of the power of an informal blacklist is revealed in the case of corporation lawyer Joseph Rose.

JOSEPH ROSE AND THE ASSOCIATED MILK PRODUCERS

In 1973 Joseph Rose, a thirty-five-year-old attorney with five children, joined the Associated Milk Producers in San Antonio as in-house counsel. His wife's serious illness had forced a move so they could be near their families. The Roses never expected that they would soon be enmeshed in a major scandal that would cost Joe his job, undermine their financial security, and isolate them in a community where his employers had

*The blacklist has been used against labor over a period of many decades. Perhaps the best-known and most documented case is the exclusion of Hollywood figures during and after the so-called McCarthy period in the 1950s.[12]

enormous influence. Rose had had a successful career with several major corporations, including Gates Rubber Company and Montgomery Ward, and had always considered himself an ethical practitioner. He admired his former superiors as men of the greatest integrity.

In his new job he examined the milk cooperative's records. To his dismay, he became aware that the AMPI was making illegal political payments to the Nixon re-election campaign in return for a commitment to retain price supports for milk producers. These covert contributions were part of a larger pattern of illegal arrangements between corporations and the Committee to Re-elect the President which the Special Watergate Prosecutor and the Senate Watergate Committee were investigating. Rose had walked into a major scandal.[15]

He immediately approached his superiors with his suspicions but they rejected his concerns, hoping to ride out the investigation. He knew, however, that if he did not take some action, he would become implicated in an ongoing criminal conspiracy. Perhaps, as one AMPI official humorously suggested, Rose was already implicated because he had been signing checks as one of his duties. Rose was far from amused. As he weighed his options, he believed that going outside the organization with his allegations could be personally risky since he might be charged with violating the attorney-client privilege.

His wife, Linda, a strong, intelligent, and articulate woman, remembered the stress they both felt as he pondered his alternatives:

> The real world was not turning out to be in any way like the theory that we both grew up with when we were young. I can remember Joe coming home and saying as he walked in the door, "I can't believe these things have happened. You're not going to believe this." I'd see him pacing back and forth and finally when he did come in and sit down, he said, "There are some things that are going to happen that are really going to have an impact on us." Joe had already made up his mind. He knew the direction that he was going in.

Linda Rose strongly agreed with her husband's decision not to participate in illegal activity. They had raised their children with profound religious and ethical commitments and felt that, as parents, they could never face them honestly if they did not act on their beliefs. At the same time, Linda Rose felt that she had unwittingly put excessive pressure on her husband during those trying times:

Do you know that I was so naive I can remember saying one evening that if all the dairy farmers would be made aware of this situation, it would be all right. Now I realize that the dairy farmers had severe economic pressures of their own because milk prices were sliding so precipitously.

I honestly thought that it was in Joe's power and his capability to end the illegal activity simply by reason and by his demand that it be shut down. When Jack Kennedy was running for office, he said the individual could make a difference. Well, I bought it hook, line, and sinker. I thought you could.[16]

Both Joe and Linda Rose believed that professional ethics and religious beliefs required a firm stand. In the fashion of many of those who had come to maturity in the 1960s, they also accepted a conscious commitment to changing the nation's moral climate. Linda Rose fully believed that her husband could make a profound difference because of his faith and will.

Joseph Rose was more aware of the dangers ahead. Realizing that he was vulnerable, he decided to seek advice and counsel:

I consulted a lawyer and former judge here in San Antonio, who had had many dealings with the Associated Milk Producer people and knew that they were rather disreputable. He urged me to start keeping notes on everything I did, to gather all of the documents that supported my position, to bypass the general manager, and to take the evidence to the board of directors. I was never allowed to do that.

Rose met with several members of the board during the annual meeting but was refused permission to address the entire group. Obviously, they decided to take no action but informed the general manager of his charges. The results were predictable: there was no change of policy, and the messenger who brought the bad news was immediately dismissed: "When I returned to work, I found a guard posted at my door. The locks had been changed. The general manager demanded to see me. My services had become very, very unsatisfactory. I was fired and felt a great sense of relief."[17]

Rose thought his relationship with the Associated Milk Producers had come to an end. He was mistaken. The executives of AMPI had taken seriously his earlier threats to go to their constituents:

While I was still employed, I had indicated to AMPI executives that if the board would not listen to me, I would go right to the dairy farmers, and they obviously felt my career and credibility had to be completely destroyed to protect their own tails.

When I was fired I was glad to be out of it, and I planned to keep my mouth shut. Then I had a call from a lawyer involved in an antitrust suit against AMPI. He said, "They are really slandering you—making some very vicious attacks on you."[18]

Events quickly moved out of Joseph Rose's control. He was subpoenaed to provide evidence of AMPI activities by the Watergate Special Prosecutor's Office and the Senate Select Committee investigating the Watergate scandals. He raised the issue of attorney-client privilege in both forums but was overruled. When he realized that he would be forced to testify, he informed AMPI about his pending appearances. The company put out the word that he had broken attorney-client privilege and successfully blacklisted him in San Antonio. Without a job, Rose became a pariah as other attorneys in San Antonio were unwilling to assist him in any way, fearing they would be tarred by associating with a "disreputable" lawyer: "All of a sudden friends began to disappear. I can remember that there was one particular attorney in town to whom I went for help. I was looking for a job and he was absolutely no help. In fact, he shunned me as much as he possibly could."[19]

The ostracism left him without any source of employment. The Roses and their five children were forced to move from a large, comfortable house to a two-room apartment. Joe decided he had to accept a promising position in another part of the country—but hope quickly turned to disappointment. He could not escape the tentacles of those seeking to break him:

There was an attorney up in New York, and I answered one of his ads. It turned out that he was a friend of an executive of AMPI, and, indeed, his secretary was a niece of one of the executives. I accepted that job in New York, and he and I went out on one case. He said right in front of a client, "He does not know it yet, but at Christmastime I am going to fire him." I thought he was kidding, and I did not pay any attention to it, and then—lo and behold!—right at Christmastime, he fired me. Great psychological warfare.[20]

The actions of Rose's colleagues were a severe blow. He had always felt fortunate to work with people whose ethics he respected. Their good opinion of him had solidified his view that one could practice law with integrity. Now when superiors had acted with dishonesty and vindictiveness, colleagues in the legal community, who should have come to his defense, were defining him as the culprit. The pressure became increasingly intense for a man who just a few months before had considered himself a successful attorney and a good provider with a secure future. The Roses lived on beans and salad and frequently received anonymous threatening phone calls. The family was terrified: "I literally had a judge tell me I should be armed because people had been found with bullets in their backs for a hell of a lot less than I did."[21]

Rose became deeply bitter. Beyond the loss of job and home, he felt betrayed by the American Associated Milk Producers, by his colleagues in the legal profession, and even by relatives who had suggested to his children that they were unlucky to have him as their father. Only his wife, his children, and his own father stood by him. They all paid a price, but the children were Rose's special concern:

I think children are damaged even worse than the person who takes the stand. That is one thing over the years that I have tried to make up to them because I understand and saw the damage and the pain they went through. The children see their father as unable to function, and they start saying, "Why?" They can't come up with any good answers. I would not like to have been in their shoes. My shoes were bad enough, but theirs were far worse.

As with other resisters, religious belief provided the Roses with some sustenance in those difficult times: "I don't think I would have been in the place I was at the time I was, had it not been part of God's plan for my life and I think the good that came out of it, came in a very strange way because what came out of it was a lot more self-sufficiency."[22]

Rose did have the satisfaction of knowing that his allegations were proven correct. The charges against the AMPI for making illegal political payments were ultimately tried in federal court in 1974, and several of its executives were convicted and sentenced to prison.[23] There was, however, no legally constituted third party or external authority to mediate the conflict between Rose and his former employers or to protect him from continuing reprisals. With only one exception, even the government officials who directly benefited from his cooperation were not forthcoming in assisting him when he was virtually blacklisted. Linda Rose was particularly adamant about this, feeling that they had been totally discarded by those who should have come to their aid, including the federal authorities who needed Rose to testify in order to make their case:

> I resent the fact that when so much assistance can be made available by our Justice Department to criminals who cooperate with them, why in hell wasn't it made available to a guy who wasn't a criminal? I mean assistance with his career. Absolutely none. If he had been a criminal he probably would have been relocated, new name, new position, it all would have been there for him, wouldn't it? I can't think of one person within the Justice Department that, by the time the dust had settled, hadn't used us, and used us badly. . . . The people I expected the most help from . . . the other attorneys that he was working with, the Justice Department—those were the people who in the end really helped us the least.[24]

Despite the most difficult times and the isolation they experienced, the Rose family held together until Joe could re-establish his law career. In part, this was possible because of Linda's traditional attitudes toward the marital relationship. Her profound conviction that it was the wife's duty to be submissive to her husband and to define her role as the supportive one served to lessen the conflict between them. She continued to believe that "he was some kind of hero." Yet this loyalty often exacerbated her own feelings of guilt and inadequacy. Her anger at the family hardships was sometimes directed at their situation, sometimes at her husband, and frequently turned on herself. Her husband was thankful that she had never mentioned the possibility of divorce, even during the years when he was unable to support the family and was the target of criticism from relatives and friends.

CHUCK ATCHISON AND THE COMANCHE PEAK NUCLEAR PLANT

The pattern of ostracism suffered by Joseph Rose, whose professional competence and integrity were maligned, is also graphically illustrated by the experience of Chuck Atchison, a nuclear worker who was the first whistleblower at the Comanche Peak plant in Glen Rose, Texas. He had initially approached the Nuclear Regulatory Commission in confidence in 1980 when he realized that there were serious safety violations in the construction of the plant. For two years, Atchison remained an anonymous whistleblower, a role that normally provides maximum protection.[25] Increasingly he doubted management's integrity and believed it was too eager to have the plant go "on line," or begin operations, even if quality control had to be compromised.

Atchison's profile was not unlike other nuclear whistleblowers whom we have discussed. He fully believed in the goals of the organization and in nuclear power. He had been well rewarded and had done supervisory work and quality-control inspections. Yet his fear of potential disaster to his community led him to approach secretly the responsible government agency.

His turnabout surprised many of his friends, but was reminiscent of the changes Dobie Hatley had undergone (see pages 125–30). When he first started working at Comanche Peak, Atchison was even reluctant, according to a friend, to see the film *The China Syndrome,* which dramatized the events leading to a near meltdown. After the screening, Atchison scoffed at the idea. Surely such an accident could never happen. He became more concerned after the near catastrophe at Three Mile Island in 1979, but remained committed to nuclear power and felt he had a place in helping to build this important energy source. Atchison, a friendly, confident, and energetic man in his forties, had earlier been in business for himself. He was a firm believer in an individual's ability to achieve. His friends consider him a natural teacher, someone who seldom gets angry. He seemed, therefore, suited to the demanding job of quality assurance inspector with responsibility for training new inspectors. Apparently, he did his job too well.

In April 1982, Atchison was suddenly fired by Brown and Root, the construction company building the Comanche Peak plant. As a quality assurance inspector, he had recently been involved in reporting serious construction and welding problems that required the company to have the work redone and reinspected.[26] While dismissal for such actions was not uncommon, Atchison was shocked when he was "let go."

His superiors charged that he had overstepped the boundaries that concerned him as an inspector, and maintained that he was incompetent in evaluating the welds in the plant construction. Contrary to management's assessment, Atchison was sustained by a subsequent NRC investigation that supported his allegations of poor work that could be dangerous in the event of a natural disaster.[27] Furthermore, a Department of Labor report later found that Atchison had acted within his area of responsibility.[28] Despite these confirmations of his actions, he was out of a job.

Immediately after his dismissal, Atchison again contacted the NRC. This time officials informed him that his anonymity as a whistleblower could not be protected since he was no longer employed at the plant. NRC documents later revealed that on the very day of his termination, one of the NRC inspectors violated his confidentiality and identified him to plant officials.[29]

With the end of Atchison's job, the legislated guarantee of protection for nuclear workers was now openly denied to him, making him much more vulnerable as he sought new employment. His decision to file a suit with the Department of Labor for unfair firing escalated his difficulties with Brown and Root, which seemed determined to make Atchison suffer for reporting violations to the NRC. In moving from providing information to taking direct action against the construction company, Atchison had become a more dangerous adversary. Like Joseph Rose, he suffered for the threat he represented: "I was on unemployment for twenty-six weeks. Meanwhile I went to job fairs in Dallas, took subscriptions to a job shopper magazine that lists all the jobs in the nuclear industry. I updated my resume and started cranking them out through the mail." Atchison could not find a job. Yet he refused to accept such punishment passively and sought to strike back by testifying publicly against Brown and Root and the Texas Utilities: "I read they were going to have a hearing to license Comanche Peak, and wrote a letter to the NRC. I walked into that hearing and the people I knew from Texas Utilities just came unglued. They were just about ready to get their license granted."[30] Atchison had now become a major witness against his former employers. He would not be silenced by intimidation or by hopes of getting another job. He had committed himself to fighting the plant and exposing its problems.

Atchison's actions led to a new level of retaliation which followed him to work sites far from his home—a situation aggravated by his falsification of his educational credentials in his application to Brown and Root.[31] Louis Clark's advice to all whistleblowers has been proved accurate. "If there's anything in your background that is less than perfect, it will probably come out."[32] Atchison was finally hired by a contractor at a

Louisiana power plant but had been there for only three days when management learned of his testimony about Comanche Peak and fired him. While they claimed that the revelation of his having lied about having a college degree led to his dismissal, Atchison and his attorney believe it was an excuse for blacklisting him, a belief that was confirmed in a Department of Labor hearing that is now under appeal.[33] Finding himself *persona non grata* in the nuclear industry, Atchison became increasingly depressed as he struggled to survive economically. Although his wife, a bookkeeper, now provided the family wage, one income was insufficient:

> Everything that wasn't nailed down with the mortgage was sold. We lost our Visa and MasterCard rights and our gasoline credit cards. Finally we lost the house in July 1983. My wife, Jeanne, has always been employed as a secretary-clerk bookkeeper. That was the only thing that really kept us going. We let someone take over the payments on the house and found a trailer we could take over the payments on.

The company's reach seemed so pervasive that he even feared physical assault. The ambiguous circumstances of Karen Silkwood's automobile crash in 1974 (see pages 27–28) reinforced his fear of possible organizational revenge:

> Silkwood hit the headlines again. I became paranoid if things happened like a car following me. I'd make several turns and the car would keep up with me. I feared that the company could hire gunmen that would kill someone for big dollars and get back across the border without anyone knowing it.[34]

A resister's sense of personal safety is fragile and easily shattered. The wife of another resister employed as a federal police officer told us angrily how frightened she had become for the safety of her young children after her husband had charged his superior with beating patients and visitors in a veterans hospital. Sue Berter could not rest easily once she knew that the superior had reason to take revenge on her husband.[35] While nothing had occurred, she fantasized the worst. Even Atchison, older and tougher and with years of experience in pulling the bodies of drowning victims from the waters near his hometown in Texas, conjured up images of impending harm. Not only the Silkwood case but also later the unsolved shooting of Judith Penley, who died after raising questions about the safety of nuclear plants built by the Tennessee Valley Authority, further fed the fears of the Comanche Peak workers. They knew that a shotgun blast had ended Penley's life shortly after she had met with interviewers from Quality Technology Corporation, a private firm hired by the government to investigate complaints at the nuclear facility.[36]

Atchison had now lost his job, his home, his credit rating, his sense of personal safety, and his self-esteem as a breadwinner. Forced to leave their familiar surroundings and to live in a mobile home without most of their possessions, the family no longer felt like respected members of the community. Atchison became a living symbol to other workers of the cost of resisting large corporations.[37] The pressure and humiliation penetrated deeply into his sense of self. He dreamed of striking a major blow against his adversaries when in reality he had to settle for the small pleasure of knowing that they had suffered a few defeats in their rush to obtain a license and make good on their investments: "My emotions went the full gamut from deep depression to hostility. Now most of that part is gone. The main emotion I still get is tickled to death if I see an article in the paper that makes them look a little bit worse as they go along."[38]

Atchison was not content with these small victories. To fight his case of illegal firing, he contacted the Department of Labor and the press, engaged lawyers, worked with the Government Accountability Project— using every possible means to confront Brown and Root, the construction company that had fired him, and the plant owners, Texas Utilities. The reprisals enacted against him for whistleblowing extracted a heavy toll but simultaneously resulted in his developing a new reference group of environmentalists organized to fight against unsafe nuclear plants. He became a principal witness in the campaign of a local grass-roots safe energy group against the plant. He was nationally recognized in 1984 when the Government Accountability Project and the Christic Institute* nominated him, along with Dobie Hatley, Sue Neumeyer, and several other ethical resis-

*The Christic Institute describes itself as follows: "The Christic Institute, a non-profit, inter-faith public interest law firm and public policy center, was formed in 1980 by the group of people who coordinated the public education, investigation, trial, and Supreme Court victory of the Karen Silkwood case. The Institute is best known for its vigorous investigations and court challenges of corporate and government injustices. . . . The Christic Institute's daily work is grounded in the Judeo-Christian tradition of social justice and builds on the American tradition of political democracy and constitutional rights."

ters, as the first winners of the Karen Silkwood award for exposing dangerous working conditions.* The citation that accompanied the award was yet another sign that the blacklisting had failed to silence him.

The blacklisting of Atchison was a classic response by industry to an employee who threatens the production schedule or a company's potential for profit. Even the legal protection that was to be guaranteed to nuclear industry employees failed to shield him. As long as Atchison remained an anonymous whistleblower, he was able to maintain his position and still bring safety issues to the attention of the Nuclear Regulatory Commission. Once he was fired and identified as a whistleblower, he was blackballed throughout the nuclear industry. The company also attempted to estrange him from other workers by claiming that his criticisms could cause a plant shutdown and a loss of jobs. Coming from the largest and highest-paying employer in the area, these were no idle threats. By controlling the employment market and the definition of Atchison's actions for other workers, the company successfully squashed any possibility of worker solidarity.[39] As a result, Atchison and other whistleblowers constantly feared physical attack from both the company and irate co-workers.

Dobie Hatley, Sue Neumeyer, and several other workers later followed in Atchison's footsteps only with great trepidation, knowing that he had lost his home and had been unemployed for months. They believed that many of their fellow workers wanted to report flagrant violations of safety regulations, but had learned the lesson of Chuck Atchison's fate too well. They felt that the company would go to any lengths to assert its control, and that for many workers the price was simply too high. What management did not accurately predict, however, was that the severe punishment that discouraged many workers drove a handful, like Chuck Atchison, to continue resistance and to forge new alliances—efforts that contributed to preventing the plant from going "on line."†

---

*The awards were announced on the Personalities page of the *Washington Post,* 13 November 1984. The presentation coincided with the tenth anniversary of Karen Silkwood's death.

†A 1988 report by a former NRC commissioner details the poor quality of the Comanche Peak design and construction. It faults inexperienced management with the failure to meet the increasingly rigorous standards of the NRC. Although the report never refers to Atchison and the other Comanche Peak whistleblowers, their allegations are substantially confirmed.[40]

Dismissal

Dismissal is the most common form of retaliation foisted upon ethical resisters. It affected two-thirds of the whistleblowers we studied. The results are almost always devastating. The bitterness, anger, and depression suffered by the Roses and the Atchisons characterized other families of resisters; some resisters were so humiliated at losing their jobs that they experienced severe emotional withdrawal. Spouses had to use all of their energy and ingenuity to devise strategies to maintain communication and solidarity while creating a semblance of normalcy for their children. Mary Howard was a wife who understood her husband's sense of betrayal and his fury at having been rudely discarded by his employers. His emotional withdrawal from her and their children was a great burden, yet she remained determined to convince him that she was on his side.

TERRY HOWARD AND THE ZACK COMPANY

Terry Howard had been a science teacher in Massachusetts public schools for twenty-five years before he decided to change his career. The Howards both described Terry as a person who knew his own mind and would not cater to the wishes of superiors if he felt they lacked integrity. Mary put it simply: "Terry has always been an individual. I've always admired that in him."[41] While they both knew that there was a risk in leaving the security of a teaching job to forge a new career, they were willing to take a chance on being able to support their family of ten children, four of whom were still living at home.

After several false starts, Howard met a good friend who helped him secure a job at the Zack Company, an Illinois contractor that built heating, air-conditioning, and ventilation systems (HVAC) for nuclear power plants. Howard's friend, John, extolled his science background to Zack's owner who needed someone to run the quality-control division to avoid problems with the Nuclear Regulatory Commission. Howard seemed like a natural choice. Beyond his years of teaching, he had earned a Master of Arts degree in educational administration and had forty-five hours of postgraduate work, mostly at Holy Cross College, funded by a grant from the National Science Foundation.

The Howard family moved to Illinois in the fall of 1981, where Terry underwent a brief period of training in quality assurance and was appointed a quality assurance engineer in documentation. But, while he had been hired precisely to help reorganize the company's files, Howard soon concluded that his superiors were ignoring his reports that many documents were missing, falsified, or inaccurate. When there were no records indicating the quality of materials, or verification that there had been proper purchases from vendors to ensure the safety of the nuclear power plants under construction, the company expected Howard and his staff to produce bogus ones.[42]

When Howard continued to press his superiors, they dismissed his concerns and suggested that he might look for another job. In earlier informal conversations with the managers of Consumer Power, the utility company that had subcontracted the ventilation work to Zack for the building of the Midland, Michigan, plant, he had learned that they were aware that Zack had had serious problems in quality assurance in the past, and he believed there was some possibility that they would be vitally concerned about safety defects. Thus, in April 1982, fearful about the safety of the Midwestern plants that had Zack heating, ventilation, and air-conditioning systems, and angered by his superiors' unwillingness to let him do his job, he approached Consumer Power with his allegations about Zack's practices. Mary Howard believed that her husband had no choice but to make this move:

> He could not live with his concerns and I couldn't live with him. He had to do something. So he made the allegations of wrongdoing to Consumer Power, the utility company. Terry felt better after he had done it. He was not living with it any more. They are not supposed to let anyone know who made the allegations until the investigation is done, but they all knew who it was. I'm sure it was all set up.[43]

Believing that the utility would seriously investigate his charges, Terry Howard did not realize that such an inquiry could roll back the utility's schedule for going "on line"; and it would completely work against the utility's self-interest to uncover falsified records or poorly designed heating or ventilation systems. Howard would quickly learn that the utility companies using Zack systems were not ready to take any determined action.

There were immediate consequences. When he had told his friend John of his intentions to notify Consumer Power utility company, his friend at first promised "to go to the wall" for him, but the Howards believe that after John received a substantial raise, the first signs of a breach became evident. Mary Howard recalled those troubling days: "We still thought he was our friend, but from that day on, he wasn't. I had been very close to his wife, but I never saw her again after the allegations were made. We lived in the same city. I tried to call her and never got an answer."[44]

After a cursory, on-site investigation, the utility company decided that no further inquiry was necessary. While they never contacted Howard, it appears that they informed his employer of the serious allegations he had made. In a voice that cracked long after the event, Mary Howard explained how Terry's boss set him up for dismissal:

> His employer asked him to make an outline proposing how some of the problems could be corrected. He came home and he was so excited about it. He said, "I think I finally got through to her. She is going to correct this." He worked on it the whole weekend and then presented it to her. She gave him back a scathing letter. It said he had no business in business; that he had no managerial ability and was the incarnation of the Peter Principle. And it hurt him very much. It hurt me, too.

Terry's days at Zack were over. The dismissal was both peremptory and humiliating. Howard and his entire team were ordered out:

> They followed me out of the office and told the other people to leave everything where it was and to leave, because their services no longer were needed. They were reorganizing. This is what companies do. They immediately advertised and put in another department of clerks just like us.[45]

This ritual of dismissal, which was reported by other workers, engineers, and physicians, was intended to undermine Howard, to expose him as incompetent, and to denigrate him in his own eyes and those of his fellow employees.[46] It was a carefully orchestrated effort designed to ensure that his allegations were discounted, and that he would be defined as erratic and unreliable. Mary Howard saw the devastating consequences: "The whole thing did an awful job on Terry. His self-esteem, his self-worth, his confidence was shaken terribly, and now he is like a workaholic. He has got to prove himself because they demeaned him."[47]

Terry Howard had trusted his superiors; they had hired him for his competence, personal qualities, and enthusiasm. They promised to reward him for good work and, indeed, had given him an early promotion. An articulate, strong-willed man, he generates confidence as he talks of his work or family. Yet, despite these personal characteristics and years of previous successful employment, the dismissal and the feelings of betrayal undermined his confidence and changed his relationship with his family. Painfully, Mary recalled those bleak days:

> I still think of him sitting there in the kitchen of that house. He'd get very upset—almost violent sometimes. Just pick up something and throw it. He was very angry. I was angry, too, but I couldn't get angry the way he could. Somebody had to stay calm. Sometimes I think he thought he was all alone, very much alone. It did an awful job on him. It really did. He was so upset. He started drinking, too. What are you going to do? It bothered me and it still does. It changed our lives. Sometimes I think he thought that I didn't understand. But I did. I felt everything he felt. . . . There is sometimes a bitterness in Terry that I can see, and he pushes himself, and he doesn't take the time to understand other people.[48]

Terry Howard's story encapsulates that of many resisters. Retaliation erodes their confidence and sense of security. They do not expect such treatment and cannot accept it. It is simply unjust and rocks their definition of a predictable social order.[49] They often feel alone and humiliated, and doubt that anyone, even their own wives or husbands, can fully comprehend their sense of loss and betrayal. For some, depression is the most characteristic response. But often anger takes over and becomes the vehicle for continued resistance. They believe that their superiors have to change and recognize that their cause was just. For Howard, as for many of the resisters we studied, anger fueled his determination to achieve vindication.

As Terry Howard dealt with his feelings of loss and dislocation, Mary, like many spouses, had to reorganize the finances of the family and assume a far greater burden than in the past for the family's economic survival, while simultaneously absorbing the emotional shock. The wife or husband witnessed the resister's greatest failures and often served as the available person on whom to vent anger and frustration.

Even under these adverse circumstances, however, many spouses reached out and found mechanisms for communication. Mary Howard spoke for many others when she detailed the ways that she maintained the bond with her husband. She totally identified with him emotionally—"What happened to him, happened to me"—and learned about the facts in the case—"I knew the documents as well as he did." Yet, because she saw herself as the key to the survival of the family, she had to repress some of the anguish: "I wouldn't let it knock me down. And I think that sometimes Terry couldn't understand that. It hit me the same way, but I just kept myself active. I had to for my children. I couldn't be defeated." When Terry's situation deteriorated even further, and Mary felt that neither she nor the children could reach him, she devised other means of communication: "When I couldn't talk to him and he got to the point that he'd take everything the wrong way, I would write down what I meant, and that way he could understand me. It was my way of communicating with him." Although Terry found no sustenance in religious faith, it was crucial to Mary's ability to survive: "This whole situation tested my faith. It has stood by me very well and brought me through a lot of it. I suppose I knew God would not abandon us. We hadn't done anything wrong. I wish Terry had some of the faith I have, but I can't seem to give it to him and that bothers me."[50]

Yet Terry Howard was not defeated. He knew he was right. Immediately after being terminated, he and his assistant, Sharon Marello, went to the Nuclear Regulatory Commission with a briefcase full of documents and spent a full day presenting the material. The NRC officials appeared impressed with their allegations and promised action. Nothing happened. Still determined, Terry and Sharon took their case to a Chicago television station, which mounted an intense investigation and then, in July 1982, aired a lengthy report on the case, supporting the charges of the dismissed workers.

The full-page newspaper advertisement for the program included a large photo of Terry Howard and Sharon Marello. The caption read: *These people were so concerned about safety at the LaSalle nuclear plant, they lost their jobs to bring you the truth.* The station's investigative team supported Howard and Marello's charges of missing and forged documents and of potential dangers in plant control rooms because of inappropriately constructed ventilation systems supplied by Zack. Reporter Paul Hogan of Chicago's Channel 5 News pointed out that the NRC had had access to the crucial documents for a full three months but had taken no action. The regional administrator vehemently argued on camera that Howard and Marello had supplied no documents relevant to the LaSalle nuclear plant, which had recently been granted a license to operate. When the reporter pressed the point, the interview was interrupted while the official allowed the reporters to examine the relevant NRC files. Much to his consternation, they produced the key documents proving that there was a serious lack of quality control at that plant.[51] This event and the continued probing by the media led to the NRC decision to delay the license until an independent audit team could review the quality records and order appropriate repairs.

The controversy at both the LaSalle and Midland plants continued long after the Howards returned to Massachusetts in 1982. Criticisms mounted and, in 1984, the Midland plant had the distinction of being named the "worst in the Midwest." It never opened.[52] The LaSalle plant eventually did go "on line" but only after a GAP petition on behalf of Howard and Marello led the NRC to require several months of repairs.[53]

"MARGARET HENDERSON" AND THE DISRUPTION OF FAMILY LIFE

Margaret and Harry Henderson (not their real names) were another couple in which a previously successful husband withdrew from family relationships, despite his wife's best efforts to provide emotional support and keep him engaged. Margaret Henderson told us in detail of Harry's transformation. He had joined the federal government after working several years as a business executive in the South. When he protested waste of substantial amounts of government funds, his superiors ordered him to remain silent and threatened to ruin his career if he spoke outside the agency. When he would not retreat, they initiated a campaign to isolate and later to dismiss him.

Like the Roses, the Atchisons, the Howards, and other families of resisters, the Henderson family remained intact. They fought for several years in a campaign that ultimately led to Harry's public vindication. While outwardly cheerful and devoted to each other, the Hendersons suffered the damaging effects of Harry's obsession with his case and with the people who had victimized him. He could not come to terms with his sense of betrayal and his need to expose those who had deprived him of his job and forced him into several years of debilitating unemployment.

According to his wife, he became increasingly removed from her and their young children. While they lived in the same house, the couple no longer shared the close relationship they had enjoyed for all their married lives. Harry simply could not "let go." He could not accept that the battle was over, and that his former superiors who had deeply injured him had continued to build highly successful careers in the government. Margaret Henderson described the impact on the family:

Nineteen years ago, I married a man who was outgoing, secure, bold, and optimistic. About his career he was self-confident, enthusiastic, and ambitious. As husband he was interested in and supportive of my activities. Later, as father, he was involved in the lives of his five children and made every effort to spend as much time with them as possible.

From an outgoing person who was involved in the interests and activities of his family, he became withdrawn, spending whatever hours he could in isolation, poring over and over his documents, compulsively reading and rereading every memo dealing with his work situation. When he and I did sit down to talk to each other, he could speak of nothing but what was happening at work and what his supervisors were doing to him, with the pain and suffering he was going through evident in the slump of his shoulders and strained quality of his voice.

All of this, of course, had an effect on the rest of the family. We were afraid to approach Harry with our own needs and concerns, having come to expect his rejection and withdrawal because he no longer had time for or interest in us. One of our children was referred for psychological counseling. I found it necessary to seek work outside the home, having to escape from his oppressive presence and influence. His sleeplessness disturbed our night's rest. We all observed the profound effect of his work situation upon him: the bold man become fearful and intimidated; the aggressive person become reticent and insecure; the optimist become hopeless; the relaxed and outgoing person become tense, withdrawn, and isolated; the well-rounded man become obsessive, paranoid, and neurotic. No longer was he the loving spouse and father. He was the stranger who, although living among us, was not with us.

How do I see my husband today? He is no longer the self-confident executive. Indeed, he evidences no hope or desire to ever pursue his career again. Just two nights ago he woke me by talking in his sleep in a recurring nightmare about the horrors he suffered in his agency. If his supervisors had set out with the intention of destroying his personality and ego as well as his career by subjecting him to their threats, harassment, abuse, intimidation, and humiliation, they were totally successful. He who only wanted to do what was right was instead the victim of many wrongs.[54]

The distress described by Margaret Henderson reflects the experiences of other families.[55] Like Joseph Rose, Chuck Atchison, Terry Howard, and Harry Henderson, many other whistleblowers were successful husbands with good careers. Confrontation with their employers severely challenged their ideas about fairness and the rewards for hard work, as they found themselves in a position traditionally reserved for women and members of minority groups. These formerly successful men were shunted aside, no longer taken seriously, and told that they could easily be replaced, and their careers were unexpectedly truncated. The anger that drove them forward threatened to overwhelm their lives, leaving them permanently scarred. The return to productive work was the central component in re-establishing a resister's sense of stability and order. Harry Henderson suffered the most chronic effects because he was unable to work. He nursed his bruises rather than accept the reality of his loss and rebuild his career. Since his wife's income gave the family a modest financial base, he was able to devote himself almost full-time to battling his tormentors. He now plays a prime role in helping West Coast resisters evaluate and fight their cases. As adviser and committed witness, he has given others encouragement and counsel.

Many women and minorities know that their career possibilities can all too easily be jeopardized by prejudice; for a successful white, middle-class man, this realization is a wholly unanticipated jolt. They feel humiliated and emasculated by a process that leaves them powerless, frightened, and facing an unpredictable future. Joseph Rose astutely compared his situation to less advantaged groups when he spoke of his anguish at not being able to play the role of father and husband adequately: "What you have in effect is a father who has lost the capacity to support his family."[56] For males who have grown up with traditional expectations of family life, the rejection by employers and the inability to support the family mean one has failed as a man.

Transfer

The blacklisting of Chuck Atchison and Joseph Rose and the peremptory dismissal of Terry Howard occurred in private industry. Although recent labor law has developed a series of limitations on the private sector's right to dismiss at will, only industry can so swiftly fire employees, giving no notice and no explanations.

Since workers and managers in the public sector are ostensibly protected against such precipitate and arbitrary acts, ethical resisters in government agencies are normally punished by demotion and transfer. They are often relegated to positions outside their areas of expertise and assigned tasks well below their level of competence, as a constant reminder to the dissenters of their powerlessness in the hands of the bureaucracy. These reprisals often serve as a first step in a long process of retaliation culminating in dismissal.

In response, resisters can accept the humiliation associated with the new position or fight back by contacting lawyers, the press, the Congress, public-interest groups, or the inspector general's office. Not infrequently, the transfer of a dissenting employee transforms an internal protest into a full-scale public act of whistleblowing. As the conflict escalates, management feels even more compelled to bring new charges in order to warrant dismissal and counter the negative publicity. Jim Pope's case illustrates this pattern in government whistleblowing.

JIM POPE AND THE FEDERAL AVIATION ADMINISTRATION

Pope, a pilot and inventor, joined the Federal Aviation Administration in the 1960s. A highly respected engineer, he had responsibility for the department in charge of both airport and airborne safety of private, noncommercial planes. A decade later, he became embroiled in a controversy about two systems designed to prevent midair collisions. He believed that the evidence clearly pointed to the advisability of an Airborne Collision Avoidance System, while most high-placed FAA officials advocated the alternative Beacon Collision Avoidance Systems. The Airborne system was located in the aircraft under the control of the pilots, while the Beacon system would be controlled from the ground. Pope argued that the Airborne system was more effective and cheaper, and could be more quickly operational. He believed his opponents were against it because it had been developed by a private company, Honeywell, in competition with the FAA's own system. He further charged that there was a cover-up of an FAA-commissioned study by the Mitre Corporation documenting the superiority of the ACAs.[57] FAA officials, favoring the ground-based system, insisted that it was less susceptible to false alarms.

This sensitive issue became particularly heated after a disastrous 1978 midair collision over San Diego in which 144 people died. Pope argued that the collision could have been avoided had the airborne system been used. The chief administrator did not agree and later testified that neither he nor any member of his staff had knowledge of an industry report evaluating the airborne system as superior and cheaper.[58] The controversy over the crash avoidance systems led to the decision to disband Pope's unit, the General Aviation Department, and transfer him to Seattle. He was the only one who was not given a choice of location, although a number of colleagues later testified that there were several appropriate positions available in the Washington, D.C., area.

Pope reluctantly accepted the transfer and the promise that an exciting new job awaited him. Despite her protests, he decided to go without his wife, Florence, convincing her that she should stay in their recently completed house in Virginia until he was settled in Seattle. But the new and challenging position never materialized. While Pope was allocated office space, with an impressive title, and continued to receive his $51,000 annual salary, the job description was fictitious. He had virtually no work.[59]

His new supervisors did not want him, and colleagues were warned to stay away from him if they valued their careers. For Jim Pope, the transfer to Seattle was a trap, a dead-end position, a punishing form of dismissal with pay. He sat at an empty desk day after day while his supervisors insisted that his relocation had no punitive intent. He was furious and deeply bitter:

> They separated me from my family and my kids. They made up all these stories about me in the hope that they could fire me. I didn't have any way of fighting back. I kept thinking that they would not get away with it. What they did was illegal and wrong. They are letting people get away with weekly collisions on airplanes. They are destroying everything I've worked for all my life.[60]

Pope desperately needed to see himself as someone tough enough to fight back; and in 1981, after a year and a half in Seattle, he contacted a local newspaper. Like many ethical resisters, Pope went public when he had exhausted all of his agency's internal mechanisms. He received coverage in the Seattle press and in professional aviation journals,[61] and appeared on "60 Minutes" in March 1981. His public disclosure about airport safety problems and his claim that he was receiving $51,000 of public funds for a nonexistent job embarrassed the FAA. His superiors responded by inundating him with so much work that they could justify a flood of memos criticizing his work performance and set the stage to fire him. For the first time in his sixteen years of government service, Jim Pope was defined as an unsatisfactory employee.[62]

The new effort to break him took a heavy toll. He was in great emotional turmoil and began to suffer from chest pains. His wife urged him to see a psychiatrist, who recommended that he enter a hospital where the physicians suggested that he apply for a disability retirement from the FAA. When Pope began these proceedings, the FAA charged him with being AWOL and fired him.[63] Under this provocation, Florence Pope later concluded that "this country has some characteristics which make it no different from Russia"[64] a harsh comparison that reveals the depth of disappointment many resisters and their spouses experience. Florence Pope was reacting against a powerful bureaucracy which could exile her husband, punish him with no work, and seek his dismissal because their efforts had led to his collapse. The abuse of policy troubled her deeply. Like the Soviet government, the U.S. federal bureaucracy could, without the least human compassion, effectively label a dissenter a danger who had to be removed for the sake of government stability.

Once again Jim Pope refused to back down in the face of reprisals and appealed his termination to the Merit Systems Protection Board. In August 1982, the FAA agreed to drop the dismissal action, to purge his personnel file of all charges and allegations, and to approve disability benefits for him.[65] Despite this victory, Pope pressed his case, and in 1985 the Office of the Special Counsel of the U.S. Merit Systems Protection Board found that there was a "substantial likelihood" that his initial charges about FAA mismanagement of air-safety issues were true. The Department of Transportation was ordered to undertake an investigation of the failure of the FAA to certify collision-avoidance systems that had been found to be inexpensive and safe. When the DOT cleared the FAA of all charges without ever interviewing Pope, the OSC was not satisfied and took the unusual step of ordering a reinvestigation, at which the DOT reasserted its initial findings.[66]

A 1986 midair collision in California, involving a commercial airliner and a private plane, rekindled interest in the Airborne Collision Avoidance System. The chairman of the National Transportation Safety Board recently complained about the FAA's inability to mount its own system: "The FAA told us in 1981 that it would be ready in 1985. Now it tells us that we will have it by 1988. . . . If it's a voluntary program it's safe to assume that a majority of our fleet won't have a TCAS [traffic-alert collision avoidance system] by the end of the century."[67] Pope reappeared on "60 Minutes" (7 September 1986) and the "McNeil-Lehrer Newshour" (27 October 1986) to present his version of the controversy.[68] He is currently advanced development technology integration manager with NASA and, though pleased with his new position, continues to promote a viable and safe collision-avoidance system.

Transfer is an ingenious bureaucratic device which transforms a conventional organizational procedure into a punishment accompanied by multiple symbols of humiliation. Some government whistleblowers have found themselves in offices with no windows and no heat controls, as did Demetrios Basdekas after he testified before a congressional committee about problems in the Nuclear Regulatory Commission. While transfer may not always lead to termination, it is designed to result in isolation, as in the case of Jim Pope. It often exacerbates the conflict and serves to expose issues that previously remained hidden from public view.

Personal Harassment and Sexual Exploitation

Destroying a person's career, either through blacklist, dismissal, or transfer, is by far the most frequent form of retaliation. Although there are many variations in the applications of these punitive measures, all ethical resisters receive the message that their career aspirations are no longer valid, that they have been cast aside.

There are less common but by no means less destructive instances in which these measures alone are not deemed effective and other, more personal forms of retaliation are invoked. No whistleblower can forget the fate of Karen Silkwood; or of Marie Ragghianti who, after exposing corruption in the governor's office in Tennessee in 1976, faced trumped-up charges of drunk driving, endured false rumors about alleged sexual promiscuity, and feared for her personal safety.[69]

Both of these resisters, in their aim to challenge powerful men in industry and government, provoked immediate and severe reprisals that went far beyond a threat to their careers. Angry employers, seeking any possible means to retaliate against "difficult" workers, can easily resort to gender-specific attacks, as these women experienced. To destroy their credibility as witnesses and to intimidate them further, they were threatened with physical reprisal, as were Ragghiante's children. Billie Pirner Garde had similar experiences.

BILLIE PIRNER GARDE AND THE CENSUS BUREAU

Billie Pirner, born in the northern Wisconsin city of Appleton, was raised as one of five girls in a conservative German Lutheran family. During high school she joined the Civil Air Patrol and hoped to apply to the Air Force Academy. Since the academy did not yet accept women, she settled for enlisting in the U.S. Air Force, a route followed by many of her male friends who went on to fight and die in Vietnam. She believes that her background prepared her to face the severe crisis that she met later in life as an ethical resister:

> We react to stress with the emotional and psychological tools that we have. I think the tools I got served me in pretty good stead, although I wish none of it had happened. I grew up with the stoic German character and with the strong independent heritage that my grandparents passed along. They are very moral people. Those were the traits that developed during high school and through my extracurricular activities in the Civil Air Patrol.
>
> It was a kind of military experience that was very important in reinforcing independence and in helping me to learn to control my emotions. That was probably the only reason I didn't go crazy when all this happened to me. That and my Air Force experience had a lot to do with reinforcing independence and discipline and helping me survive this whole emotional trauma.[70]

During her four years in the U.S. Air Force, Billie married Larry Garde, and they had two daughters. The family returned to Larry's hometown in Oklahoma where Billie finished college, earned a Master's degree, and taught in the local high school and in a junior college. With her marriage's deterioration, Billie divorced her husband and at age twenty-seven was planning to go east to Pennsylvania to study for a degree in clinical psychology when an attractive job offer changed the course of her life:

In January 1980, I was almost ready to leave the state when I was approached by the local congressman and his aide. I've always been politically active and had been the head of the volunteers during his campaign. They asked me to take the assistant directorship at the Census Bureau. The census itself was to begin in April 1980. The offer itself had a lot of good things in it, or so I thought. So I balanced out immediate education versus earning some money and administrative experience as the number two person in a big office.

I decided to take the job, which had some very interesting parts to it. I was supposed to hire people consistent with the ethnic composition. The idea was to have minorities counting minorities . . . Indians counting Indians which in eastern Oklahoma was a very big segment of the population. The various Indian tribes are big because the Trail of Tears is where we dumped all the Indians in Oklahoma, so you have eighty or ninety tribes in little pockets in Oklahoma. Eastern Oklahoma had been severely undercounted in the 1970 census and federal funds are assigned according to that count so the area got much less money for schools and hospitals. I thought it was an important job to do and would give me good experience for the East Coast. Otherwise, I was just going to be this little Oklahoma schoolteacher. As it turned out my boss had a whole other agenda.[71]

John Hudson, a thirty-two-year-old regional manager, was part of the local power structure. He intended to use the census for his own political purposes and thus directly influenced Garde's work. First, he wanted to make sure that she hired only those people who would be useful to him, who would owe him favors. He even instructed Garde to change civil service test scores if necessary to ensure that the right people passed. She was taken aback by his order, changed the scores on three papers which she kept in her desk, and raised a question about it shortly afterward at a regional training session in Denver. The instructor told her to follow the orders of her supervisor.[72]

She ignored this advice and, upon her return to her office, changed the test results to their original scores. In the light of later events, she was fortunate that thirty-five people had heard her ask about the propriety of Hudson's orders. If Garde was disturbed by the score changes, Hudson's other demands totally alienated her. Not only did he make sexual overtures to her but he also told her she had to sleep with local political leaders. She put him off as she had others during her years in the air force. She was less inclined to dismiss his designs on her former students, for she felt that these youngsters were far more vulnerable than she:

John Hudson wanted me to hire a harem of young women from among my former students who would sleep with visiting political officials. Now he could not have been more explicit about what he wanted to do. I just thought he was nuts. I did not think he would ever try to implement that. As disgusting as it may seem, what he said was "I know which politicians like little girls, and which ones like little boys, and which ones drink and which ones run around, and which ones take bribes, and that's how you control them." He pretty much got away with it, and in the beginning he was searching for my Achilles' heel.[73]

After six weeks, Garde spoke with the local congressman's staff and with the Census Bureau's regional director. No one wanted to get involved. Since Hudson spent so much time pursuing his political ambitions, the census maps were not being properly done, which Garde maintains resulted in an eventual serious undercounting of the population and a loss of some $2,500,000 in federal funds. Alcohol and marijuana were also being used in the office, whose atmosphere Garde likened to "Sodom and Gomorrah."

When Hudson learned that she had complained of his activities, he developed an effective strategy to intimidate her:

He called me in and said that my ex-husband wanted custody of our two children, and he was going to help him get it if I didn't conform. I didn't cry in the office, but I went home and I was absolutely terrified. I knew Hudson had the political clout to harm me. It was a small place, and he had a lot of influence. It would not be hard for him to spread false rumors about me in the community.

Hudson did precisely that by casting aspersions on her sex life and her fitness as a mother. Even though the accusations he made were not true, she felt increasingly vulnerable. On one occasion her daughter waited outside her day-care center for two hours because someone called and said that Billie would pick her up for a dentist's appointment. Billie was horrified that anyone could be that mean. It was only the beginning:

> To break me down there would also be calls in the middle of the night saying things like "I saw you screwing so-and-so." And it terrified me. At every turn, there was something about my kids. I called his [Hudson's] boss and then his boss's boss and everyone said they would take care of it.[74]

Finally, several other workers in the office also complained of Hudson's sexual exploitation, use of drugs, and dereliction of duty. One woman put all of her observations in writing. Hudson was given three weeks to prepare for an inspection by the regional office. Singling out Garde as the ringleader, he immediately fired her.

While outraged, Garde was actually relieved. As a temporary employee, she decided not to fight the dismissal. Like Joseph Rose, she was willing to walk away. She felt she had done all she could and had already suffered enough. She prepared for a move to Washington, D.C., to get on with her life. Her children were spending the month with their father in Muskogee and were to join her on 27 June 1980. Within a few days after her arrival in the East, Garde received a call from an Oklahoma newspaper reporter who wanted her to confirm the story he was writing on the Census Bureau scandal. He had spoken to many bureau employees who all said that Billie Garde was a principal witness. She refused to talk, still hoping that the investigation by the Denver office would result in a just solution: "So I called the director of the regional office, who had investigated and had heard the whole story from many others. He said that he was not going to do anything. He hoped Hudson would resign, but if not, the census office was going to close in a month anyway."

Garde could not believe that the bureau would not take action despite such an abundance of evidence of gross misbehavior: "It was so outrageous. In the heat of my anger, without giving any thought to the fact that I didn't have my kids, I called back the newspaper and said, 'Let me tell you the story.'"[75]

Garde had immediate misgivings, recalling Hudson's warning that he would help her husband get custody of her children, and asked the reporter to delay publication. But he convinced her that it was impossible. She was also reassured by earlier conversations with her former husband: "Larry said that he had heard through the grapevine that if he wanted to keep the kids, that Hudson had enough authority to do that; but he said that I shouldn't think that he would do that, . . . that he wanted what was best for the kids, and . . . I believed him."[76]

The newspaper story appeared the day the children were to leave Oklahoma for Washington.[77] They never arrived:

> Within a couple of hours, Larry and Hudson had gone to a lawyer in Muskogee. Then Larry and the lawyer went to the courthouse. The judge was getting off the elevator, and Larry's lawyer said to the judge, "This is Larry Garde. He's married to the woman involved in the census scandal. He doesn't want to send the kids back." And the judge didn't say a word, and he signed the order and changed custody from me to him.* No notice, no hearing, no nothing . . . just *boom!* And so then, when I called later that day to make sure everything was OK, he said, "You're never going to see the kids again."

After Garde overcame the initial shock, she managed to ask Larry what had happened:

> He said that Hudson had told him that I was the one that was going to go to jail and I was guilty of all these sins and crimes and political abuse. He claimed that I had had an affair with Hudson and others and that I was using drugs. Everything Hudson had said that he was going to make sure people believed about me then came out of Larry's mouth. And I of course thought, "He got to me."[79]

Through blatant falsehood and political connections, John Hudson punished Billie Pirner Garde. In her case the typical work-related retaliation would have been ineffective, since she was planning to leave the area and relocate more than one thousand miles away in pursuit of a new

*The subsequent inquiry by the Department of Commerce did not sustain Garde's allegations that the judge had been improperly influenced by Hudson in transferring custody to Larry Garde. The Commerce Department investigator claimed that Garde's evidence was circumstantial, and the judge denied that Hudson influenced him in any way about this matter.[78]

career. Since distance was no guarantee that she would not return as a witness against Hudson, he stigmatized her as an unfit mother and hoped to destroy her credibility in the community.

As in the cases of Silkwood and Ragghiante, Garde's gender was central. When she came on the job, her superior attempted to involve her in a nefarious sexual arrangement. When this failed, he systematically tested to find where she was most vulnerable. As a woman and a single mother, Garde felt nothing could be more threatening than harm to her children.[80]

Hudson's campaign against Garde backfired, for she became ever more determined to testify against him. Other people who had worked in the office also came forward, some willingly and some when they realized they had no choice but to tell the truth before a grand jury. On 25 June 1981 John Hudson was indicted by a grand jury for conspiracy to defraud the United States, promising employment or other benefits for political favors, making false statements, and obstructing justice.[81] As the case was about to go to trial, Hudson pleaded guilty to one count of conspiracy to defraud the United States and five counts of violation of the patronage-hiring section of the Hatch Act. He was the first person ever to be sentenced for patronage abuse under the Hatch Act passed by Congress in 1948.[82] Hudson's penalty was a one-year term in federal prison and three years probation.

Billie Garde regained custody of her daughters after Larry Garde learned that all the charges against his former wife had been a fabrication. This emotionally grueling experience initially involved futile efforts to get the Muskogee judge to reverse his ruling; a kidnaping charge against her when she kept her daughters for an extended Christmas stay so they could receive medical attention; a highly restricted visitation order that during one six-month period allowed only one visit with her daughters which had to be held under armed guard. These hardships were complicated by an attempt by the Justice Department to indict her because she had admitted in an affidavit that she had changed the three test scores under orders from Hudson.*

The spiral of retaliation started by Hudson brought her to the edge of

---

*Jack Anderson noted President Reagan's outrage during a cabinet meeting in 1981 when he heard about the case of Billie Garde and the punishment she had suffered. "Tell me this couldn't happen! Not in my country! Not in my country!" he is reported to have said.[83]

her own endurance. She spoke of "slipping off the raft" when she faced indictment, and felt she had neither the financial nor emotional resources to fight on. She wanted to plead guilty just to have the ordeal over. Only her attorney's insistence that she would never get her children back if she gave up kept her going. Assistance from the Government Accountability Project and a generous donation from a church were crucial factors in enabling her to continue her fight for vindication. Although Billie Garde believes that, with the help of psychological counseling, her daughters have adjusted to their past ordeal, the entire experience has markedly influenced her own life, as we shall discuss in chapter 7 (see pages 217–19).

Conclusion

The retaliation against ethical resisters reveals the dark underside of American bureaucratic life. Just as the resisters personify the continuing presence of conscience and individual responsibility, so do the reprisals mounted against them expose the lengths to which management will go to crush dissent. By their actions, ethical resisters become disturbers of power, challengers of the status quo that all too often benefits a few corporate managers and government bureaucrats. While the resisters often evoke sympathy, they have no shield adequate to protect them. Professional associations, churches, and community groups are seldom available to facilitate a resolution of the conflict between ethical resisters and their adversaries. The resisters usually find that they either have to accept defeat or undertake a lengthy and expensive fight.

Nonetheless, they are not totally without help. Alternative authorities in American society stand ready to join their struggle—authorities who provide a social foundation for the courageous behavior necessary to confront large organizations. In the next chapter, we shall discuss how the media, congressional investigating committees, state legislatures, and public-service organizations have become the prime vehicles in the resisters' battle against intimidation and discharge.

Chapter 6

Allies in the Struggle: The Press, Legislators, and Public-Interest Groups

THE WHISTLEBLOWER'S determination to continue the battle cannot be understood only as an act of individual courage. Such a struggle requires assistance from others outside the workplace who are willing and able to aid the resister.

In distinctive ways, members of the media, Congress, state legislatures, and public-interest groups comprise a set of alternative authorities outside the orbit of the organizations seeking to destroy the whistleblower's reputation. These men and women have substantial influence in the larger society and vested interests in nurturing ethical resistance. Their own careers and ideological commitments are served when knowledgeable insiders are able to provide detailed information about lawless behavior. Their contributions to the encouragement and protection of ethical resisters are crucial to the whistleblowing process.

Without the attention of independent reporters, many resisters would be forced to end their protest after the initial reprisals. The willingness of journalists to listen, evaluate, and publicize allegations of wrongdoing is often a central component in facilitating whistleblowing. From the reporters' point of view, whistleblowers are excellent informants capable of contributing to a major scoop. Some journalists have built national careers investigating and publicizing their allegations. Such reporters often encourage employees to come forward with material that will assist them in uncovering and developing a story. In chapter 2 (see page 48), we described how Jack Anderson and Drew Pearson knew that congressional staff members James Boyd and Marjorie Carpenter would have to gather incriminating evidence against their former superior by secretly obtaining keys to his office, a controversial effort that led ultimately to the historic censure of Senator Thomas Dodd for financial impropriety.*

In a later case, reporters went beyond publicizing wrongdoing and demanded reinstatement for the whistleblower. After Irwin Levin, a New York City social worker, had been exonerated in an inspector general's investigation which validated his charges that reports of widespread child abuse had been neglected by the Office of Special Services for Children, aggressive reporters confronted Mayor Edward Koch with the fact that this vindicated employee remained at a lower rank and salary as a result of earlier demotions by his superiors. The reporters' prodding at a press conference in 1984 led the mayor to order full reinstatement. Levin, who had been publicizing the deaths of nine children for five years, was finally given the recognition and protection he deserved. Without the reporters' intervention, he would have remained in the shadows, vindicated in an official report and yet the victim of superiors who vented their wrath on someone who exposed their dereliction of duty.[2]

By going beyond the presentation of the story and undertaking their own inquiry, journalists have provided independent validation of whistleblowers' allegations in newspaper columns and television programs. That such validation can be crucial in building public support for official action is clear from the case of the *Kansas City Times*, which investigated the misuse of patients in a drug study at the Veterans Administration hospital

*The significance of strategically placed individuals may also be seen in other times and other societies. In the Dreyfus Affair, a crucial whistleblower within the French military, Lieutenant Colonel Georges Picquart, came across evidence that Jewish army officer Alfred Dreyfus had wrongly been convicted of treason in 1894. Picquart was determined to force the military command to proclaim Dreyfus's innocence. Later, journalist Emile Zola and Socialist leader Jean Jaurès also took leading roles in Captain Dreyfus's defense against a military hierarchy motivated largely by anti-Semitism. "Had Dreyfus stood alone, however, he would undoubtedly have shared the fate of Hitler's victims, Stalin's opponents, and the Argentine *desaparecidos*. Dreyfus was saved because others came to his rescue. They too are the heroes of the Dreyfus Affair."[1]

in Leavenworth, Kansas. The *Times* reporter not only spoke to Dr. Mary McAnaw and her colleagues about their complaints about the study but also continued his own probe. He published a series of articles questioning the hospital's decision to use VA patients as subjects for testing an antidepressant drug.[3] The articles generated congressional pressure that the physicians themselves had been unable to create. This pressure spurred an investigation by the Food and Drug Administration which subsequently determined that the protocol of the study had been violated. Although the media have no legal authority to implement change, their persistent attention can often prod official bodies to stop "dragging their feet" and take action.

Prominent elected officials are another group of strategically placed individuals who can aid resisters. Legislators frequently invite whistleblowers to testify at well-publicized hearings if their own staff investigations convince them that a significant political issue underlies the whistleblowers' complaints. When the hearings confirm the whistleblowers' stand, they gain more than publicity. Legislators often become allies whose publicized support legitimizes the resisters' credibility at a time when organizational superiors may have intensified a plan of vilification. The support of well-known politicians provides a vital infusion of hope, offsetting a sense of despair and isolation. Vows of protection and the introduction of legislation to encourage and shield resisters serve as potent symbols of their devotion to the public welfare.

One brief example will suffice. For more than twenty years, legislators have sided with Pentagon whistleblowers in pointing out large-scale waste of government funds. In recent times, this congressional intervention has resulted in public scrutiny of the entire defense establishment. Under the leadership of senators William Proxmire of Wisconsin and Charles E. Grassley of Iowa, overcharging by defense contractors has become a bipartisan issue. Democrats and Republicans, liberals and conservatives, have joined forces to protect whistleblowers from unwarranted transfers and forced resignations.

When George Spanton, an auditor for the Defense Contract Audit Agency, suspected that Pratt Whitney had charged millions of dollars in excessive salaries and expenses to the government, he asked for access to additional data. His superiors did not support his request and arranged a punitive transfer. Spanton appealed this decision to the Merit Systems Protection Board and sought assistance from the media and several key members of Congress, who kept him from slipping into oblivion. Senator Grassley, in particular, took an active role in the Spanton case and even went directly to Ronald Reagan. When disappointed by the president's lack of response, Grassley continued his advocacy by making public statements to the press.[4] His continued intervention kept the highest officials in the government involved. Spanton was ultimately vindicated, and his superiors were forced to defend their actions against him.

A third significant form of support for the whistleblowers comes from public-interest groups, which offer legal assistance, advice on which actions are most likely to garner publicity and recognition, as well as personal and emotional sustenance. Such activists have often eschewed more lucrative careers in order to build organizations that protect the public welfare. Their commitments validate the significance of whistleblowing as much more than a struggle of a single individual against his or her employer. Public-interest activists confirm for ethical resisters that their actions defend health and safety, protect against environmental degradation, and help preserve the integrity of government agencies.

In an early case, committed activists carried the torch for vindication even after the resister's death, when public-interest and political groups fought for an investigation into the mysterious circumstances of Karen Silkwood's death in 1974. Later the National Organization for Women supported the successful lawsuit that charged her former employer, the Kerr-McGee Corporation, with negligence that caused plutonium contamination (see pages 27–28).

In a more recent controversy, the Coalition to Stop Government Waste waged a campaign on behalf of an imprisoned government whistleblower, Mark Price, to prove that his incarceration was an act of unconscionable reprisal orchestrated by his former superiors in the Department of Education (see pages 106–17). The coalition lobbied members of Congress to investigate this punishment and supported Price during his trying months in prison, reassuring him that he had not been forgotten. On 8 October 1986, as a symbol of their belief in his integrity and the importance of the issue he had tried to bring before the public, the coalition presented him with their annual award, previously bestowed upon some of the nation's best-known and most reputable whistle-blowers.*

---

*Previous winners of the Whistleblower Patriot Award include George Spanton and Vincent Laubach.

The whistleblowers' quest for vindication normally begins with three basic goals. First, to have some formal body, such as the courts or an investigating committee, officially declare that the initial charges are true. Second, to have one's name cleared, through public confirmation that one is a moral person and a good worker. The third major goal is to recover what was taken away during the retaliation period: they seek reinstatement, eligibility for promotion, serious work assignments or some financial compensation, and the right to find another position without prejudice. As a relationship develops between ethical resisters and strategically placed individuals who can assist them, the resisters' "private problems become public issues."[5] The struggle for personal vindication is joined to a larger agenda of exposing irresponsible behavior and demanding the changes that will ensure public accountability. This is the first major victory over the whistleblowers' superiors whose efforts, until this time, have been directed at containing the protest and defining the issues as mere personal problems.

The following cases show how strategically placed individuals in the media, the legislature, and public-interest groups have helped resisters bring to light major instances of bureaucratic wrongdoing: unsafe maintenance of nuclear bomb factories, the dumping of toxic wastes, the neglect of mentally ill patients, and the failure to collect millions of dollars owed the government by mining corporations.

The Seattle Times *and Casey Ruud's Battle with the Hanford Nuclear Reservation*

Like his father and brothers, Casey Ruud made a career working in nuclear-plant quality control. At age thirty-one, Ruud was employed by the Rockwell Corporation, a private contractor at the government-owned Hanford Nuclear Reservation in the State of Washington. As the lead auditor, in 1986 he earned $32,000 annually and was highly committed to the importance of nuclear power for both civilian and military purposes. He had ten years of experience and by all accounts was tough and independent. Ruud was also a stickler for following rules: "After all," he said, "we are not making TVs or cars."[6]

In the early 1980s, with the Reagan administration's policy to expand the U.S. supply of nuclear armaments, the government issued contracts that resulted in increased production at Hanford and other plutonium-producing plants. Most of the facilities, built hurriedly during the 1940s, had been poorly constructed even then and had outlived their projected productive life. After Ruud's audits revealed that the plants had improper safeguards to prevent a catastrophic accident, he filed two reports detailing the problems of engineering design, "a badly flawed security system," and "improperly documented transfers of plutonium from one place to another." Ruud believed that the problems were serious; he recommended that the plants close, and filed another report indicating that the required repairs had not yet taken place.[7]

His disenchantment intensified as he realized that the Department of Energy was not sufficiently vigilant in monitoring the facilities. Nonetheless, he was not yet ready to publicize his reports or to seek outside intervention. The case took a dramatic turn in August 1986 when Eric Nalder, an investigative reporter for the *Seattle Times,* received an anonymous letter alerting him to the existence of Ruud's critical audits. Nalder believed that if these charges were substantiated, Hanford posed a great danger to the State of Washington and the surrounding area.[8] The disaster at Chernobyl, which only a few months earlier had destroyed a nuclear power plant, killed several workers, and contaminated an area of hundreds of miles in the Soviet Union and some European countries, gave credence to his fears. Nalder had written several reports, indicating that Hanford closely resembled the Chernobyl nuclear facility in design.[9] To Nalder, a similar tragedy seemed to be in the making on his own doorstep.

Nalder was strategically placed to pursue the story. He had lived in the state since the mid-1960s when he attended the University of Washington. In 1983, after working at several small local papers and magazines and for the *Seattle Post-Intelligencer,* he became a reporter for the *Seattle Times.* Nalder was attracted to the challenge of stories requiring intensive probing. The search for hidden events put him in contact with many anonymous informants, some of whom later became whistleblowers. He had a reputation as one of the toughest investigative reporters in the Northwest. After the Chernobyl accident in April 1986, Nalder was assigned to examine parallels between the design of the plant at Hanford and that of the ill-fated Soviet facility. One of the excellent contacts he had developed provided him with copies of Ruud's audits after the Rockwell Corporation refused to release them.

When Rockwell's managers learned that the *Seattle Times* planned to publish a major series on their inattention to Ruud's audits, they alerted the U.S. congressional delegation about Nalder's upcoming stories and provided a few details of the audits. Senator Slade Gorton, who was involved in a close re-election campaign, immediately made the material public. Simultaneously, Rockwell's management responded to Nalder's published accounts by claiming that Ruud's audits greatly exaggerated the plant's problems, that some modifications had already occurred, and that many of the auditor's findings were merely a matter of opinion.[10]

Nalder and the *Seattle Times* pressed on. The day after the Rockwell denials, he wrote another front-page article citing an earlier 1985 audit by Casey Ruud that detailed serious safety problems caused by improper welding. According to this audit, "virtually every area checked disclosed items of non-compliance which leads to the conclusion that control of welding and associated inspection activities is less than adequate." These allegations drew a rapid response from several West Coast congressmen who called for an investigation. Rockwell continued to insist that the plant operated safely. This assessment was supported by a Department of Energy manager who questioned the validity of Ruud's reports.[11]

Meanwhile, the *Seattle Times* continued to pound away with Nalder's front-page disclosures. SECURITY FLAW AT HANFORD IS RE-VEALED: PLUTONIUM WAS OPEN TO THEFT read one headline. The story, which underscored the dangers of plutonium and its casual treatment at Hanford, revealed that the Department of Energy had been concerned about plutonium security as early as 1984 and had ordered the plant "to correct all flaws in the system." Yet, Nalder charged, recent audits documented continuing problems and substantial health hazards. They were sufficiently serious for Ruud to recommend that Rockwell stop all movement of plutonium in the plants, a move that would have terminated operations. The *Seattle Times* minced no words in explaining the lethal properties of plutonium to the public: "Plutonium is an extremely dangerous radioactive material that could be used by terrorists or smaller countries to build an atomic bomb. Extremely small amounts of it can cause cancer if inhaled."[12]

The issue came to a head the following day, 8 October 1986, when Casey Ruud finally agreed to an interview. Rockwell's management wanted Ruud to support its claims that he had not recommended that the plants be closed, but he refused to compromise his integrity to protect the company. When one of the vice presidents publicly made that pronounce-ment, Nalder called Ruud, who decided to make a public statement of his own views.[13]

Ruud recognized that he could "lose his job, his career, and possibly all his material possessions." Although he had four young children to support, he felt he would not be destitute since he owned a small frozen yoghurt business and could work as a welder, if necessary. In addition, his wife and older brother wanted him to do the "right thing" and shared his view that Eric Nalder could be trusted. That belief was crucial. Ruud had been impressed by Nalder's tenacity and his straightforward manner of pursuing information from Rockwell: "I have been involved with many correspondents, and I'll tell you that there isn't a single one who can hold a candle to Eric Nalder."[14]

The same day, the headlines in the *Seattle Times* read: HANFORD AUDITOR BREAKS HIS SILENCE: RUUD BACKS UP REPORTS, EXPECTS REPRISAL. Knowing well the danger of speaking out ("I believe if I am not fired after doing this, I will probably be stuck in a corner office working on the United Way Fund"), Ruud nevertheless sharply criticized his own company and the failure of the Department of Energy to provide proper oversight of problems of security, welding, radioactive waste disposal, and design. Disillusioned by his management's response that the *Times* had "bent the truth," Ruud came forward to stand behind the veracity of his reports: "Either management is totally misinformed of what action takes place, or they twist the facts to reflect their viewpoints," he claimed.[15]

The day Ruud's name appeared on the front page of the *Seattle Times*, the DOE's on-site manager, Michael Lawrence, closed the two pluto-nium-processing plants at Hanford. He claimed that this decision had nothing to do with Ruud's audits or the *Times*'s stories, but rather re-sulted from "inadequate safeguards against the possibility of a nuclear chain reaction." Lawrence cited a 29 September incident that prompted him to take decisive action.[16]

Nalder, of course, doubted Lawrence's explanation and believed that the DOE official had responded to the pressure created by the *Times* series. He was satisfied that his reporting had achieved a speedy and effective result. A dangerous facility had been exposed, and a first step had been taken by a government agency that had been reluctant to act. While pleased with the impact of his series, Nalder emphasized that it placed a special burden on him: "Any time you encourage an employee to come forward to challenge his superiors publicly, you have to show that you can be counted on. If not, future whistleblowers will not trust you with their stories." Nalder told us that he would publicize any future attempts by Rockwell or the DOE to retaliate against Ruud. "I'll never stop watching," he vowed.[17]

From the ethical resister's point of view, Nalder was the ideal reporter. First, having worked on a series of articles about the possible dangers of nuclear facilities, he was in a position to investigate the seriousness of Ruud's audits and to provide prolonged coverage of the crisis. Second, the articles characterized Ruud as a man of integrity and competence and emphasized the ineptitude and even irresponsibility of both Rockwell and the Department of Energy. Finally, Nalder's articles paved the way for recognition of Ruud by influential political figures who could set the stage for his complete exoneration.[18]

After he made the decision to come forward, Ruud felt that "it became easy. I wasn't vindictive. I wasn't angry. I did what I wanted. Fortunately, it was Eric who wrote it the right way and put it out on the streets. Without the publicity they would have shuffled me off and never have fixed anything."[19] Within days of the first published reports, he was interviewed for nine hours in Washington, D.C., by staff members of the House Energy Subcommittee. Later Ruud told Nalder:

> After a while I was very comfortable to tell them my story. Everything just flowed as well as could be expected. When I walked out when we were all done, I knew that everyone in the room understood the big picture clearly. . . . I believe that something really great could come of this; ultimately we could end up fixing the system.[20]

Ruud had been invited to Washington by representatives Ron Wyden (Democrat-Oregon) and Al Swift (Democrat-Washington). Later, Wyden criticized the DOE and extolled Ruud: "Let me put it this way: This [Ruud] may be one of the most important people in the region." The congressman was aware of the serious reprisals Ruud might suffer: "He's had the courage to come forward and we're going to be very watchful over his employment status."[21]

In a remarkable turnabout, the DOE then joined with an endorsement of Ruud's work. He was assigned to assist the department in an investigation of the Rockwell facility. The DOE's director of environment, safety, health, and quality assurance became the first DOE official to praise Ruud publicly. "From what I have heard from a number of different sources," said Ron Gerton, "Casey Ruud was right on. He is a good hard-hitting auditor."[22]

Ruud had achieved the three goals of vindication: his allegations had been proven well founded, his superiors had been publicly chastised for their insufficient attention to major safety concerns, and he had remained in his job and even been given additional responsibilities. What elements contributed to this outcome and prevented his reports from languishing in a file drawer? Once it became clear that neither Rockwell nor the DOE was planning to take action to correct the serious and potentially lethal problems at Hanford, it was essential for his reports to gain widespread and sustained public attention. While Ruud himself proceeded cautiously, the reliability of his audits convinced Nalder and other *Times* staff that the issue was serious and Ruud a crucial witness. By revealing his findings, they laid the groundwork for his public testimony. The ultimate success of an investigative reporter is measured by his or her ability to expose hidden problems of grave public concern and effect responsible action by accountable officials—goals impossible to achieve with a one- or two-day story. Almost every day, from the beginning of October 1986 through January 1987, articles on the situation at Hanford appeared as lead stories in the *Seattle Times*. Other newspaper and television stations throughout the country also reported on the story. As the immediate questions surrounding the audits faded, Nalder and the *Times* initiated a follow-up series on safety problems in the "bomb factories" throughout the United States. This was now a major public issue and could no longer be buried by discounting the reports of one auditor. In an hour-long, prime-time documentary aired on 24 April 1987, "The Bomb Factories," ABC powerfully and provocatively highlighted the major problems in these plants. Casey Ruud was among those featured.

At first Ruud enjoyed a favorable outcome after challenging a major corporation and a recalcitrant government agency. It seemed fortunate that the story broke while he still held his job and was not in the defensive position of fighting for reinstatement. His natural allies in the press and Congress knew of his vulnerability and were committed to protecting him. They kept the spotlight on him and on the serious issues he had exposed. When DOE officials closed the plants, they in effect admitted that the time for stonewalling was over. They acknowledged that Ruud was right, and that they needed him to regain credibility with Congress and an increasingly concerned public. Much to Ruud's surprise, the positive reaction from the Hanford community far outweighed the criticisms. There were many phone calls and letters from people who lauded his courage: "You don't know me, but I feel the same way you do"; "You're my hero"; "I couldn't do it myself, but you're what life is all about."

Initially, both the DOE and Rockwell sought to benefit from Ruud's reputation for toughness and integrity. Instead of firing or isolating him in the face of media and legislative investigations, management enlisted his services in order to rebuild public trust in their operation and oversight of the plants. The organizations feared that they might lose the congressional support vital for the continuation of their programs. Ruud believes that without Nalder and the *Seattle Times* hammering away at the potential dangers of these plutonium plants, there would have been little incentive to reward him for his insistence on maintaining standards against the wishes of upper management, who saw him as the bearer of bad tidings. He reflected that the "system is so corrupt that even top management will be rolled over if they attempt to change it." It is "human nature" to attack those who are controversial and don't play the game. At Hanford and elsewhere, the plants are so old and the dangers so great that those who manage the operation would rather wish the dangers away than face the overwhelming task for which they would be held responsible. They will deal with the problem, Ruud maintains, only under the sternest pressure.[23]

In early 1988 the Reagan administration decided to close the plutonium-processing plants permanently. That February Ruud lost his job when Westinghouse (the company that took over management of Hanford) laid off three hundred workers. Ruud believes he was refused transfer to another project because he had testified before a House of Representatives Committee on Energy and Commerce the previous October. The Department of Labor subsequently ruled that Westinghouse had illegally fired Ruud, violating a statute that protects whistleblowers. Westinghouse has offered him a new job on the condition that he drop all prior claims for damages against the company. Ruud refuses and vows to continue his struggle, taking his case to the press and to Congress. Nalder remains a staunch ally in this second phase of Ruud's resistance.[24]

Congress versus the Environmental Protection Agency and Dow Chemical

Complete vindication is reserved for only a handful of ethical resisters, a rare success experienced in 1983 by officials from the Region 5 office of the Environmental Protection Agency when they testified before a congressional committee. These Chicago-based officials had been deeply disturbed for two years about the collusion they claimed existed between Reagan EPA appointees in Washington and the Dow Chemical Company—an inappropriate relationship that, these officials believed, had resulted in the continued discharge of chemical wastes such as dioxin into the river near Dow's Midland, Michigan, plant.

The issue had its inception with the election of Ronald Reagan to the presidency in November 1980. Throughout his campaign, he had advocated far less government control over industry as the best means to encourage business growth and to revitalize the American economy. The implementation of this ideology had particularly serious implications for those who worked for the Environmental Protection Agency. The president appointed Anne Gorsuch Burford as administrator and gave her a clear mandate to reduce government oversight in order to demonstrate to business that the government was now an encouraging partner rather than a watchful monitor.

The situation had almost immediate ramifications for Dr. J. Milton Clark, a thirty-year-old scientist who had recently joined the Chicago Region 5 office and been assigned to write a report on dioxin contamination. Clark had been concerned with issues of environmental degradation ever since his days as an undergraduate and graduate student at the University of Kansas. He hoped that his work in the Environmental Protection Agency would enable him to fulfill a personal commitment to help preserve the nation's precious resources, and was particularly concerned with the poisoning of the water, the threat to aquatic life from acid rain apparently caused by factory emissions in Midwestern states carried to Eastern sections of the country, and the dangers to people exposed to highly toxic industrial wastes. Clark had been aware that the Food and Drug Administration had already issued an advisory for people living downstream from the Dow Chemical Company in Midland, Michigan, about the possible contamination of fish from the lethal chemicals. Although Dow scientists had denied that there was serious danger to humans from dioxin, and rejected the charge that their plant was responsible for contamination of the water, Dr. Clark felt otherwise:

> Much of the scientific community was alarmed, concerned that Dow scientists were not being forthright in their interpretation of the data even that they had generated. I felt, at the time that I was writing the report, there existed a real risk of having very powerful entities in society misusing or twisting the information.[25]

Given the significance of the issue and the freedom his immediate supervisors had provided, Clark wrote a strong report in 1981 that pointed directly to the responsibility of Dow in creating an environmental crisis. He charged that people eating fish caught downriver from the Midland, Michigan, plant could be in serious jeopardy. His report concluded with this serious warning:

> Dow Chemical of Midland, Michigan, has extensively contaminated their facility with PCDDs [polychlorinated dibenzo p-dioxins] and PCDFs [polychlorinated dibenzofurans] and has been the primary contributor to contamination of the Tittabawassee and Saginaw Rivers and Lake Huron. . . .
>
> The consumption of fish from the Tittabawassee River, the Saginaw River, Saginaw Bay, and possibly other sites in the Great Lakes should be prohibited.[26]

Clark's report created a furor in EPA headquarters in Washington, whose administrators were especially angry because someone leaked the report to a Toronto newspaper. Dr. John Hernandez, the second in command, then sent the report to Dow Chemical Company for "peer review." Milton Clark was outraged over such a breach in procedure:

> We never heard of a situation where you have an internal report of the EPA that went to a chemical company that we were in the process of regulating. The pressure mounted to the point where the vice president of Dow called Valdas Adamkus [the acting head of the Chicago office] and said that if we agreed to take out certain lines of the report, they would endorse it. The middle management people here in Region 5 were very worried that there could be reprisals re-

sulting in loss of jobs. Certainly even Adamkus's position was in real jeopardy.[27]

The leaders at the Chicago office now faced a major dilemma as they confronted terms dictated by Dow and supported by headquarters in Washington, terms that violated their professional values and their definition of the mission of the EPA. While a Republican himself, the acting administrator, European-born Valdas Adamkus, intensely disliked the current administration's policy of weakening his agency. He recalled the early days of EPA when he joined a group of enthusiastic pioneers of government workers devoted to environmental protection. Adamkus knew that the goals of EPA had changed drastically when "told by the second highest official in the ranks of EPA in Washington that I should not even mention the word 'acid rain' *ever* in his presence because no such thing exists." Adamkus, passionate in his commitment to the EPA, put his dilemma thus:

We had national as well as international problems. They included chemical contamination like the one involving Dow, the issue of acid rain, and the phosphorus-loading situation [the amount of phosphorus that is permitted to be discharged into lakes to prevent environmental damage] specifically related to the detergent manufacturers. The situation at Dow was only one of the many issues that were debated by the specialists who were being prevented from pursuing environmental problems by policies and directives from Washington. And that led to a moral question being raised by people on my staff and myself: "Should I just act according to my conscience and commitment to the job or should I willingly accept those directives which are contrary to the mission of the agency and the intent of Congress?" Some people simply gave up and left because they probably could not take the pressure. Yet there were those of us who decided to take the more resistant way by trying to do whatever we could under the circumstances—to protect what was protectable.[28]

Adamkus and his colleagues firmly believed that the Washington administration deviated from the goals for which the EPA had been founded. They mistrusted this leadership and deplored policies they believed endangered the public. They debated public disclosure, but decided that disobedience would be futile. What congressional figure or which newspaper would be willing to push for an investigation when the Reagan administration was at the height of its power and prestige? They counseled patience and more subtle forms of resistance.

Their opportunity for public disclosure arose in dramatic fashion two years later when, in the spring of 1983, several congressional committees, under the control of the Democrats, mounted an investigation into the misuse of Superfund dollars allocated by Congress to clean up the nation's worst toxic waste dumps. Environmentalists had already challenged the commitment of EPA administrator Anne Gorsuch Burford and her closest associates. There was considerable suspicion by members of Congress, particularly in the Democrat-controlled House, that several of the highest officials at the EPA, who had come to Washington directly from industries that were among the worst violators of environmental standards, were condoning violations of EPA regulations. Burford, who had publicly announced her intention to lessen the agency's oversight of industry, maintained that excessive federal regulations had hampered the enactment of the Reagan administration's policy of reducing the burden on the business community. Her controversial and combative stance made her a perfect target for the Democrats, who seized the opportunity to take center stage by attacking the administration's policy as dangerous to the environment. Congressional committees raised questions about the possibility of "sweetheart deals" with corporations, the misuse of Superfund money to clean up toxic waste dumps, and harassment techniques invoked to eliminate critics within the EPA, such as Hugh Kaufman, who was followed into motels in an unsuccessful attempt to cast aspersions on his private life (see pages 135–36).[29]

Various facets of the EPA program came under intense scrutiny by at least six separate congressional committees.[30] Among those most interested was Congressman James Scheuer of New York who wanted to revive the Subcommittee on Natural Resources, Agriculture Research and Environment of the House Committee on Science and Technology, which he chaired, and make it a base for investigating the mounting environmental scandals reported in the press. The subcommittee's staff included the chemist Jim Greene, who had held a fellowship from the American Chemical Society to provide Congress with scientific information. He later decided to give up college teaching and remain in Washington.

With active direction by Scheuer and the committee's staff director,

George Kopp, Greene was strategically placed to investigate dioxin contamination of the nation's waters. He acquired the names of government officials who were expert on this issue and ultimately contacted Jack Houser (not his real name), an EPA employee who wanted to reveal information anonymously about the dioxin issue. Houser believed the Reagan appointees were treating dioxin as a "political football" rather than as a serious health and environmental issue. Greene was supportive of Houser's desire to remain unidentified: "Maybe he would not be fired if his name were revealed, but he would be relegated to some broom closet for the rest of his career."[31] Making documents available to congressional oversight committees became highly charged after Anne Gorsuch Burford herself withheld substantial numbers of subpoenaed documents, citing certain files as "enforcement-sensitive." Although initially backed by President Reagan's claim of executive privilege, Burford's actions proved to be politically explosive. She became the first high-placed official in history to be charged with contempt of Congress. Burford ultimately relented and transmitted the documents under orders from the president.[32]

In this atmosphere, Greene became convinced that Houser had important information. As their relationship evolved, Greene could ask specific questions, and Houser would indicate whether documents were available about the EPA's role in that particular issue. Events took a decisive turn when Houser escalated his risk by inviting Greene to his home in the middle of the night to give him several documents, among which was the censored Chicago report.

This report was critical in accelerating the investigation, for, with the resignation of Anne Gorsuch Burford, John Hernandez had become acting administrator and her likely successor. Houser's documents showed that Hernandez had been influential in intervening on behalf of Dow's right to "review" the Chicago report two years earlier. Greene knew that he had uncovered a potentially explosive issue, and approached the Chicago group to testify before Scheuer's committee on the alteration of the report and Hernandez's role in that episode.

This was precisely the opportunity the Chicago EPA professionals had been awaiting. The committee staff found that Valdas Adamkus, the regional administrator, Milton Clark, the report's author, and other staff members in the Chicago office were willing to testify publicly before Congress. Although Clark and his Chicago colleagues had been upset when Washington superiors had required alteration in the report, Adamkus had decided that the best strategy was to keep his group intact, resisting inappropriate Washington directives where possible, and continuing the investigation of cases of environmental abuse in the hope that a day would come when enforcement would again become a paramount EPA strategy.

The intervention of Congress transformed the situation, making corrective action a real possibility. At the same time, the Chicago group members were aware of their own continued vulnerability. They knew that the agency was under strict surveillance and that their professional futures were at stake. Since they had decided in 1981 not to protest publicly the alteration of the report, they were open to accusations that they had violated their public trust despite their disagreement with their Washington superiors and their readiness to provide public testimony now.

Their fears were not unfounded. While Congressman Scheuer and committee staff members may have been sympathetic to their accounts, the outcome of the actual hearings was not predictable. The congressmen who would be questioning the Chicago group had their own political agenda and might use the occasion to accuse them of dereliction of duty. Dr. Milton Clark, the principal author of the original report on dioxin contamination, who had long wanted the censorship issue to become public, expressed his own anxiety as the actual hearings neared:

I knew the Dow Chemical/dioxin issue had come to a head. The information had to be accurately presented. I felt at that time that I could have been under some sort of surveillance because the White House had ordered an investigation immediately before we were to appear before Congress. I had been involved with the Dow Chemical and issues of environmental pollution for many years. I was really obsessed with having this thing come to fruition. I knew that we might win or we might lose. I really did not know where the testimony would go or what sort of backlash might occur in Washington.[33]

Adamkus and his staff testified twice. The first time they appeared before Representative John Dingell's Subcommittee on Oversight and Investigation, their testimony was well received, despite some intense questioning by Congressman Edward Markey (Democrat-Massachusetts).[34] Several days later, on 23 March 1983, they were called before the

Scheuer committee. After his opening statement, Adamkus was closely questioned by Congressman Robert C. Torricelli (Democrat-New Jersey) who, taking the approach the Chicago group had feared the most, accused Adamkus of knowingly suppressing significant health information, "given what you knew about the impact dioxin could have on the American people, the evidence from Midland, where 111 children had birth defects, the possible carcinogenic nature of dioxin." Pointing an accusing finger directly at Adamkus, Torricelli said, "It is hard to believe that you really did your best efforts to protect the American people, isn't it?"[35]

Torricelli, continuing on this line of attack, was impatient with Adamkus's attempt to separate his Chicago group from the Washington office. Adamkus argued that he had, in fact, initiated the report, insisted on its completion, and done everything possible to resist the withholding of vital information. But Torricelli was determined to link Adamkus to the Republican-controlled EPA, the primary target of the congressman's wrath: "We have seen birth defects. We can suspect cancer. You know some people are going to die, and no one was there to protect them, all because you were concerned about Mr. Hernandez, Mr. Hernandez was concerned about Mrs. Burford, and Mrs. Burford was concerned with Ronald Reagan."[36]

Adamkus was so taken aback by the vehemence and intensity of the attack that he could barely respond. He defined himself as a responsible official who had done everything possible to avoid undermining the integrity of his group. Now he was being tarred with the same brush and accused of everything he resented in the Washington administrators. At this moment, the atmosphere of the hearings changed as the chairman, James Scheuer, interrupted Torricelli's line of questioning. Other committee members supported Scheuer, who emphasized the limits of the authority under which Region 5 had operated and thus helped remove any accusations of their irresponsibility.

The shift in tone was finalized in Scheuer's closing remarks to the Chicago witnesses, which dominated the hearings and were widely quoted in the press the next day:

> I want to express my admiration for the way you stood up far beyond the call of duty, in resisting the relentless and unremitting pressure from Washington to change your report and to change the regulatory policy as to dioxin, as to phosphates, in ways that you felt were inconsistent with the public interest. . . .

The fact that under our form of government in Washington they make the final decisions is in no way a reflection on the good fight you made to serve the public interest in a way that you felt was consistent with the scientific data that was available and the way the public interest should be served. . . .

I congratulate you for your conduct in the field and also for your cooperation with this committee in coming and telling us the truth as you see it . . . so that the Congress in its wisdom and the new Administrator in his wisdom can take the actions that are necessary to prevent this kind of egregious misconduct from happening again.[37]

Despite Torricelli's blistering criticism, the political interests of the Democratic committee members had coincided with the needs of the Chicago group and provided them with a sympathetic forum to explain their actions.

Media accounts presented Adamkus and his colleagues in a heroic light. In a lengthy article, the *Wall Street Journal* in particular emphasized the pressure on Adamkus's group and the tactics they had utilized to continue their work under adverse administration policy.[38] Milton Clark expressed his enthusiasm for the outcome and his belief in the importance of a strong system of checks and balances:

To me it really demonstrated the concept of the separation of powers. Congress does have particular powers which help check the federal government from going in a direction that may not be in the best interests of the people. That is very good, as information is brought forth and is presented by those with opposing viewpoints. Dow people were brought in. We were brought in. All of us entered our information. I look at the larger picture and I think it is extremely valuable to have these open hearings with the people participating from the scientific community, from business, and from the EPA representing their views. All of this is then evaluated by Congress and then disseminated to the public. Maybe you lose something once it gets to the press, and maybe there are congressmen who have political interests in what they are doing, but nevertheless the information is still getting out to the public as a whole.[39]

The case of the Chicago EPA illustrates the vindication all ethical resisters seek. They presented their position in the glare of national publicity and, despite the controversy generated by their earlier caution, were supported by several influential members of Congress. It was critical that their adversaries within the EPA were forced to resign and were replaced by others having a stronger commitment to the environment and public health. The Chicago group was publicly lauded as part of the tradition of strong individuals standing up in the public interest against opposing forces. Unlike other resisters, they could not simply be characterized as foolish idealists who had risked all in a vain fight for principle. In essence, their vindication consisted of maintaining a sense of their professional selves, achieving congressional and media recognition and acclamation, and participating in the re-creation of purpose in their organization. Valdas Adamkus was elated:

> Only two months ago, the morale of this agency was at the very bottom. People stood in the hallways wondering if they would have a job tomorrow. Nobody was talking about the program or how to improve the work. In two months there has been a total reversal. People are enthusiastically coming up with new ideas and looking for the best solutions to problems. I don't know if anything could be more rewarding and satisfying. Sometimes I think I'm still dreaming.[40]

The actions of the Scheuer committee in investigating collusion between high government officials and the Dow Chemical company illustrate the various roles that congressional committees can play in facilitating public disclosure. First, committees use their own staffs to investigate questionable practices both in the federal government and in private industry. Without the serious inquiry mounted by the staff members George Kopp and Jim Greene, there is little likelihood that the censorship of Milton Clark's report would have been uncovered and publicized. It took long, deliberate conversations with an anonymous whistleblower and subsequent discussions with Adamkus, Clark, and the others in Chicago to prepare the necessary documentation for the Scheuer committee hearings.

Second, the hearings themselves provide a national forum for testimony by witnesses from all sides of a dispute. In this case, the committee heard representatives from Dow as well as statements by the Chicago EPA. While this was not a legal proceeding in which they had the right to cross-examine, the committee members did closely question witnesses. Although there was a partisan tone to much of the interrogation, the participation of both Republicans and Democrats assured that these hearings were not simply a one-party device.

Third, while ethical resisters testifying before congressional committees have no ironclad guarantee against retaliation, members of Congress can publicly monitor any punishment of those who appear before their committees. This cloak of protection is more effective for federal employees than for those working in the private sector. Several whistleblowers, including Hugh Kaufman, who played a prominent role in the Superfund investigation, report that their ability to continue to function in their agencies has depended heavily on the watchful eye of several interested members of Congress.[41]

When staff members feel that they cannot provide this form of protection, they act much more cautiously. While preparing for the hearings, the staff had been approached by the spouse of a Dow employee, who was ready to testify about the increased rate of birth defects among residents of Midland, Michigan, where there was active discharge of waste from the Dow plant. Knowing that she would endanger her husband's standing at Dow and that she might not be able to protect the confidentiality of the thirty women who had given her information, Congressman Scheuer's staff cautioned her about the dangers of coming forward publicly. She responded that the health and well-being of the children were more important than any personal recriminations she or her husband might suffer. Scheuer believed that he could present the evidence against Dow's policies without involving her, and decided not to bring her to Washington. In the end, such judgments are made by members of Congress and their staff who must weigh the personal risk of public testimony against its value in exposing serious problems.

An examination of the success of the Scheuer committee in vindicating and protecting the Chicago EPA employees reveals that congressional committees can be most effective in providing a shield in highly specified circumstances. Like journalists, committees are far more effective in helping employees who have remained on the job. Once dismissed, whistleblowers have found that it is much more difficult to achieve reinstatement. Furthermore, while Adamkus and Clark fought for the right to continue investigations of environmental hazards, their ultimate success was guaranteed by the total shake-up of the EPA leadership in Washington. The appointment of William Ruckleshaus as EPA administrator solidified their position and had a braking effect on those in high-level management who had a stake in evening the score. It is not always so.

The protection of Congress should not be overestimated. While it is the only forum for certain whistleblowers to reclaim public legitimacy, Congress cannot serve as a widespread remedy. Most whistleblowers cannot get the attention of a congressional staff person. Hearings are designed to gather information for potential legislation, to oversee government agencies, and to spotlight serious problems in the government or in industries subject to government regulation. Congressmen do not necessarily want to become adversaries of industry or government agencies or to enmesh themselves in long-standing conflict unless it serves their own political needs. There are many bona fide whistleblowers who could not attract the attention of congressmen because their protests did not occur in a context that served the legislators' agenda, and there are others who testified but feel they were not provided the promised shield against retaliation. Jim Pope (see pages 156–59) provides a deeply somber note on the interest and reliability of Congress:

As the #1 whistleblower on FAA's mid-air collision program "TCAS" [Traffic-Alert Collision Avoidance System] hoax, I was *subpoenaed* to testify on March 31, 1981 by [a] U.S. House of Representatives member . . . As a result of my lengthy and fully documented revelations, that hundreds of people have been killed in mid-air collisions which FAA could have prevented, I was soon thereafter fired on the basis of quickly trumped-up charges. I received absolutely NO protection from [the] Representative . . . ; and worse yet, after testifying, . . . [the] Subcommittee took absolutely NO action on FAA's gross misbehavior. Since that 1981 hearing, 288 MORE people have been killed in preventable mid-air collisions, including those 84 over Cerritos [California] on August 31, 1986.

I stood up, testified, was fired, and all for naught. Future whistleblowers, BEWARE![42]

California Legislators Pass a Protective Law

In the cases of both Casey Ruud and the Chicago EPA officials, strategically placed individuals in the press and Congress were able to illuminate the national issues the resisters had attempted to expose. In both instances, the testimony of the resisters contributed to significant changes within their organizations. There are other situations in which the struggle for vindication has significant political consequences. In one dramatic instance briefly introduced in chapter 4 (see pages 117–20) in the discussion of the religious views of Dr. Zalman Magid, several professionals refused to stand mute in the face of dangerous mental health practices. Their actions ultimately led to the enactment of ground-breaking state legislation in 1987 which outlawed retaliation against whistleblowers employed in the public sector in California.

The case unfolded in San Diego in 1984 and 1985 at the San Diego County Hillcrest Mental Health Facility (CMH), a ninety-two-bed acute psychiatric hospital. Dr. Martin Schorr and Dr. James Hardison, psychologists with years of service, observed a pattern of patient neglect and poor medical practice which they believed would ultimately lead to unnecessary tragedy. They became particularly disturbed by the murder of a comatose patient by his roommate, and joined to confront their superior with their allegations. He did not act and clearly indicated that he believed that Schorr and Hardison were more the problem than alleged patient abuse. Outraged by his rejection, both psychologists felt that their superior had deteriorated badly in recent years. Despite their earlier friendship, Schorr said that he could no longer defend a service chief who neglected his duties and joked about the death of patients.[43]

When Schorr approached the *San Diego Tribune* with the material about CMH, he was referred to Betsy Bates, who began covering the story.[44] After an independent investigation of the hospital, she asked Schorr and Hardison whether they would be willing to meet with a member of the County Board of Supervisors, which had overall responsibility for all county facilities. The request put the two psychologists in a delicate position. Up to now they had not gone to "outside agencies," and they worried about the implications of such an action. Yet, believing that the problems at CMH had escalated dramatically, they did not feel they could defer action. Schorr explained their decision:

This was a very big step. Hardison and I had never taken anything out of channels. Yet we were getting nowhere with the head of clinical treatment, and more incidents of patient abuse had already occurred. Jim and I talked about going to a board member for hours and finally came to a decision. We would go but we wanted Betsy Bates to be present. We also felt that two lone psychologists would not get very far without additional clout. We decided to invite Dr. Zalman Magid, board-certified in child and adult psychiatry.[45]

While Schorr felt that Magid would be hesitant and anxious about becoming involved, Schorr had deep respect for the psychiatrist's strong sense of justice, concern for patient care, and his own integrity: "We knew that he would not lie and he would be loyal to his ideals in pursuit of a fair deal for the patients and staff. We also felt that, once he was committed, he would stay the course and become emboldened by the experience. In the end this is exactly what happened."[46]

The arranged meeting with the staff aide of one of the supervisors of the board went well. The three CMH professionals outlined the problems, and the aide told them that the matter would be investigated and they would be protected against retaliation. Neither promise was fulfilled. No remedial action was taken, and the protesters became increasingly alienated from their superiors as harassment against them intensified. Betsy Bates, who had by then written several articles about CMH in the *Tribune,* made a crucial recommendation. She singled out the Republican state assemblyman Larry Stirling as the man to contact, for his office had called her and indicated a willingness to help.

Although Schorr and all staff members had been ordered to refrain from approaching outsiders, he was determined to push forward. His colleagues were somewhat more hesitant: "Since we had been burned once, there was considerable ambivalence about going on. Hardison wanted to drop the whole thing. Magid was willing to do whatever we two decided, but was also unwilling to go on if one of us dropped out. I got Hardison to hold off until we all had more time to think about it."[47]

In April 1985, Schorr found a way to inform Stirling of the problems at CMH. Schorr, Hardison, and Magid pointed to several deeply troubling events. In September 1984, for example, the police had brought a patient to the hospital after preventing her from committing suicide. She was released within forty-five minutes by the screening psychiatrist who deemed her nonsuicidal. Twelve hours later, she returned to the bridge where the police had originally rescued her, and killed herself. A subsequent report revealed that the woman had a history of suicidal behavior and had been admitted into the CMH only three weeks before for similar problems. The chief of the Adult Mental Health Service defended the hospital by arguing that there had been no problem with the screening psychiatrist's decision to release the patient, and claimed that "people say they are going to kill themselves all the time; if someone really wants to kill themself, there isn't much that we can do about it."[48]

The problems surfaced even more clearly in January 1985 when police brought to the hospital another seriously disturbed patient, who was admitted by the screening psychiatrist and diagnosed as paranoid schizophrenic. Despite serious depression, the patient was not given medication or seen by a psychiatrist for fifty-six hours, allegedly because of reduced staff on the weekend. On early Monday morning, the patient strangled his comatose roommate.[49]

Less than two months later, a third patient died from an overdose of a drug. An investigation revealed that the staff had failed to take the patient's vital signs as soon as possible after admission. Zalman Magid, drawing upon his own medical knowledge, became convinced that if appropriate procedures had been followed, there would have been a clear indication of the need for additional treatment that could have prevented an unnecessary death.[50] Magid, the two psychologists, and the social worker Sid Rhodes, who now joined the group, felt that these deaths were deeply disturbing but not surprising given the severely overcrowded conditions, the inadequate state funding, the poor training of many staff physicians, and the insufficient attention to professional credentials that characterized hospital personnel procedures.[51]

The "Four Musketeers," as they came to call themselves, had found a tough and knowledgeable ally in Larry Stirling, although no other government official seemed willing to investigate the strange events at CMH. An attorney in his mid-forties, Stirling had been elected as assemblyman in 1980 after serving on the San Diego city council. He saw his post as enabling him to serve his constituents "who had run out of options. When people come to me they are usually in trouble."[52] At the time the CMH professionals contacted Stirling, his staff was already overextended in an investigation of a geriatric health care facility,[53] and could not take on the crisis at CMH. Instead, Stirling made the crucial decision to contact Art Letter, who had previously worked with him and had two decades of experience in state government in both New York and California. Stirling had a high regard for Letter's assessment of people and for his investigative abilities, and thought he could help evaluate the allegations. For his part, Letter, though a Democrat, knew and respected

Stirling from an earlier time when they had served together on a Comprehensive Planning Organization for San Diego.[54]

At Stirling's request, Letter attended the initial meeting at the home
of Martin Schorr where, for several hours, Schorr, Hardison, Magid, and
Rhodes described the events and the irresponsibility they alleged existed
at the hospital. Later that evening, after listening and pressing their hosts
to clarify the situation, Stirling and Letter huddled alone and made several
decisions. They concluded that underneath the stream of complaints and
some bickering and tension—the "shrubbery," as Stirling called it, that
can be attributed to the usual infighting in any organization—the four
professionals had revealed personal knowledge of a pattern of neglect that
Letter felt was "potentially explosive."[55] Letter recalls this observation:
"If these guys were right, then we had the makings of a real live *One Flew
over the Cuckoo's Nest.* It's probably going to be very difficult to be able
to distinguish the patients from the staff." Second, Stirling decided that
the case ultimately rested on the testimony of Zalman Magid. This man
who remained silent for most of the evening, until asked by Stirling
whether he agreed with the charges, deeply impressed the legislator.
Magid was the psychiatrist, the medical man with the most prestige and
credibility. He was that rare physician who was willing to criticize irresponsibility of his colleagues publicly. Stirling sensed that Magid had the
empathy and courage to stay the course in order to save lives and prevent
patient neglect. Stirling and Letter further concluded that Schorr, Hardison, and Rhodes also had the tenacity to keep supplying them with
essential information despite the risk.

With this assessment, Stirling appointed Letter as a part-time member
of his staff with primary authority to pursue this case. According to Schorr,
each man had a special job:

> I was asked to be the point man, and Jim Hardison was backup. Each
> of us divided up areas of responsibility. We all agreed to say nothing
> on hospital phones. In a moment of levity, we each had coded numbers.
> Since I had 007 on my license plate, Magid became 6 and 9/10. Rhodes
> was 005, and Hardison 004. When Larry Silver [a young social worker
> at CMH] joined our group two months later, he became 003.

Schorr looks back on it all with some amusement: "We had to have
some fun. What was going on at CMH was so deadly that we needed a

change of pace somewhere, and this was part of it. In time, our humor saved many a situation for us."[56]

As a first step, Letter met with the four resisters and pressed them to reveal any "skeletons in their own closets" that might come out in the course of an investigation of the hospital administration. Letter sought assurance that there were no criminal records or anything else that could be used to discredit these men publicly:

I wanted them to know that even though they had faced difficult times before, that this was a true struggle to the end. It could have profound effects on their lives. Their careers and marriages were at stake. I asked them if they were willing to go through with it. A day later they came back and said, "We are willing to do it."[57]

Letter then asked each to write a critique of the hospital, in order to separate the most important issues from less serious grievances that were not actionable. This was also the beginning of a relationship in which Magid, Schorr, Hardison, and Rhodes would become a continuing source of information to Stirling. He saw them as "Deep Throats," men who have the acumen to observe problems and the courage to communicate them. Letter subsequently reported to Stirling that the case rested on the two deaths in the hospital and on three suicides that had occurred in the community during a one-year period from April 1984 to April 1985. Stirling immediately informed the proper authorities of the deaths so they could investigate for criminal wrongdoing.

The assemblyman also notified the county Board of Supervisors in April 1985. He received no response, and the chairman of the board later denied that he had received any notice of the allegations. Despite these statements, Stirling and Letter had written office receipts and had also sent copies of their initial investigation findings to the district attorney, the grand jury, and other state and federal agencies. The county Department of Health issued a response a month later indicating that it believed that 95 percent of the allegations were untrue and that the other 5 percent did not result from "poor patient care problems, rather they were problems with administration, medical records, and inadequate personnel."[58] Letter, who believed that the county staff and the Board of Supervisors responded out of fear of potentially costly lawsuits, now speculates, "I assume they were advised by counsel to maintain that they did not do anything wrong and therefore no dismissals or changes were required."[59]

Unsatisfied by the "whitewash and the cover-up" of the county officials, Stirling requested a review by the California auditor general's office and by the state's health agencies. Within the next few months, three separate reports by state and federal regulatory agencies concluded that substantial problems did, in fact, exist at the hospital. One state investigation concluded, "The facility is plagued with poor staff morale, questionable clinical practices, ineffective management and supervision, inadequate treatment programming and an inefficient health care delivery system."[60] Stirling was deeply impressed with the state auditor, who was a nononsense former combat officer in Vietnam with no ax to grind. The evidence, Stirling knew, now went far beyond the resisters' passion or his own political concerns.

In January 1986, the federal investigation released an even more devastating decision. The office of the inspector general of the Department of Health and Human Services notified the County of San Diego that the CMH hospital was to be excluded from the Medicare program for three years. This unprecedented step was followed by exclusion of the facility from the federal military health-care insurance program, a disciplinary action that effectively curtailed a major source of funding on which the hospital depended. One county staff psychiatrist who had been of great concern to the whistleblowers was also personally excluded from the Medicare program. He resigned and then, ironically, was able to secure employment for a short time in a Veterans Administration hospital in Battle Creek, Michigan. The Veterans Administration, when made aware of his Medicare exclusion, summarily dismissed him.[61]

Despite all the flurry of investigations and confirmation of the resisters' allegations, their plight worsened. CMH administrators escalated their retaliation. Zalman Magid was taken off clinical practice, put in an isolated room, and assigned only the lowest clerical duties.[62] In November 1985, Dr. Magid was brought up on charges of neglecting his medical duties, in an effort to destroy the credibility of the key witness. Stirling could not believe that this inquisition was happening in San Diego in the mid-1980s. "The bureaucracy would protect its own and root out its critics no matter how outlandish the reprisals," he concluded.[63] Martin Schorr retired under a cloud of controversy after completing twenty-seven years of county service.[64] After a heart attack and subsequent surgery, Sid Rhodes concluded that the pressure was unacceptable and he, too, retired.[65] For a short time, Jim Hardison remained in the system but he left in early 1987 when he found an attractive position that allowed him to pursue his career. Neither Stirling nor Letter could adequately protect the resisters when no other member of the medical staff came forward to support Magid's allegations. Other witnesses were necessary to "bring down the administration." Letter speculates that these physicians simply felt too married to the mental health community to risk their well-paid jobs.[66] One staff physician told Jim Hardison that since problems existed in all hospitals, professionals had to work around them rather than risk their careers by attacking the bureaucracy.[67]

Deeply troubled by how few resources the ethical resisters had against determined retaliation, Stirling directed Letter to comb the law looking for a code that would provide them with direct protection. When none was available, Stirling felt that further action was required: "We had to protect those who had gotten into the boat with us." He initiated legislation to protect all public employees by introducing an amendment to the state's Government Code that extended existing protection for state workers to all employees in the public sector, including those at the county level.

Citing the injustices against the ethical resisters at CMH, Stirling campaigned for legislation making it a crime to retaliate against public employees who "blow the whistle" on improper conduct at their workplace. One section of the new law provided that:

> any person who intentionally engages in acts of reprisal, retaliation, threats, coercion, or similar acts against a state employee or applicant for state employment (or any employee or applicant for employment who files a complaint with a local agency) is subject to a fine not to exceed $10,000 and imprisonment for a period of up to one year, is subject to discipline by adverse action by the appointing power or the State Personnel Board and is liable for damages in an action brought by the injured party.[68]

Co-sponsorship with several Democratic assemblymen, strong support from many public and private lobbying groups, including the Union of American Physicians and Dentists, and substantial news coverage of the CMH scandal all contributed to the unanimous passage of the bill in the California legislature. Governor George Deukmejian signed it on 16 July 1986, and it became law on 1 January 1987.[69]

No one could hope for better assistance from public officials than

Magid, Schorr, Hardison, and Rhodes received from Assemblyman Larry Stirling and from his staff member Art Letter. Committed to public disclosure and actions against patient neglect at the hospital, they used every local, state, and federal agency review board possible to investigate and bring action against responsible officials at CMH. They kept in close contact with the whistleblowers and were aware of their plight. Magid, for instance, never believed that the state officials were simply using him for their own political purposes; rather he "respected their insight, sensitivity, and determination to pursue justice."[70]

Stirling's involvement did not cease with the passage of protective legislation. He and Letter continued to monitor the fate of Zalman Magid who, among the original four resisters, remained a target for further punishment as he sought other employment with a state facility. In 1987, he applied for a position as staff psychiatrist at Patton State Hospital. At the interview the acting medical director grilled Magid about his appearance on a "60 Minutes" program some weeks before that had exposed the unnecessary deaths: "He said he wanted to know what was going on inside my mind when I spoke to '60 Minutes.' He said that there were sometimes deaths at Patton, and that he was concerned that maybe if I were a staff member I would report them and cause trouble." The acting director concluded the meeting by informing Magid that it would be considered not an interview but an information-gathering session. Magid "felt stunned and shocked by such unprofessional medical attitudes and considered giving up the practice of medicine."[71]

After Magid reported this interview to Stirling, the latter wrote to the director of the Department of Mental Health demanding an investigation of the hiring discrimination to ascertain whether the acting director at Patton had violated the new Whistleblower Protection Act. Stirling's strong statement was released to the press:

> Should these charges, which are contained in the enclosed letter and background material provided by Doctor Zalman Magid, prove to be correct, then I would expect you to take disciplinary action against the Acting Medical Director. Quite frankly I am tired of hearing about a "good Old Boys" network of psychiatric professionals who appear to spend more time punishing members of their profession than carrying out their public safety duties. I have known Dr. Magid to be a courageous and caring psychiatrist who simply told the truth about conditions at this workplace. Dr. Magid and other professionals at the County Mental Health Hospital in San Diego

simply reached a point where their professional consciousness would not allow them to sit back and watch as their superiors repeatedly mismanaged their workplace.... Your Department's own investigation confirmed in part that the original charges brought by Dr. Magid and others were correct.[72]

Larry Stirling kept his promise to help guard against reprisals[73]—a promise motivated by principle and self-interest. Both Stirling and Letter firmly believed in the importance of professional integrity and courage. Not only did their work on behalf of such employees contribute to their vision of a good society, but they also saw their own careers benefit from their involvement in the CMH investigation. They took a risk initially in backing the four dissidents and calling for extensive investigation by several state agencies. Of course, they made enemies along the way; but once their allegations were proven valid, they enjoyed extensive press and television coverage and solidified their reputations as a formidable team.

Stirling was re-elected by the largest majority in his career in the next election and has developed a growing reputation in the Assembly. In February 1988, he decided to run for the State Senate. Art Letter became a permanent member of a key legislative committee. Although both men felt deservedly satisfied about the role they had played in supporting and guiding the CMH resisters and in affecting legal change for others who may follow, they also recognized the limits of their influence in confronting government agencies determined to continue operations as usual despite the intervention of legislators in alliance with ethical resisters. The energetic and articulate Stirling spoke from extensive experience when he concluded that resisters will always be vulnerable to severe retaliation; and that the "bureaucracy, once in motion, will not be stopped."[74] Dr. Magid and his fellow whistleblowers learned this lesson all too well.

The Government Accountability Project and Vincent Laubach versus the Department of the Interior

Few Americans are more involved with ethical resisters who blow the whistle than Louis Clark, who became director of the Government Accountability Project in 1978 (see pages 61–63). He quickly helped devise a new direction for GAP, moving away from a strictly educational orientation to an emphasis on political activism and legal defense of whistleblow-ers—a dual orientation that makes GAP unique among public-interest groups. Clark and his associates believe that those who call attention to serious problems must be staunchly defended while the issues are publi-cized and social change sought. Clark had been a Methodist minister prior to becoming an attorney, and his experience in the civil rights movement and his pastoral counseling skills significantly influenced his career choices. He wanted a career that would combine religion and law and be compatible with his commitment to social change.[75] His earlier work in civil rights had a profound effect on him:

> I was in Mississippi on a Saturday morning in 1968 playing cards with a black couple on a beach. They were friends and we had come down there to enjoy the weekend. All of a sudden we were arrested for vagrancy and held in jail for two days without being allowed to make a phone call. The cell was filled with people. They could sleep about fourteen people on steel beds that had no mattresses or pillows, only burlap blankets. There were people lying on the concrete floor. The food literally came from the remains of a local restaurant. It was horri-ble food and I did not eat it. Everyone else was in a lot worse shape than I was. . . . I felt that if I had a law degree I wouldn't be as powerless as I felt I was at that moment. And then my Ministry came through. We had been kept in complete isolation of what was happening to us and all of a sudden we were free. This Washington lawyer had come from our center in Jackson and met with the head of the Longshore-men's Union. The two of them went to the mayor and got us out of jail. I was very impressed with the power of the law and with the fact that a lot of people didn't have that power. I thought a law degree would be really very useful.[76]

In analyzing the allegations of a whistleblower, Clark evaluates their significance, the possibilities for reform from a particular case, and the emotional ability of a resister to sustain himself or herself during the lengthy ordeal that will ensue. When he is willing to accept a case, he first counsels the client about the consequences of public disclosure:

> The people who come forth are making an ethical decision. Most would prefer not to make the decision; it is almost always one that is thrust

on them, not one they seek. I am very conscious about not treading on this decision. The people who are thinking about blowing the whistle need to know what kind of support they are going to get. I encourage people who are religiously involved to talk to their religious counselor. I always advise them to discuss it with their spouses or significant others. The person who comes through the whistleblowing experience is a different person from the person who entered it; and, to some extent, the spouse might not like this new person.[77]

This evaluation process sometimes leads a prospective whistleblower to decide not to come forward, as when a supervisor in a federally funded project in the construction industry brought tape-recorded evidence of bribe taking by federal inspectors. While Clark felt the sums were not large, the issue was important to publicize:

I told him to go home and talk to his family. That weekend there had been a murder in the construction industry of one of the subcontractors to the government. While the murder was not related to this project, it threw the potential resister and his family into fear. He had teenage children, and they told him not to do it. I returned all of the material he had brought in.[78]

Usually it is not the client but Clark himself who decides against taking a case because of GAP's limited resources. In making this determination, he has to weigh several factors. First, how significant is the information? Second, is it worth risking the client's career? Third, will anyone care? Even in a case he may consider important, he may conclude that he cannot interest reporters or a congressional committee in bringing it to public attention.

Where the case does seem to have a potential to bring about reform, Clark must assess whether anonymous whistleblowing is preferable. If so, he contacts a reporter and provides a briefing and available documentation. Most clients would like to remain unidentified, but many stories lose their power without a witness to back them up. Human interest provides follow-up stories in the press for days after the initial revelations. Print journals, says Clark, are much more valuable than television coverage, which tends to be quick and short-lived. A determined reporter, even with a small city newspaper, can pursue a story for days or weeks.

Many prospective clients approach GAP for legal assistance after they have blown the whistle and are facing serious retaliation, including job loss. At this point, Clark and his colleagues have to develop a strategy to win reinstatement or appropriate damages. Among the numerous whistleblowers whom Clark has advised, Vince Laubach remains one of the most compelling. Laubach, educated in Catholic schools, graduated from college in 1962, attended Gonzaga University Law School in Spokane, and spent most of the 1970s working for state and federal governments. He reported that he gained valuable experience working in the Justice Department for four years on tax fraud cases. He particularly enjoyed his three years as assistant U.S. attorney in Detroit, where he was in charge of investigating cases of fraud in the Department of Health, Education and Welfare and the Internal Revenue Service. "It upsets me how people, especially at higher levels of government, were cheating and defrauding the American taxpayer. They were getting away with it, and nobody cared. I was given a free hand to go after them by my superiors, who were extremely reputable and honest."[79] In 1975 Laubach convicted fifty-five IRS employees for fraud on the government.[80]

When a Democratic president was elected in 1976, Republican Laubach's program was ended by his superiors. Later he and his family moved to Reno where, as deputy district attorney, he prosecuted cases of physician abuse of Medicaid, stock fraud, and food-stamp and welfare violations. With the election of Ronald Reagan in 1980, Laubach received an opportunity to do something about fraud at the national level. He was appointed a senior attorney in the solicitor's office of the Interior Department and assigned to investigate the failure of strip-mining companies to pay required fines and reclamation fees for the use of public lands. Since Reagan had campaigned on the pledge of cleaning up fraud, waste, and abuse, Laubach felt he was in friendly territory in the Office of Surface Mining. He had extensive experience in fighting white-collar crime and a dogged determination to root it out. He could not be sidetracked and would not compromise once he felt he had a mandate to do his job.

Upon his discovery that the Carter administration had left tens of millions of dollars uncollected, Laubach fully expected that his superiors would act quickly to accept his recommendation that special efforts be made to retrieve funds and impose heavy fines on recalcitrant strip-mine operators, a move that could only embarrass the previous Democratic administration. To his dismay, he learned that the Interior Department, under the leadership of Secretary James Watt, had no intention of collecting the fees or the fines, although the inspector general's office had already issued a report calling for more timely collection.[81] Laubach's appeals to his superiors were without result, but he continued to issue memos calling for stringent action and even criminal sanctions against those who violated the law.

Like many other employees, Laubach had to decide whether to retreat or to resist by taking his findings outside the department. Vince Laubach's familial, religious, and educational background had solidified his strong views on the importance of individual responsibility and personal integrity. He was highly influenced by his father, a conservative and service-oriented Catholic businessman, and by his teachers in the Benedictine college he attended. Laubach saw law as a calling to service. Although a successful businessman for several years, he felt law was more challenging and provided a better opportunity to help others. The values learned early in life were reinforced when he clerked for two judges whom he admired and found to be people of great integrity:

> I learned that there are some really decent people out there who are public servants. I clerked for Judge Thompson, a federal district court judge in Nevada. He made some difficult and courageous decisions in cases of political corruption and school desegregation. He had the courage to do what he thought was right without backing off, even though there were threats on his life. We had a very close relationship.[82]

Once Laubach decided not to accept the instructions to back off from his investigation of the uncollected reclamation fees and fines, he approached colleagues on Capitol Hill and later the inspector general's office of the Interior Department. Despite legally guaranteed confidentiality to any employee who brings a charge to the I.G., the inspector general promptly reported Laubach's allegations to his superiors, who ordered Laubach to refrain from any further contact with outside agencies. They further signaled their displeasure by assigning him to perform only clerical duties. This was only the first stage of his troubles. Laubach had been labeled a dangerous dissident whose influence could damage his superiors.[83]

A serious car accident, exacerbated by a job-related injury when he was ordered to move a heavy typewriter, left him with a crippling back injury. He received verbal permission to go to the Mayo Clinic in Minnesota for special treatment, but once gone his superiors declared him AWOL and fired him. Despite his debilitating physical problems, Laubach decided to fight his dismissal and, in May 1983, filed a grievance against the Interior Department—only to find that a former superior appointed the examiner who would hear the case.

"Frightened to death," as he later said, about the prospect of huge legal fees, Laubach spoke to the Pentagon whistleblower Ernest Fitzgerald, who advised him to approach GAP. Louis Clark and his colleagues evaluated Laubach's case and found it met the criteria for acceptance on all counts: his allegations pointed to a serious instance of government neglect in regulating a private industry, and the issue could clearly be understood by both the media and the general public.[84] Equally important, they viewed Laubach as a fighter who would stay the course in a protracted battle. From his perspective Laubach appreciated the efforts of GAP on his behalf, especially the work of their leading litigation attorney, Lynne Bernabei, an honors graduate from Harvard Law School who has fought many legal battles in Washington on behalf of the poor and the disenfranchised.

His wife, Kathy, though fearful of the impact on Vince and their four children, strongly supported his undertaking the battle. She had returned to work to help support the family, and her religious convictions encouraged her husband's commitment not to blink at a major skirting of the law. Yet, unlike him, she was ready to condemn the Reagan administration for failing to live up to its public commitment to pursue anyone who defrauded the government. She wondered why Vince had been hired when everyone knew he was incorruptible and aggressive. Perhaps, she thought, it was as simple as wanting to reward a fellow Republican:

I think there was political support for him. Actually, I also believe that the solicitor at that time was a Reagan Republican who liked Vince. They didn't evaluate whether it was a good spot for him given his strong background in fighting fraud. They assumed he would be loyal and true, one of the good old boys. It would all work out.[85]

At one point, the Interior Department offered Laubach a compromise: if he would accept a reprimand for the AWOL offense, he would be reinstated. Clark advised Laubach to accept, reasoning that the allegations against the Office of Surface Mining were now well publicized, Laubach's health and career were in jeopardy, and a quick settlement would allow him to get on with his life. Laubach refused. He would not countenance any punishment while his superiors, who were culpable, would get off scot-free.[86]

As Clark continued to negotiate with the Department of the Interior, a House subcommittee report in 1984 gave Laubach's charges a full measure of credibility. The subcommittee and a federal district court had concluded that the Interior Department had "flouted the law" and "failed miserably" in enforcing strip-mining legislation. The department had also misled both the Congress and the public.[87] GAP attorneys now pressed even harder for a settlement. Finally, in 1985 an agreement restored Laubach's right to his job, paid him $24,000 for damages and legal fees, provided a clean employee record, and offered a satisfactory job reference should he seek other employment.[88] Laubach felt vindicated by the victory, the sustained support he had received in the Congress, and the coverage the case had received in the media. Louis Clark believes that the combination of publicity and political support markedly strengthened his hand in his negotiations with the Solicitor General's office, and that the many newspaper articles and two national television broadcasts on Laubach's victimization put pressure on the Interior Department to settle. Clark also observed that it was easier to reach a settlement because most of Laubach's former superiors had by then moved on to other positions, and the new leadership had little stake in denying Laubach any vindication.[89]

By Clark's definition, the case had all the ingredients for a successful outcome. The failure of the federal government to collect millions of dollars in fines and fees pointed to a larger national issue of waste of natural resources. It was a prime example of government-industry collusion which victimized citizens in areas where strip-mining companies ravaged the land and ignored their responsibility to restore it and thus safeguard the rights of local residents. Furthermore, far from being engaged in a solitary battle, Laubach was, inadvertently, in the forefront of a national movement to protect the environment. Suits filed by environmentalist organizations had alerted him early in his struggle to the necessity of government action, and he had come to believe that coal company executives could be held criminally liable for filing false reports.

Clark and Laubach developed a close working relationship even though they were an unlikely pair. Laubach, a conservative Catholic, had always been in government service and placed a high premium on loyalty to his organization and success on the job. In contrast, Clark had a background in the civil rights movement and was identified with the struggle for social change. Despite these differences, they formed a strong alliance. They agreed on the significance of the issues in the Interior Department.

Clark, however, had an agenda that went beyond defending resisters. He also wanted to expose government-industry collusion and challenge major corporations and government agencies that defraud the public purse, destroy the nation's environment, or threaten the safety of communities. Resisters like Laubach are crucial in this effort, providing inside knowledge and serving as witnesses to wrongdoing.

To achieve their goals, GAP and Clark not only draw upon the Congress for its law-making and investigative potential and develop close links to committee staff members, but also form contacts in the media who will assist in publicizing the abuse of employees of integrity. A symbiotic relationship thrives among these groups. For the press, Clark and GAP and others in the public-interest sector provide insights into cases, background briefings, and quotable statements. Similarly, congressional committees turn to public-interest groups when they need witnesses and expert testimony to pursue an investigation or prepare legislation.

Conclusion

With the help of people in government, the press, and public-interest agencies, ethical resisters have aired significant social issues: bomb factories in the State of Washington *were* a major threat to public safety; the dumping of chemical wastes by Dow *did* poison the waterways and endanger public health; inadequate patient care *did* result in unnecessary deaths; tens of millions of dollars of funds *did* remain uncollected from mining companies. The whistleblowers we have described in this chapter were widely recognized for their determined stand: Casey Ruud identified by both the press and Congress as one of the most important figures in the State of Washington; Valdas Adamkus, Milton Clark, and their associates publicly congratulated by Congressmen Dingell and Scheuer;

Martin Schorr, James Hardison, Zalman Magid, and Sid Rhodes applauded on the floor of the California legislature; Vince Laubach featured on several national television programs.

The influence of the whistleblowers' allies rarely, however, extends to control of hiring and firing. Public pressure can defend those who have remained on the job, such as the Chicago EPA officials, but cannot ensure reinstatement for those who are fired. In this respect, Vince Laubach was fortunate, benefiting from his relationship with GAP, the press, and key members of Congress. But, as both he and Clark recognize, this is a rare convergence, unavailable to most ethical resisters.[90]

Finally, no amount of personal vindication or activity by public figures has solved illegality in government and industry. Bomb factories are still so poorly maintained that several were closed in 1988.[91] Poisonous chemical wastes are still being illegally dumped. Patients still die from inept hospital care. And the Interior Department has moved but slowly to collect the outstanding funds and bring suit against the worst offenders. Industry and government still collude, and a bureaucracy has many ways to sabotage an agreement.

Chapter 7

Remaking One's Life:
Aftermath of Retaliation

MILTON CLARK and others at the Chicago office of the Environmental Protection Agency retained their jobs despite prolonged conflict with their superiors. When they were vindicated and the EPA leadership ousted, they were in an excellent position to resume productive lives and to put their difficulties behind them. Of the sixty-four whistleblowers we studied, twenty were able to hold on to their positions; of these, all worked in the public sector. Unlike the Chicago group, most of the others paid a heavy price for staying on. They felt marginal and isolated and believed that their careers had been severely curtailed. Since their superiors could never forget that they had put principle above loyalty and disobeyed orders from the top, the resisters suffered from chronic retaliation. Several graphically described the dangers of taking on the bureaucracy. "My advice to potential whistleblowers," wrote Al Louis Ripskis, who continued in the federal government, "can be summarized in two words: 'Forget it!' "

> But if you can't forget it, then leak the information—making sure that your name isn't associated with it. Finally, if you can't do the above, then at least find out what it takes to be a successful whistleblower and the possible consequences. Be prepared to be ostracized, your career coming to a screeching halt, and perhaps even being driven into bankruptcy.

It's a hell of a commentary on our contemporary society when you must be ready to become an insolvent pariah if you want to live up to your own ethical standards by "committing the truth" and exercising your First Amendment rights.[1]

These ideas were echoed by another ethical resister, who has managed to remain in the EPA, even though he is an outspoken critic of the government's failure to deal with hazardous wastes. Despite his pride in the role he has played in apprising communities of potential danger, William Sanjour never underestimates the high costs of blowing the whistle. He has pointed instructions for those who believe that they have the courage of their convictions:

Remember that whistleblowing will most likely ruin your career, so if you are young and have a career ahead of you, and you feel you must blow the whistle, good for you—but do it anonymously.

Don't make the mistake of thinking that someone in authority, who, if he only knew what was going on, would straighten the whole thing out. This can be a fatal mistake.

In the words of Hugh Kaufman [a well-known whistleblower in the EPA], if you have God, the law, the press, and the facts on your side, you have a fifty-fifty chance of defeating the bureaucracy.[2]

Despite this hard-headed reality, both Ripskis and Sanjour, as well as virtually all of the others who remained at their posts, continued to fight against policies they felt endangered citizens and weakened their agencies. Ripskis, in particular, believes that those in government who dare blow the whistle must do so with the care and planning that characterize the approach to any military campaign: understand your adversaries; make sure you have active allies in the press, media, and public-interest groups; and plan your steps so that you are ever on the attack. With this strategy, he asserts, you can avoid the inevitable role of maligned victim who is isolated and doomed to remain a passive recipient of bureaucratic recriminations.[3]

Bill Bush, a NASA engineer, stayed on the job long after he lost his case in the Supreme Court. He had sued the director of the Marshall Space Flight Center for depriving him of his freedom of speech in challenging the agency's decision to limit the work assignments of engineers over forty. The 1983 *Bush* v. *Lucas* decision was a devastating blow to Bush personally and to ethical resisters in the federal government as a group.[4] The Supreme Court by a unanimous vote let stand a lower-court decision that government employees do not have the right to sue their superiors since the 1978 Civil Service Reform Act has established internal grievance procedures through which they can seek remedy. The Court believed that this limitation was necessary to prevent excessive litigation and paralysis of management. Bush has continued to argue that a prohibition on the right to sue is an infringement of his constitutional rights.

Isolated at NASA for over a decade in a position that had no responsibility and little work, Bush spent his days developing a computer data base of thousands of dissenters including whistleblowers. He became the hub of an information network about resisters throughout the country, corresponding with hundreds of people, and occasionally serving as an expert witness in the trials of whistleblowers. Bush's volume of mail is an enlightening indication both of the range of dissent that exists in American society and of the desperate need of citizens for emotional sustenance and legal advice. The correspondence also provides additional evidence about the significance of the media. Bush's correspondents learn about him and his database from television programs and newspaper accounts of his one-man effort to record dissent. Bush shares his data readily. He also directs those who need legal advice to the Government Accountability Project, those who require emotional counseling to Dr. Donald Soeken, and others to specific journalists and legislators if their cases merit further investigation (see Appendix, "Who Can Help"). He has paid a high price for his involvement with his "family of whistleblowers," suffering for years from a debilitating stress-related nervous condition that has affected his speech. Yet he continues his crusade while denigrating his past commitments:

An objective assessment of my life of sixty years has disinterred a sad conclusion: I've taken much more than I have been willing to give! Many opportunities for me to be of service to others have been missed because of my obsession with the pursuit of trivial interests and submission to peer pressure to conform to the dronish ideal. My twin rules of existence were: "Don't rock the boat!" and "Me first!" As a consequence I became a rudderless ship on a purposeless journey to No Place.

Then in 1974 and 1975, I publicly criticized my federal employer for being guilty of illegal discrimination and waste. With that fatal development, I abandoned my cardinal rules forever. Good riddance! Anyone who has studied the history of dissent can guess what transpired after my having spoken out. Nonetheless, only since then have I made any favorable progress toward balancing my deplorable "taking-giving" tally sheet.

Becoming a more "giving" person has been a great source of pleasure and satisfaction to Bush, especially now that he has become an outcast in Huntsville, Alabama. His colleagues and other townspeople have not taken kindly to his attacks on the major local industry, the Marshall Space Flight Center:

> In spite of the avalanche of hatred I brought upon myself, I learned for the first time the pleasures of assisting others in trouble. My associates began to confide in me about their concerns, both in regard to personnel matters and to those of public welfare. As a direct result of those contacts, I interceded in several matters in which I had no selfish interest. Helping others and participating in non-violent activism are personally more rewarding than selfishness and passivity.[5]

In one particularly dramatic instance, a distraught caller told Bush that he had a pistol and was going to commit suicide. His superiors had transferred him to a nonexistent job and his new co-workers resented his presence. The pressure was more than he could bear. Bush successfully pleaded with the whistleblower to reconsider and quickly dispatched Dr. Betsy Brothers who lived forty-five minutes from the man's hotel. Brothers drove down immediately and talked to the despairing resister. Feeling that the action saved the caller's life, Bush is proud that he was able to send a concerned colleague to intervene. He retired from NASA in 1987, but still stands ready to help those who need him.

Finding a Job

Work is a central source of self-esteem in American society. It provides income, family security, the basis for future planning, and an important social dimension. Colleagues, clients, superiors, and subordinates form a complex web of relationships that permeates one's daily life. For these reasons the loss of work was a grueling punishment to the remaining ethical resisters. It left them financially insecure, unconnected, and uninvolved in what had previously been central to their lives. Many who lost their jobs experienced a profound sense of grief, characterized by physical debilitation, emotional depression, and an obsession with the case and its potential resolution. In order to rebuild a sense of purpose and direction, they had to re-create their work lives. Only when meaningful work was restored could the process of emotional healing truly begin.

Ten of the forty-one ethical resisters who lost their jobs were fortunate in finding work almost immediately. Their new positions provided needed income, recognition of their skills, and a life beyond their cases against their former employers. For twenty-eight resisters, somewhat fewer than half of the total sample, work was not easily replaced. Some were unable to find another position because they had been blacklisted. Others awaited legal resolution hoping to regain the job they felt was rightly theirs. The long periods of idleness deeply affected these resisters and their families. Only when they gave up on the idea of reinstatement could they enter the final stage of the ethical resisters' odyssey which meant getting on with their lives and securing new situations which were emotionally comfortable and financially viable.

Eighteen of these twenty-eight whistleblowers eventually did forge new careers in fields unrelated to their previous work. For them, flexibility and the development of additional skills were required to restore their work lives. Despite their best efforts, such a career switch usually meant a loss of income. One long-term cost of ethical resistance has been a reduction in their standard of living. But the price is small compared to the ten whose lives were "on hold."[6] Some of these were continually denied employment wherever they applied, their reputations as "troublemaker" apparently following them everywhere. Others were so heavily involved in fighting their legal battles that they had little time or energy for forging new careers or contemplating a move to another area where prospective employers might be less hostile. Not surprisingly, even those whose careers were destroyed found meaning in their loss. They became activists in the causes that led to their dismissal and dedicated themselves to assisting other ethical resisters in the struggle for vindication. In this chapter, we trace the various paths that led resisters to an ultimate resolution of their battle or to a painful realization that closure was still beyond their farthest reach.

Avenue to a New Career

The experience of resistance was often so profound and consuming that for several resisters, including James Boyd, Frank Camps, and Billie Garde, it became the avenue to new employment. While there was a painful period of uncertainty, each created satisfying and fulfilling professional opportunities. Boyd drew upon writing skills he had developed as a congressional aide; Camps directly applied knowledge he gained as an automobile designer; and Billie Garde completely changed careers in the wake of her devastating personal experience. All remained centrally involved in exposing and seeking to remedy major social, political, and economic problems.

Once he blew the whistle on Senator Thomas Dodd in 1965 for illegal use of campaign contributions (see pages 46–53), Jim Boyd knew that his career in the legislative branch of government was over. Although Boyd and Marjorie Carpenter believed that they had been fully vindicated when the U.S. Senate censured Senator Dodd in 1967, they also recognized that no congressman would ever hire staff members who had exposed their own employer. Congress has helped vindicate other resisters, but has closed the door on those who have dared challenge its own ethical standards.

The period following the battle to censure Dodd was a difficult time emotionally and financially for Jim Boyd: "I would dream of myself with no place to go and with only a few days left on the job. I had no money and the people who depended on me for support were going to be ruined. And then I would wake up and remember that I still had three days of income or something like that." With extensive documentation compiled for his Senate testimony and with drafts of some preliminary material, Boyd met with a literary agent who became interested in the idea of doing a book on Senate corruption:

> I went to one of the best agents in New York City and showed him a couple of sample chapters. The agent read them and then immediately contacted a publisher. The agent asked if I could stay overnight so we could draw up a contract. I had eleven dollars in my pocket and fortunately the publisher agreed to take my check and not cash it for a few days. That's how tight things were.
>
> I got the contract and an advance which covered several months of

living. Then my great financial break came. *The Saturday Evening Post* bought the rights to serialize the book in three issues. They paid me twice as much for doing that as I had gotten as an advance for the book. I was tickled about that for it was a mass audience magazine going to people all over the country, especially to Connecticut where the Dodd affair was particularly important.[7]

Boyd's progress from maligned Senate employee to widely read and respected author was unique among resisters. His ability to convey the tragic quality of Thomas Dodd's fall transformed the case from a single tale of corruption to an indictment of a legislative system that erodes the values of its elected members. Published in 1968 at a moment when many Americans, influenced by the civil rights and antiwar movements, were questioning the integrity of their leaders, Boyd's book was well received for its explanation of the human and institutional forces that generate corruption. His judgment was harsh and convincing, and he remained determined to expose the abuse of power and decision making in Washington. A new foundation provided just such an opportunity:

Then an offer came for me to go back to Washington to direct a new, experimental foundation to support investigative journalists. That was in late 1968 and it is still operating today. Marjorie was not working then and she took a part-time job on the staff. So we worked out of our house [they married in 1967], and for the next five years we had a financial base.[8]

In launching his new career, Boyd drew upon his writing skills, his knowledge of Washington, and his commitments as a social activist, encouraging the exposure of major problems and scandals. His years as Senator Dodd's assistant had given him insight that he could now apply to journalism. The publicity and positive reviews of his book drew other job offers to his door. The *Washington Post* and the *New York Times Magazine* both asked him to do profile stories on Washington figures. As the stigma from the Dodd case was slowly replaced by an appreciation of his insider's knowledge, his reputation became less associated with that of former whistleblower and more as a writer who published in prestigious organs.

Boyd's financial situation also benefited by his association with Jack

Anderson. In 1973 Anderson received a substantial sum to write an autobiographical account of his years as a muckraking journalist, but the writing dragged on fitfully until he asked Boyd to assist him. They spent the next decade collaborating on a book detailing Anderson's career and on another exposing the political miscalculations that led to the 1973 oil shortages. Boyd had become an analyst of the country's major economic and political problems.[9]

In reflecting on the years since the Dodd case unfolded, Boyd counted some of the costs and gains of his decision to challenge a powerful U.S. Senator. Like virtually all resisters, he lost a secure financial base. He also ruptured friendships with close associates:

> I have friends from that period of my life who are now retired. If I had done that, I would have been retired now for three years, and I would have been getting thirty-five thousand dollars a year. I realize that there is a tremendous material loss involved. Also, there's something in an institution—various supports, professional, friendship, life-support type things—that you lose when you are separated from that institution.

There were less tangible benefits from his breaking loose from the moorings that had secured his life for twelve years: "What I have gained is a whole new outlook on life—a feeling of independence—of 'being my own man'—working at my own hours—and all that sort of thing, which I find enormously attractive."[10]

Marjorie Carpenter could not conceive of another path they might have taken. Given her ethical standards, Senator Dodd had to be exposed. She recalled the pain of friends lost, of newspaper articles referring to her as a "curvy, green-eyed blonde," and the sense of deep embarrassment when her life was publicly examined and often distorted by the national press.[11] For a young woman from a small southern town in Arkansas, that kind of publicity was anathema. Yet she had grown to accept it and appreciated the support of new friendships from some of the journalists who covered the hearings. She also emphasized how her shared experiences with Jim Boyd played an important part in creating and strengthening their relationship:

> When you go through something like that, you know that here is a person that you can depend upon. I think you learn to respect one

another's abilities. There are things that Jim does very well and maybe some things that he doesn't do so well, but you can complement one another. When you are under a lot of pressure, you learn to respect one another. That is very important because deep down you are attracted to someone because you like the way they approach things.[12]

The Dodd case had tested her character, and she met the challenge. Her sense of self and her belief in her own values, her confidence, and her relationship with Jim Boyd have all been enhanced by their ordeal. She has spoken to her children about those years; and while she, like all parents, wants to protect her family, she hopes they will have the insight and ethical fortitude to expose wrongdoing:

I hope my children won't flinch if they get into similar situations. I hope that, knowing about our situation, it will be easier for them to accept the challenge. I see so many parents who feel they can protect their children. They can't. If children are prepared for making a hard ethical decision, that is one of the best protections you can give them. Suffering for your beliefs is not wrong. It is not going to be fatal. And it may be necessary in some cases.[13]

Boyd was not alone in utilizing his whistleblowing experience as an entrée into a new career. Frank Camps, who had worked for the Ford Motor Company for most of his adult life, retired when it became apparent that his objection to the design of the Ford Pinto and his vocal concern about the death and injury it had caused had effectively ended his advancement in the company (see pages 18–20). He sued for age discrimination and for protection against legal action by those who had suffered from Pinto accidents. His action received front-page coverage in Detroit and other cities where major Ford plants were located.[14]

Camps soon found that others were interested in his skills and eager to hire him. He began to consult for attorneys litigating product liability cases that involved defects in automobile design and manufacturing. He underscored how important those relationships were in re-creating his career and his sense of himself:

When I filed my suit, six months before I left Ford, it gained wide publicity, not only in the Detroit papers but in many papers and on many television stations in the cities where the Ford plants were located. It also got into the *Wall Street Journal.* I began getting calls from attorneys all over the country, and I couldn't quite comprehend what they were driving at until one of the attorneys said he would like me to help him on a case. He came up with an hourly figure and a retainer that was absolutely staggering, compared to what I was making at Ford. He became my mentor.

Camps went on to explain how his new work as an expert witness dissipated the emotional residue of the painful confrontations with his long-time employers at Ford:

All of those feelings I had—the anxiety, resentment, anger, helplessness—that's all gone, because of what I now accomplish. I am now doing what I want to do, when I want to do it. I can speak my mind truthfully and openly in a court of law. There is nothing more gratifying than to know that you are now involved in due process. Incidentally, in all of the cases I have been involved in, I have seldom been on the losing side.[15]

Camps has continued to enact his long-standing concern with issues of auto safety, and is particularly irate when major automobile companies design and produce cars with defects that could be avoided with proper testing. He believes that corporations continually weigh the costs of additional testing and redesign against the potential damages they might have to pay to injured parties who bring suit. Camps described one such case in 1983 in which he was a central expert witness:

In this case in San Antonio, a 1980 Chevette [General Motors] came to an intersection and was hit on the left-rear quarter panel by a four-wheel-drive truck. On impact the Chevette hatchback door popped open, and two young passengers were ejected out the back door. One was killed and the other suffered severe head injuries. I was called to San Antonio to look at the vehicle and I noticed immediately that there was a lack of protection on the side. The car had been built to make it as light as possible to get good gas mileage. As I got into the case, I found that the lock on the hatchback door had been used previously in a 1971 Cadillac. General Motors did not want to go through the expense of tooling up another lock and simply took this shelf item and put it into the Chevette. They knew full well that the lock would pop open if there was an impact on the left-hand side of the car because that was the kind of lock it was. G.M. never tested the left side. Can you imagine that? They build more than a million Chevettes and never tested that vehicle by hitting it on the left side until July 1983 when they were preparing to take the case to trial. We saw their movies of the test crash and we found that immediately on impact, just as in our accident, the hatchback door popped open.

Camps was certain that the injury sustained by the young people could have been substantially less had the car been safely designed, for two youngsters sitting in the front had suffered only minor injuries. He is certain, too, that this situation with the Chevette is part of a larger pattern of irresponsibility found in all automobile manufacturing:

It is more or less a cost-benefit analysis that they go through. They say, how much is it going to cost us to design a new lock for that door, tool it, and put it in the vehicle? X number of dollars. How many lawsuits will we have regarding this car? X number of dollars. Which seems the best way to go? Put the old lock in because maybe we'll have five lawsuits, maybe we'll settle in each for one hundred thousand dollars, and we'll come out of this five or six million dollars ahead. I have nothing against the corporation making money, but I really feel strongly about them making money at the cost of safety of the occupants and the safety of their customers.[16]

Government regulation of automobile safety, which had served as a central backdrop to the Pinto fiasco, now helped Camps carve out a new career. Prior to the development of such legislation, he would have been forced to retire to a quiet life in a Detroit suburb, his last years at Ford a bitter memory. Now that automobile companies are liable for violations of federally mandated safety regulations, Camps has become a valuable witness, testifying on behalf of accident victims. Thus, another insider has benefited from changing regulations that provide a public forum for debates that have traditionally been restricted to corporate boardrooms:

Before I testify I'm a bundle of nerves. Once I get up on the witness stand and they swear me in, I am completely calm. My wife is absolutely shocked because I was never like that. I guess it's because I think I am doing something worthwhile. You know, those kids in that accident . . . one shouldn't have been killed and the other should not have had serious head injuries. It wasn't that heavy an impact. I just feel like it is something I should be doing and I feel good about it. When I am up there testifying, it is a new world. I just feel like I was made to do this.[17]

As Frank Camps based his new career on the very issues he confronted at the Ford Motor Company, another ethical resister devoted her working life to serving whistleblowers. Billie Garde had benefited from the services of several organizations when she fought her former superior at the Census Bureau in Muskogee, Oklahoma (see pages 160–66), and, in the legal battle to win back her children and to clear her name, she turned to public-interest organizations in Washington. Chief among them was the Government Accountability Project, which conducted an independent investigation of her case and helped her take it to the Merit Systems Protection Board. After the conviction and imprisonment of her former superior and the subsequent decision of her ex-husband to relinquish the children to her custody, Garde had to decide what to do next.

At the age of twenty-nine, she enrolled in law school and became the director of the Citizens Clinic for Accountable Government, part of the Government Accountability Project which was expanding its staff at precisely the moment she was looking for a job. As a lawyer Garde continues to assist whistleblowers, particularly those in the nuclear industry. She negotiates with employers, conducts investigations to provide evidence for administrative hearings and court trials, and litigates to prevent unsafe plants from receiving licenses.

Several whistleblowers emphasized how helpful Billie Garde had been when they were in the throes of their cases. For example, Anne Jennings (not her real name) was dismissed, ostensibly on a drug charge, from Comanche Peak nuclear power plant. She had been a member of the team ordered to change the records so that the Nuclear Regulatory Commission audit would proceed without incident. The irregular procedures were very difficult for her. She felt under great pressure to perform illegal acts and, as a single parent, worried about her ability to support two small children. While she initially went along with the orders of management, she believed she was let go because her superiors did not trust her to remain silent after the head of her group was fired.

When the company discharged Jennings, she found herself drinking too much, passing bad checks, and frightened about the future. Her mother came to live with her, and slowly Jennings began putting the pieces of her life back together. Billie Garde was a central person in that effort: "I called Billie Garde, who is one terrific lady. If it hadn't been for her, I don't know if I could have gone through all of this. I called her collect, and if I need anybody to talk to, I still call her."[18]

Garde went to Texas and helped Anne Jennings apply for unemployment insurance and file a grievance for illegal firing with the Department of Labor. Jennings had not yet received any unemployment benefits:

> At first I was just so stunned that it didn't even dawn on me, and I was busy looking for a job. I met different lawyers, and they have all been really good, but Billie Garde was a person that inspired me to get up and move. I filed my petition with the Department of Labor, and there was supposed to be a hearing in August. In June, Brown and Root's lawyers called me up to take a deposition and to get ready for the hearing. I talked to their lawyers for about four hours, and then my lawyer had to leave for California because of family illness.

By the time Billie Garde returned to Texas the following week, Anne Jennings had real doubts about going on with her case:

> Billie came out and we started talking, and I told Billie that by this time I had started to work and had my mother come down and was getting it together, and I said, "I don't want to put my kids through it. It's my name, my kids grow up in this town, go to school here. For what they are going to do to me, it is not worth what I am going to get out of it." And Billie said, "You are exactly right. I hate to see you go through it. Do you want me to go see what I can do?"[19]

After a day of negotiations, the corporation agreed to pay $3,500 legal expenses for Jennings and to end their dispute over her right to get unemployment. They further agreed to seal her file at the plant. Nobody would ever know that she had been fired. The letter would simply state the dates she had worked there and report her job title and her hourly pay rate. Jennings now hoped she could get a better job than the part-time work cleaning condominiums she had been forced to take. She credits

Billie Garde's crucial assistance in helping her to move out of a disastrous personal situation.

In most instances, Garde did not negotiate personnel settlements but, rather, became deeply involved in preparing for licensing hearings. Like Frank Camps's new career, Garde's, too, depended on the foundation provided by laws passed in the 1970s to regulate the construction and licensing of nuclear plants. During the last decade, the complaints of engineers and workers have led to the closing of several nuclear plants and the postponement of licensing for others. Major controversies have swirled about the safety of plants dispersed throughout the country. Environmental groups have published lists of the nation's most dangerous facilities.[20] As the industry established twenty years before in the glow of enthusiasm for solving the nation's energy needs now became the focus of anxiety about accidents that could adversely affect millions of people, hundreds of workers began to believe that their testimony could have an important impact.

Billie Garde has become a central figure, traveling throughout Texas and other areas to take depositions from quality-control inspectors, iron workers, and welders. Her own whistleblowing past, her compassion for the dislocated lives of resisters, and her competence in dealing with the Nuclear Regulatory Commission make her particularly effective, as she provides legal services, emotional support, and a political ideology for workers willing to put their paychecks on the line to challenge management's failure to comply with mandated safety regulations.

Opening a Private Practice

For most people, the experience of whistleblowing did not readily lead to a new career but was a liability that they had to overcome. The diversity of American economic institutions allowed some professionals who had worn out their welcome in the bureaucracy to escape the retaliation of their superiors by moving to self-employment. Fortunately for Dr. Grace Pierce, who challenged drug testing she considered harmful (see pages 93–96), several medical colleagues invited her to join their clinical practice. Giving up a research career of several decades was not easy, but the offer did provide an outlet when her suit against the pharmaceutical company made her *persona non grata* in that industry.

"I really lucked out," she says. Her skills, the support of several colleagues, and the receptiveness of her patients have provided a positive continuity to her work and personal life. She does, however, harbor many troubling questions about whistleblowing and its effectiveness in changing organizational policies:

> Now that the whistleblowers have been re-established or resettled into other pursuits of living, what has happened to the persons, institutions, or corporations that created these dilemmas? Have there been corrective steps taken to avoid similar episodes of employee disenchantment? Have those offenders to the whistleblowers changed in any way? Have there been any recriminations? Is there less deception or corruption, or is it better concealed? Have the pathways of whistleblowers been kept open or even broadened for other employees who may be confronted with similar ethical issues? Are the courts any more or less supportive? Were these struggles really worth it? Have our little pieces of this world actually improved because of these actions? Are there other ways and means available to resolve the whistleblower's conflicts—perhaps more effectively and perhaps less painfully with less personal sacrifice? Is there still a place for "idealists" in a world quite full of "realists"?[21]

Dr. Betsy Brothers (see pages 82–92) continues to fight for the changes Pierce desires. Brothers has re-established her career and remains deeply involved in the battle for whistleblowers' rights and for greater organizational sensitivity to ethical concerns. Like Pierce, she moved into an established practice. She began to work with her father when she was rejected for a permanent position at the Veterans Administration after her superiors suspected she had written to the inspector general's office to complain about the treatment of Dr. Mary McAnaw. Brothers now practices occupational medicine, a specialty quite distinct from her earlier VA work:

> In the process of fighting our case against the VA I began to reorder my priorities. As I was forced away from a career in general surgery, I became much more interested in occupational medicine. I get the biggest thrill out of sitting down and doing patient teaching. For example, doing what I did with an elderly veteran who came into the office the other day. I sat down for an hour and talked to him about

his problems. Not every physician will take the time to do this kind of thing. You can do much more of this kind of patient teaching in occupational medicine than in surgery.

Brothers's situation is not perfect. "It's not the easiest thing working with your father. But we have a better relationship than most."[22] As he cut down on his time in the practice, she assumed greater responsibility. She has not, however, stepped back from the fight over ethical standards. Even as she won her own case against her former VA superiors in January 1987, she continued to struggle for whistleblowers' rights. She appeared on television and testified before Congress on behalf of the new whistle-blower protection bill. Like most resisters, Brothers was particularly critical of the Special Counsel's office (OSC) established in 1978 presumably to protect whistleblowers. She maintained that the office did so little for whistleblowers that it had to be disbanded or totally revamped. With the *Bush* v. *Lucas* decision preventing government employees from using the courts, she argued that it was imperative that the civil service system offer better protection for its workers. In concluding her congressional testimony in the summer of 1987, she pointed out that the "OSC is totally ineffective as a remedy for whistleblowers."

In our case alone OSC consumed 5 years, seven investigators, 15 letters, 63 phone calls, and countless hours of paralegal work on my part. Investigators demonstrated preoccupation with the media interest in the case, were fixated on finding the "smoking gun," told McAnaw there was no point in OSC helping her if she would decide not to remain in the VA, and even commented, "maybe we will not do anything because the courts may do it for us." It was also mentioned that there was a need for OSC to "protect their ass," with respect to media attention, particularly after "60 Minutes" made three trips to Leavenworth. . . .

In 1983 the Supreme Court used the same argument in declining to provide further relief in *Bush* v. *Lucas*. The Bush decision was a 9–0 blow to all whistleblowers. As a result of Bush, we have been caught between the "devil of the CSRA [Civil Service Reform Act] and the deep blue sea" of the courts. Neither offers any substantial relief to whistleblowers.[23]

While Brothers's testimony was enthusiastically received by a number of the senators on the Governmental Affairs Committee, no new legislation has become law. Most whistleblowers continue to believe reform of the Office of Special Counsel is crucial if they are to receive adequate protection. New legislation must establish the OSC as an independent agency with a clear mandate to defend employees, particularly those defined as whistleblowers. Such proposed legislation augments guarantees of confidentiality, ensures timely response by the OSC, and simplifies elements of evidence necessary to prove reprisals by superiors.[24] Betsy Brothers continues to be a firm voice calling for stronger protection for government employees willing to speak up in the public interest.

Although Joseph Rose has no formal contact with whistleblowers or with his former adversaries, his unhappy experience with the Associated Milk Producers, who fired him when he refused to participate in their illegal payments to the Nixon Re-election Committee, continues to serve as an important backdrop to the re-creation of his emotional and professional life (see pages 137–42). Rose endured several years of underemployment before establishing a successful private practice. Colleagues in San Antonio had avoided him and believed the accusation that he had violated the attorney-client privilege and betrayed AMPI. Rose's life changed dramatically after a favorable article in the *Wall Street Journal* described his discovery of the illegal payments to the Nixon re-election campaign, his efforts to inform the AMPI's board of directors, his testimony under subpoena, and the severe retaliation he had suffered.[25] The article represented Rose as an attorney who had acted to serve the AMPI membership and to avoid complicity in ongoing malfeasance:

> I guess a couple of breaks from the good Lord and a lot of self-confidence finally got me back. I found a very fascinating thing along the way. Up until my entering private practice, I had always worked for somebody else and there was always a certain attitude of "here's the guy who blew the whistle on the Milk Producers, and he ought to be happy to have any job he can get."

Once the article appeared, some clients actually sought Rose out expressly because they knew of his past difficulties and admired his integrity, his emotional fortitude, and his ability to survive the most grueling punishments:

> In 1981 I made the decision just to practice on my own, pray to the Lord, instead of passing profits on to somebody else. Very candidly, the

free market has rewarded me very well so far. I think probably 99 percent of the businesses here know about me. I had a very, very interesting situation just a few months ago. One of the more wealthy and powerful families in this state had their cousin hire me to defend them in an antitrust suit. For the first time somebody finally said, "We're going to hire you because you're tough enough. We know you survived that and we believe you're clean enough." That only happened since I've been out on my own.[26]

Having re-established his financial base and his emotional strength, Joseph Rose continued to ponder his ambivalence about bureaucracies. Part of him remained deeply mistrustful:

I believe I can make a contribution to the young people in this country by continuing to respond with a strong warning that all of the public utterances of corporations and, indeed, our own government concerning "courage, integrity, loyalty, honesty, and duty" are nothing but the sheerest hogwash that disappear very rapidly when it comes to the practical application of these concepts by strict definition. The reason that there are very few Serpicos or Roses is that the message is too clearly out in this society that white-collar crime, or nonviolent crime, should be tolerated by the public at large, so long as the conduct brings a profit or a profitable result to the institution committing it.[27]*

At the same time, he had enjoyed organizational life and had frequently worked with good people. While there were substantial economic rewards in private practice, it was a solitary existence. He was sharing an office with other people and had a partner, but his situation did not provide the team effort he had known before:

I am very grateful to the good Lord for opening the doors that He has opened. My strange problem now is that deep down I have always been a corporate animal. Yet all of a sudden, all of the successes that I have achieved have come by virtue of my not being a corporate animal. So

*There is substantial evidence that even the courts tend to treat corporate managers far more leniently if these criminal acts are directed against the public rather than against their companies.[28]

I'm really struggling with that. There are still some corporations that have called me and wanted to talk to me about going to work for them. Of course, they find out about the Watergate background and shy off. I find it very strange that I have what I call a full lucrative career, and yet if I had my real choice I would probably go back if I could find a corporation like Gates or Montgomery Ward, a company that proclaims standards and practices them. Maybe I am just trying to retrieve what once was. Maybe I'm just fantasizing that once again it would be possible.[29]

Rose continued his quest to return to private industry, and in 1987 believed that his prayers were answered when a corporation offered him a job. Finding its ethical climate congenial, he accepted the position. Almost fifteen years after his ordeal began, Rose had come full circle. Unfortunately, illness has forced him to leave the job, and he is now returning to private practice.

Despite the serious and at times cruel reprisals mounted against him, Rose's ordeal provided additional evidence that professionals often have access to employment possibilities that elude blue-collar workers. The option of private practice or a return to a prestigious corporate position was not open to those who worked in the construction of nuclear power plants, walked a police beat, or sat behind a typewriter or word processor in a secretary's office. For these workers the loss of a job usually meant long layoffs and, even after they found new jobs, permanently reduced salaries, fewer benefits, and lengthy commuting.

"Making Do"

In the effort to re-create their careers, Grace Pierce, Betsy Brothers, and Joseph Rose shifted, respectively, from medical research, surgery, and corporate law to private practice. Other resisters were required to seek out entirely different career paths, leaving behind the skills and experience they had acquired in earlier positions.[30] For Bert and Pat Berube the years from 1983 to 1985 were very difficult. Bert was fired from his high-level job in the General Services Administration when he publicly protested the unsafe condition of many federal buildings (see pages 99–106). The government did everything in its power to prevent him from collecting unemployment insurance, to terminate his rights to retirement benefits, and to fight his efforts to win reinstatement.

The loss of the job permeated every aspect of the Berubes' lives. They had lived comfortably and suddenly found themselves with only the small income from Pat's part-time job. The entire fabric of their family life was under stress, and Bert had to seek new ways to adapt to changed conditions:

> I never dreamed working in a job meant so much to a family, and I never dreamed what the loss of a job could mean in completely changing your way of life, in completely making you a pauper. When your life has been a good one for fifty years, as mine has been, and it is suddenly all taken away, it really has a devastating effect on your family.[31]

While looking for another position and waiting for his case to be settled, Bert did odd jobs and for a time worked with one of his sons building cabinets in boats. The stains on his hands from the varnish gave vivid testimony to the changed circumstances of his work life. At the age of fifty, it was a rude shock to learn that all his life plans had been destroyed. He began to believe, "I'm probably going to have to work until I die rather than retire."

At the same time, Bert Berube maintains that this was a growing experience for him and that he came to some new realizations about the meaning of security:

> I know it sounds contradictory but I also believe that security is not that important. I had always spent most of the money I made so that I always assumed that if I ever lost my job, in three weeks I'd have to declare bankruptcy. . . .I haven't yet declared bankruptcy and I'm not about to for a while from what I can see. So security in that respect is not that important in that you do continue to live and you do survive and eat well and put clothes on your back and keep the house going.

His ambivalence was evident, however, as he completed his thought: "It is the long-range consequences which are the most devastating. When everything you have ever worked for in your whole life—everything you have dreamed of, everything you know, everything you went to college for—is taken away, it is a real internal blow."[32]

Berube's relationship with his wife and children has been central in sustaining him. One of his sons, who was in the navy, was proud of his father's principled stand and angry that corruption should prevail. Another son persuaded his father to work with him in the boat business, and they enjoyed working together and spending time with each other as they never did when the children were younger.

At first, the Berubes believed that they would win their case before an administrative judge. They were encouraged by the fact that the Government Accountability Project had successfully defended Bert in his fight to win unemployment benefits. There the ruling decreed that it was unlawful to deny someone benefits because he had blown the whistle. They hoped that the same reasoning would prevail on the issue of his firing. But the administrative law judge ruled against him and found that the GSA had legally fired him.[33] In his decision, the judge stated that the hardships Berube had caused his superiors outweighed the problems he was trying to address. Both Bert and Pat felt that the decision was politically motivated. They appealed their case to the Merit Systems Protection Board and awaited another long, uncertain struggle.

The decision of the judge had brought Berube to a crossroads. As Pat Berube explained, her husband had never really separated himself from the GSA and now realized that it was necessary to do so. Thirteen months after his case began, the Berubes had to make some choices about their future. In the spring of 1985, they decided to go into business for themselves, building upon the experience of the cabinet work Bert had done with his son. Their new business of cabinetmaking took him in a totally new direction from his lifetime career. The early years of the business promised to provide the avenue for rebuilding the family's economic base and for ending the frustration and sense of unfairness they had lived with for several years. Pat Berube assessed their situation succinctly, an assessment that revealed her faith, good humor, and strength: "Our new business is going well so far. We are thankful. Bert is really enjoying it as is our eldest boy. The Lord works in strange ways sometimes. Our ways are surely not His. Right?"[34] Berube has continued to assist other whistleblowers and to help them deal with the blow to their sense of self brought on by retaliation. He has also spoken at meetings of engineering associations, urging professional organizations to take a greater role in monitoring ethical standards:

I believe the challenge for the future of the engineering profession is to institutionalize a set of mechanisms to enforce obedience to ethical standards, or to protect those who find themselves vulnerable to severe organizational retaliation because they have acted according to the profession's stated values.[35]

In July 1988, five years after he was fired, Berube's dismissal was overturned by the Merit Systems Protection Board which reconsidered the case on appeal. The Board found that "the agency has failed to show, by a preponderance of the evidence, "that there were sustainable grounds for dismissal. The agency was then "ORDERED to cancel" Berube's dismissal retroactively to 30 September 1983. The GSA was further ordered to award back pay and benefits within sixty days. For Berube and the Government Accountability Project, this represented complete victory. Berube was awarded $530,000 for back pay, interest, and attorneys' fees, the largest settlement in civil service history.[36]

Berube's change of career, reduced income, determination to see his resistance in a larger perspective, and ultimate victory parallel the fate of others. Chuck Atchison, Dobie Hatley, and the other workers who lost their jobs at the Comanche Peak nuclear construction site never matched their previous earnings (see pages 125–31). They all knew they would suffer a drop in their standard of living when they were forced to leave Comanche Peak. Blacklisted in the nuclear industry (see pages 142–47), Chuck Atchison works in a defense plant and has achieved a supervisory position. While he enjoys the work, his hourly wage has been 30 percent less than he made at Comanche Peak six years ago. The pay differential resulted in a constant financial strain as he and his wife juggled house payments and other bills.

At the same time, Atchison has remained an active combatant in the battle with nuclear power companies. Despite several incapacitating heart bypass operations, he accepts invitations to speak wherever he is invited. Early in 1988, he spoke twice to the local Lutheran church, appeared at a university in Dallas before a group of graduate students, and lectured to a national conference of quality-control experts. His presentations emphasize several major points: the bad management practices and iron-fisted style of the nuclear industry; the indirect blacklisting of dissident employees and the devastating impact on their mental health and family stability; the peril of poorly constructed nuclear plants for public health in the wake of Three Mile Island and Chernobyl; and the rate increases that affect communities throughout the United States. Atchison believes that audiences are particularly receptive to these ideas because they know that whistleblowers have also shed light on the defense industry and in other areas where taxpayers have been defrauded and endangered. Like many other former whistleblowers, Atchison refuses to quit.

Atchison and Dobie Hatley have remained in communication through their ongoing suit against Texas Utilities, the company that contracted with Brown and Root for the construction of the Comanche Peak nuclear facility. The litigation dragged on for several years, and Hatley lost patience with the endless delays and the lack of information provided by her attorneys. She wanted the case settled so that she could "get on with her life." After leaving Comanche Peak in 1984, she managed a housing complex in Austin while she pursued her Department of Labor suit against Brown and Root for wrongful discharge. That suit was terminated in 1985 when she and the company "reached a mutual agreement," which she is prohibited from discussing publicly.

She actively sought other employment. It was not a satisfying time:

Beginning in January 1988, I decided I needed to go back to work. I have interviewed with the state of Texas, the city of Austin, and many industries. Everyone wants to hear my story about my termination by Brown and Root. They all know that it is important. But nobody wants to hire former whistleblowers. They are all afraid of what we would do if we were asked to tell the truth about some problem.[37]

Hatley was particularly disturbed by a job she had applied for in a manufacturing firm, where she was among the last three finalists from a long list of contenders. She could not help believing that her background played a crucial part in her ultimate lack of success. Unlike Chuck Atchison, she did not have the satisfaction of active involvement with the issues that led to her original confrontation with a multimillion-dollar corporation.

For both Hatley and Atchison, events took a dramatic turn for the better in the summer of 1988. After six and a half years of fighting Texas Utilities (the owners of Comanche Peak), Chuck Atchison, Dobie Hatley, Sue Neumeyer, and four other whistleblowers were able to claim a complete victory when Texas Utilities simultaneously signed three separate settlements in July 1988. In the first, the Atomic Safety and Licensing Board approved a joint stipulation, signed by TU, the Citizens

Association for Sound Energy, and the staff of the Nuclear Regulatory Commission, containing an agreement that Juanita Ellis, the president of CASE, will be granted a seat with full voting rights on the TU Operations Review Committee for five years. In order to monitor the implementation of a plan to improve the safety of Comanche Peak, CASE will have full access to the company's records and the right to be present at meetings with auditors and NRC inspection staff. Even more remarkably, TU has agreed to pay up to $150,000 per year for CASE to hire technical consultants.

In a second settlement, TU agreed, in recognition of the significant contribution of CASE and of the extraordinary costs borne by the organization since 1979, to pay $4,500,000 for past expenses and for establishing its oversight role. In recognition of CASE's concerns with whistleblowers who had suffered for disclosing information about the plant, the company also agreed to enter into a good faith settlement with those workers.

The settlement with the whistleblowers will allow Atchison, as well as the others, to pay back accumulated debts, to replace the home he lost when he was blacklisted, and to provide for other family needs. For Atchison, the realization of his victory came slowly. On the night after the agreement was announced, he reflected on its meaning. "I have not yet gotten excited about the news. It has been a fight that I've been in for six and one-half years. The most important thing is that the public health and safety will be met. That's why I went to the NRC originally, and now my main goal has been met."[38]

Why did this powerful company agree to this historic settlement? Juanita Ellis, who has devoted her life since 1974 to this cause, described the complexity of the situation. "All the pieces of the puzzle had to come together—the workers, the engineers, the concerned citizens. We just hung in there even when we didn't know where the next nickel was coming from."[39] In addition, Ellis believes that the possibility for a positive resolution of the years-long struggle came in 1985 when TU appointed a new executive vice president, William G. Counsil, who has proved to be cooperative and concerned. He made information readily available and reorganized the contractors and middle management, firing some who were hostile to workers' concerns about safety.

Counsil approached Juanita Ellis personally on 29 April 1988 with the draft of a letter to be read into the public record on the signing of the agreement. In the letter TU recognizes its own shortcomings in informing the NRC of problems and expresses gratitude to CASE for raising those issues. Because of CASE, the letter went on, the plant will be safer and sounder. Such a gesture convinced CASE and its lawyers, Billie Garde of GAP and Tony Roisman, formerly of Trial Lawyers for Public Justice, that a resolution was indeed possible. The letter and the subsequent agreement symbolize a profound victory for the whistleblowers and their allies.

> TU Electric recognizes that the Citizens Association for Sound Energy (CASE) and its President, Mrs. Juanita Ellis, have made a substantial, personal, and unselfish contribution . . . which assures that Comanche Peak Steam Electric Station will be a safer plant. Through the untiring efforts of CASE representatives, deficiencies which existed in the early 1980's have been revealed in the design of substantial portions of the plant which no one else, including TU Electric, the Nuclear Regulatory Commission, or other third-party experts, had fully recognized or discovered. As a result, Comanche Peak is a better, safer plant than before. . . . We commend CASE, together with its technical advisors, Jack Doyle and Mark Walsh, and other workers, public interest organizations, and supporters for their courage and devotion to CASE's goals of finding the facts and informing the public.
> TU Electric also recognizes its own shortcomings in assuring the NRC that they fulfilled NRC regulations. We acknowledge that nuclear expertise did not exist to meet those demands and that its nuclear management did not have full sensitivity to the regulatory environment. CASE, Mrs. Ellis, and her colleagues played a substantial part in achieving our current level of awareness.[40]

In reflecting on these remarkable events, Ellis said: "I am very happy, especially to have repaid the workers for their tremendous sacrifices. The people of this country do not realize how much they owe to these nuclear workers."[41]

Careers Destroyed

Among the ethical resisters we studied, a surprising number have successfully re-created their lives. In addition to the twenty who were able to keep their jobs, an additional twenty-three were able to rebuild successful careers. Despite major career disruption, they have secured new employment, maintained marriages, and recovered from the most painful period of their ordeal. An additional seven are working, although they remain dissatisfied with their current positions. A group of ten resisters remain out of work or underemployed, bitter about their punishment, and uncertain of ever being able to restore their lives fully.* Nonetheless, the solutions they have sought and their continuing identification with the whistleblowing cause reveal that they are resilient despite their setbacks. Maude DeVictor and Terry Howard are prime examples of such displaced yet committed resisters.

MAUDE DEVICTOR AND AGENT ORANGE

Maude DeVictor's parents told her she was a special child. She was born on 24 March 1940, a day that coincided with both the Christian celebration of Easter and the Jewish commemoration of Purim. To mark the occasion, her parents gave her the middle name of Esther, after the queen who saved her people from the despot who was plotting their destruction. Maude's father, a prosperous black Illinois businessman, wanted her to go to law school so she could "lead the masses." At college she had learned about racism and what it meant to be the only black woman in the college. After her second year, she joined the U.S. Navy. DeVictor finished college upon her discharge and accepted a position with the Veterans Administration, which wanted to hire minority employees in response to a class-action federal discrimination lawsuit. Maude DeVictor was not the average claims benefits counselor. Her privileged upbringing and later confrontation with racism had heightened her sensitivity and made her willing to do battle when she encountered unfair treatment. Her service in the armed forces and a bout with cancer gave her a special identification with the problems of veterans. She quickly responded to veterans' complaints about the "chemicals" in Vietnam. DeVictor began to suspect that exposure to toxic defoliants may have led to serious health problems years later.

Her efforts to expose the effects of Agent Orange, a powerful defoliant containing the highly toxic dioxin, brought her into confrontation with the VA management. She was initially encouraged by her superiors to investigate the veterans' allegations that the chemicals they had been exposed to in Vietnam caused illness. However, she soon found that her

*Three retired; one died.

superiors were reluctant to pursue this issue when they realized that it would ultimately lead to massive suits against the government.[42] The VA decided to terminate DeVictor's investigative activities, but by that time she was deeply involved with sick and dying young men and refused to end her inquiry. She continued to gather evidence that helped thousands of Vietnam veterans pursue a class-action suit against the manufacturers of Agent Orange.

DeVictor learned that one of the main problems in organizing veterans and informing government officials about the Agent Orange issue was the difficulty of translating highly technical knowledge into language lay people could understand. She found that the veterans and their families seldom recognized that those who had served in Vietnam were dying of cancer in disproportionate numbers and had no national network to communicate with one another. DeVictor knew they could not fully fathom the direct links between personal tragedies and the decision of government and corporate officials. She was able to provide some necessary information and encourage solidarity in the veterans' community. DeVictor helped afflicted veterans understand that they were part of a larger group and argued that, through united action, they would be able to make a case and get positive results. Through aggressive grass-roots efforts, the use of Agent Orange became a major national issue. The responsibility of the government and the corporations that produced the chemicals for the military came to public attention. Veterans' groups continued to press for federal government accountability for the disease and death sustained by American servicemen exposed to the deadly defoliants.[43]

A voluntary settlement of the class-action suit was reached in May 1984. Although most Vietnam veterans believe that this settlement with seven chemical companies to set up a $180 million fund did not adequately compensate them for their injuries, they all recognize the importance of the agreement.* The companies had planned to argue that there is no proof of cause and effect between dioxin and the medical problems of veterans and their families. While the settlement avoided the designation of legal responsibility, it did, at least, give some credence to the veterans' demands that the deleterious health effects of chemical defoliants be recognized.[45]

---

*About three hundred veterans who challenged the settlement lost their case when, in June 1988, the Supreme Court let stand the ruling of the lower court that the manufacturers of Agent Orange were immune from suit. This was the last legal obstacle to the $180 million voluntary settlement.[44]

The Agent Orange settlement was not cheered by DeVictor because she believed it was too limited. By this time she had lost her position at the VA in a labor dispute, having been fired in January 1984. As early as 1981 there had been threats of termination when she refused to work near video terminals lest exposure activate her cancer. She argued that it was her oncologist's opinion that she was a "high risk" cancer patient who had been previously exposed to radiation while in the military, and that further exposure could be detrimental to her health. Despite this medical rationale, there was a ruling against her when she took it to arbitration. Had she not been defined as a troublemaker, her superiors might have attempted to accommodate her, but they maintained that she had been insubordinate.[46]

After she lost her job, DeVictor felt certain that her inability to find a new position resulted from an effective blacklist against her. Prospective employers indicated that she had "a problem with management." During her time of unemployment, Vietnam veterans helped to pay DeVictor's rent and provided her with an occasional honorarium for delivering public speeches, an experience she found troubling. To make the situation worse, her doctor inquired why she had not come for the necessary check-ups after the cancer diagnosis. When she indicated that she had no medical insurance and no income, he insisted on providing the medical attention she required.

DeVictor was now in a paradoxical and humiliating position: a well-known person, she had no means of support. For twenty months, despite the national recognition for her efforts and the outpouring of affection by veterans and their families, DeVictor remained unemployed and in dire economic straits. Her entire life was consumed by the lack of a job. She could not afford any of the small niceties and worried about meeting her basic needs. She felt that she was being punished for her role in helping to expose a complex and dangerous issue: "I was just doing my job and as a result all of my basics were taken away from me. I don't know what it is to go to a concert or a play. Spring is my time of rejuvenation, and I like to go to shops and yard sales. But I haven't been able to do that. I haven't been able to have my hair done."[47]

The frustration and bitterness were debilitating. She kept going to veterans' meetings and events where she received recognition, but without work she felt that her "life was on hold." Then her prospects brightened. In August 1985, she was appointed as Veterans Affairs consultant to Mayor Harold Washington of Chicago. Part of her duties involved serving as a coordinator and organizer of the Chicago Parade Committee, which was planning a major event in June 1986 to honor Vietnam veterans. This position provided income and afforded her work in an environment surrounded by enthusiastic people who were powerful yet not vindictive.

DeVictor, who saw so much of the "ugliness of life," now spent her time thinking of the beautiful. She found that "it was a welcome change for me no longer to be thought of as the enemy."[48] She met with groups as diverse as the American Legion, Veterans for Peace, and the Conservative Vietnam Veterans. She obtained her position precisely because of her own status as a veteran and because she was trusted by the Vietnam and other veterans for her devotion to their well-being.

After leaving Chicago for California, DeVictor continued to feel her life was on a roller coaster, as she experienced both the highs from national recognition and the lows of not finding a satisfactory job. In November 1986, NBC television presented a two-hour dramatic film, entitled "Unnatural Causes," based on her battle to expose the link between Agent Orange and cancer and birth defects among Vietnam veterans and their children. The film portrayed DeVictor's sensitivity, insight, and courage, and emphasized the VA's recalcitrance. Once again, DeVictor achieved national recognition and received several invitations to speak across the country. At the same time, she continued to work in a low-paying, civil service position in a San Mateo office for adult services.

For DeVictor, the present lacks full satisfaction. She continues to argue that veterans have been asked to sacrifice their youth by political leaders who have conveniently forgotten the human costs of sending American troops to fight in foreign wars. Seeing the lesson of her whistleblowing in global terms, DeVictor has become an active promoter of world peace and veterans' rights:

> Veterans built this country. They are the citizen patriots. The country should not wait until they are sick and old. They should be taken care of now.
>
> We cannot have war. Nothing justifies killing our own breed. Even animals in the forest will protect their young. Unfortunately there is an industry based upon our having enemies. We cannot live that way any longer.[49]

A SURVIVOR: TERRY HOWARD

Like Maude DeVictor, Terry Howard has struggled to rebuild a career without sacrificing his principles. Immediately after he was fired by the Zack Company for protesting failure to meet the regulations required of the nuclear industry (see pages 148–53), he went to the Nuclear Regulatory Commission to inform it of the violations. Later he filed a suit against the corporation for illegal dismissal. As it became apparent that they could not survive financially in the Chicago area and that the suit would take years to be resolved, the Howard family returned to Massachusetts. They could not afford to wait for vindication before attempting to get on with their lives. With twenty-five years of teaching behind him and a short career in industry ended unhappily, Terry Howard soon moved into an entirely new field of work. He and several associates opened a real estate office specializing in video listings, with the idea that this use of new, widely available technology would enable clients to see a house without having to visit it personally. It was not Howard's first choice for a career, but he was enthusiastic about its possibilities:

We came back in December of 1982 thinking that friendlier territory would be better for me, and it really was in the beginning. Then I came to realize that there is no such thing as friendly territory. My associate, Rich, and I decided that we would open a real estate business. We didn't really have any money, we just kind of created a business with ideas and a little bit of money. We decided to get into video-listing properties, as part of a listing service. I believe in innovation. I believe that if you are going to live in the modern-day world you have to practice everything in the modern-day respect. It just so happens that we are what we call high-risk individuals. We have decided to surge ahead, not looking back—the fall isn't any harder from where we sit now than it would be if we sat anywhere else. Eventually this will become a big communications thing.[50]

The business did not meet Howard's expectations despite his determination to look ahead and to find a positive challenge in building a new future. The father of ten children, with several still at home, he was acutely aware of the financial burdens he had to carry. By 1985 he had decided to sell the real estate business and look for something where he would not be forced to make ethical compromises. He is not sure yet what that might be.

As an important symbolic gesture of his desire to be rid of the past, Howard no longer wants to hold on to all the materials so painfully connected with his whistleblowing experience. He gave them to us, including all the documents associated with his suit against Zack for illegal dismissal. He only reclaimed them when his lawyer contacted him for more information after the judge ruled that there were seven counts that could be litigated: "I hate discussing what went on in Chicago because it doesn't have much importance except for the history of it. I would like my grandchildren to look back and say that was the way the country used to be."[51]

The Howards have decided to face their past by emphasizing their strength as survivors. They refuse to allow their former Zack colleagues and friends to continue to control their emotional lives. For Mary Howard, as for the Roses, the Berubes, and the Laubachs, religion, family, and work have helped her to recoup and begin over again:

> We survived. I guess I am a survivor, and I have a lot of faith, which is probably what has helped me along. We'll work it out. I'm a strong Catholic. I never believed that I was as strong a Catholic as I do now. This whole situation has tested my faith and I think it has stood by me very well and brought me through a lot. I suppose it is just that I knew that God wouldn't abandon us. We had done something that was right and I think there should be more of this in people.
>
> I couldn't believe the corruption at first. People are bought and sold all the time. We can't be and I'll be happy with what I've got. I don't need the big house, we're okay with what we have. I'll always be able to take care of my children and welcome my children to my home who are in trouble. I'll find room at the table to feed them someplace. Somebody can sleep on the floor if they have to, but we'll stick together and things will work out. We'll get there.[52]

Terry Howard's main satisfaction has not come from work but from helping other whistleblowers, such as Tom Sinon (not his real name), a young worker who protested the time-card abuse by his peers at an industrial plant located in Boston. Sinon, who experienced the rejection and harassment inflicted on employees who do not remain silent, praised Howard's assistance in guiding him through the pitfalls that confront all resisters:

> I talk to Terry all the time. Just to say hello or keep him informed how management has messed up. Terry has helped reassure me and my wife that things would be okay down the road. Without him I would have been lost. He has gone through the whistleblowing experience for such a long time that it gave him great insight into labor law. He passed it on to me. His humor also lightened things up for us. I could count on him to keep us relaxed. I know my wife feels the same way.[53]

For resisters, re-establishing a normal life has been fraught with obstacles, and many whistleblowers never completely return to their former pursuits. Even as they struggle to let go of the crisis that dominated all their waking hours, many remain committed to defending ethical behavior, to helping other resisters, and to speaking out for better whistleblower protection. They are proud that they defended their principles despite the odds against them. They do not withdraw, because the battle against abusive authority is now woven into the fabric of their beliefs and lives. To turn away would be a betrayal of all they sought to achieve. Chuck Atchison sums up the experience:

> As a whistleblower you will experience every emotion known to mankind. A whistleblower will be subjected to public and private trials such as the Spanish Inquisition or the anti-Semitism suffered by the Jews under Hitler. Be prepared for old friends to suddenly become distant. Be prepared to change your type of job and life style. Be prepared to wait years for blind justice to prevail.
>
> The trials you are subject to will either cement together or tear apart a marriage. If you believe in what you are doing, do it. If you believe, be prepared to make the sacrifices that Joan of Arc and Karen Silkwood did. You may feel alone, but you blaze the trail for others, just as others have done before you. Someday the law will have more teeth, but until then I go to sleep at night with a clear mind, with my pride intact, and a purpose in life.[54]

Chapter 8

The Fight Goes On

WHEN SID RHODES, a key participant in exposing patient deaths at the County Mental Health facility in San Diego (see pages 188–97), left CMH in 1986, he quickly secured a new position as a social worker in a private mental-health organization, where he works today. Although he has much to be proud of for his crucial role in providing the momentum for a pioneering California law that makes it a criminal offense to retaliate against whistleblowers, he and his companion, Terri Richardson, now express deep dissatisfaction with their ordeal. Rhodes had a heart attack that he believes was caused by the stress of his experience at CMH; and during the height of the struggle, he and Richardson felt so threatened that they kept a gun in the house. Terri told us she had suffered from feeling emotionally isolated and abandoned when Sid became obsessed with the events at CMH. In speaking to us, they alluded half jokingly to John Wayne's characterization of the heroic sheriff in *True Grit*. Unlike the movie character, however, Sid and Terri did not ride off into the sunset at the conclusion of their adventure. And now that it is all over, they wonder what that experience really meant. Was the struggle worth it?[1]

It is a legitimate concern. We told Rhodes and Richardson that they are an integral part of a growing national movement. For, in a range of work settings, there are men and women who continue to battle in the cause of a viable democratic society where citizens will not sit idly back while lawless acts threaten the safety and resources of their communities. Although no one can sugar-coat the harsh reality of disrupted careers and family stress, the courage of whistleblowers is, nonetheless, coming to be more widely appreciated and publicly acknowledged. Indeed, whistleblowing has become more than a collection of isolated individuals. It is a nascent social movement tied together by a common ideology of accountability, emerging leaders who articulate its goals, and organizations committed to implementing strategies to bring about reforms that would lessen corporate crime, reduce government-industry collusion, and protect employees who expose dangerous and costly practices.

The forces that gave rise in the 1960s and 1970s to a generation of whistleblowers have not abated in the last two decades. The dangers of advanced technology continue to haunt a public stunned by the news of chemical explosions in Bhopal and West Virginia, of collapsed buildings and bridges in Connecticut and New York, and of oil spills in Ohio and other Midwestern states. Fear of the consequences of substandard materials, ineffective quality control, and corruption by government and industry officials continues to jar conscientious engineers, managers, and quality-assurance personnel. A burgeoning national network of public-interest groups, lawyers, legislators, journalists, and former whistleblowers is now available to employees seeking assistance in disclosing irregularities. Increasingly, ethical resisters—and the general public—are learning that in some industries the whistleblowing movement has made a difference. Thus, whistleblowers and their allies have been instrumental in closing down poorly run nuclear plants and substandard meat-packing facilities, forcing some defense industries to establish codes of ethics and ombudsmen who legitimize the right of employees to come forward internally, contributing to the effort to introduce ethics into the curricula of business and engineering schools, and lobbying for legislation to protect people who speak up in the face of lawless activity.

The movement is also facing major setbacks in its drive to force accountability in government and industry. Workers are finding an increasingly repressive atmosphere in the executive branch of the federal government. Stymied both by the Supreme Court decision (*Bush* v. *Lucas;* see pages 207–8) and by the failure of the Office of the Special Counsel and the Merit System Protection Board to act more favorably on employee complaints, resisters in the federal agencies confronted an even more difficult situation. New presidential directives have been issued, pointedly intended to silence a new generation of dissenters. Since these edicts are not reviewed by Congress, they are not subject to the normal checks and balances. They forbid personnel from speaking out and releasing materials that could help in documenting corruption or malfeasance, and are particularly dangerous because they threaten criminal indictments against anyone who discloses evidence that might later be designated as classified information.*

As a result, the future of ethical resistance in the executive branch is in grave jeopardy. While managers in the private sector of the defense industry are expressing increased sensitivity to the political pressure for greater compliance with the law, activists in the movement for integrity and accountability are pessimistic about the possibilities for disclosure of illegal acts, particularly in the Defense Department.

Dissent is increasingly dangerous. Many astute observers of the Washington scene do not believe that a change of administration will necessarily serve to legitimize public disclosure of fraud, waste, and abuse. Several of the directives handcuffing employees began under the Democratic administration of Jimmy Carter, and Ronald Reagan continued and intensified the effort to cut off whistleblowing in the executive branch. Defeating this bipartisan effort to repress dissenters is essential if federal employees are to continue alerting Congress, the press, and the public about costly collusion between government and industry.

The Importance of Whistleblowing

Tom Devine, legal director of the Government Accountability Project, has a bird's-eye view of the forces generating ethical resistance during the last decade and of the prospects for the future. As he sees it, employees will speak up when they believe they can make a difference. Scores have come forward in industries where the movement has been able to utilize their acts of resistance to produce positive change. While Devine agrees that the news is bleak in the executive branch, he argues that it is

---

*Congress responded strongly to the "gag order" and in December 1987 passed a continuing resolution amendment prohibiting any fiscal 1988 expenditures to implement standard form (S.F.) 189, or any such agreements that could prevent the flow of information from the executive branch to Congress. Senator Charles Grassley (Republican-Iowa) most actively opposed the executive branch efforts and even encouraged employees not to sign any such binding agreements.[2]

particularly encouraging in three major industries—nuclear, defense, and meat packing:

> In nuclear power the labor force has been the Achilles' heel of a corrupt industry. The Three Mile Island disaster was not sufficient in itself, since the industry actually claimed a victory. Despite the accident, they argued, there was no catastrophe. It wasn't until whistleblowers gave the inside story about shoddy construction that the industry got into serious trouble and started to panic. In the years between 1981 and 1983, we began reading the obituaries of the plants.[3]

As nuclear whistleblowers gained greater prominence, GAP received calls from nuclear workers throughout the country who came forward because they saw situations that were indefensible and believed their testimony could contribute to needed reforms. A similar phenomenon has occurred in the defense industry. Insiders protested when they saw money squandered, and pointed to vastly inflated prices for spare parts, coffee-pots, and toilet seats for the military, which became a national scandal in 1984 and threatened the largest "pork-barrel" in American history.[4] Legislators in both major parties decried the excessive waste of taxpayers' money to bolster profits and undertook extensive investigations that relied on the evidence of the resisters. This disclosure of fraud and the subsequent indictments by the Justice Department forced the defense industry itself to become concerned with the dire consequences of its failure to change its practices. To this end, industry leaders and their companies have begun to adopt self-governance programs and have publicly expressed determination to avoid future indictments or ineligibility for government contracts.

In 1985, the highest-ranking government contract lawyer for one major defense contractor warned his colleagues about the dangers the industry faced. He pointed out that the recent attention to fraud, waste, and abuse in defense contracting imposed serious pressures on those who wanted to stay in business:

> For the past three years, the U.S. government has made a public issue of fraud, waste, and abuse, in government contracts. And has taken specific, and far-reaching organizational steps to implement that commitment. . . .

In 1983 alone, there were 657 fraud convictions. Almost double the amount of 1982. Once more, in 1983, DOD collected over 14 million dollars in fines and restitutions. Pentagon sources expect grand juries to issue dozens of criminal indictments this year against major defense contractors. . . .

In short, the political role exists. The media pressure is intense. And the bureaucracy is in place to implement the new enforcement effort. There is little doubt that for at least the next four years, defense contractors like [ours] will be carefully scrutinized by DOD auditors and criminal investigators for everything involving the procurement process.

The lawyer, who prefers to remain anonymous, cautioned company managers that internal review was the key to their future:

In this environment, government contractors who fail to review, in advance of government scrutiny, their own costing, their own billing, and related contracting procedures, and to establish preventative programs, may easily make careless mistakes which could result in criminal prosecution—leading to suspensions, convictions, fines, jail sentences, and debarments.

In his final reflections, he reminded his colleagues that the fact that those who had authorized the illegal acts had not benefited personally from any of the overcharges did not excuse their actions:

Although there are no statistics available to us, I believe that the individuals, who authorized and participated in mischarging and other transgressions of this type, are not evil people, doing things for their own benefit. On the contrary, they are people who believe that they are acting in the best interests of the company. And often they are people who are succumbing to the pressures imposed upon them by higher management to show profitability in a given program. Unfortunately they are people who do not understand the consequences of their acts. I think that we have to make it clear that they are not doing the company any favors with this sort of conduct.[5]

This attorney's clear call for a changed ethos throughout the entire industry will require overhauling deeply entrenched and long-standing practices.

The National Security Industrial Association, the defense contractors' organization, also recommends that each company adopt a code of corporate conduct, review its policies, establish internal audit procedures, and enhance employee training to ensure correct implementation of contracts. In 1986, reversing earlier trends, this association wrote that it is beneficial for management to encourage employees to be vigilant and to inform appropriate government representatives of possible infractions.[6] At least according to their statements, many defense contractors hope to use ethical resisters as a bulwark against illegal actions and so have established hot-lines to encourage and protect employees who come forward. Although management believes it has taken the initiative to turn around self-destructive past policies, critics believe it highly unlikely that the new self-policing mechanisms will suddenly eliminate all long-standing dubious practices, such as mischarging and product substitution, to ensure high profits.

Their doubts were proved correct when a federal investigation into fraud and bribery in the military procurement system became public in June 1988. More than two years after an industry official blew the whistle by alerting the Naval Investigative Service that he had been approached by a consultant selling inside information, the Justice Department conducted surprise raids on dozens of contractors, looking for evidence of fraud and bribery. While Pentagon and industry officials maintain that the current watchdog system is working to expose corrupt individuals, many observers point to the latest scandal to demonstrate the depths of illegal collusion between industry and Pentagon officials and the importance of whistleblowers in disclosing wrongdoing and serving as the catalyst for major investigations.[7]

In another explosive issue, government inspectors and industry workers have blown the whistle on dangerous neglect in meat and poultry inspection. Tom Devine summarized the coordinated effort that led scores of employees to disclose illegal and disease-producing practices in that industry:

John Coplin was an isolated whistleblower in 1977.[8] He was forced to retire and was determined to push forward with his charges. It wasn't until GAP was able to develop the case for Coplin and a few others and got national television publicity that many others came forward to expose the filth in meat and poultry. USDA [the U.S. Department of Agriculture] simply looked the other way while contaminated and diseased products were being approved for the public to eat.[9]

High on the list of those who have insisted on public attention to this serious health hazard is seventy-three-year-old Dr. Carl Telleen, a veterinarian and USDA employee since 1960.[10] Telleen spoke out against slaughter and processing methods that resulted in the marketing of chicken contaminated with salmonella. He and many critics believe that the increase in contamination began in 1978 when USDA relaxed regulations in the poultry industry. According to Telleen, the industry began lobbying for deregulation as early as 1975 with the introduction of a new technology to remove the animals' intestines, because it did not want to discard chicken parts contaminated in this process. In 1978, the USDA assented to the industry's demands, allowing chickens contaminated with fecal matter to be washed off and then classified as safe for consumption.[11]

When Telleen objected to these lower standards and publicly criticized his agency, the department transferred him from Lawrence, Kansas, to Washington, D.C. Since he was sixty-five at the time and had recently redecorated his house, he believes that his superiors hoped he would retire. But he did not. Instead, once in the capital, he pounded the halls of Congress with stacks of documents providing evidence that the new technology of the poultry-processing firms resulted in the spread of fecal material throughout the carcasses of slaughtered chickens. The birds are washed in water so filthy that some federal inspectors have referred to it as "fecal soup" and the number of salmonella cases has doubled in the past decade, according to figures provided by the Centers for Disease Control.[12] Through the work of Telleen and GAP, and the publicity provided by television and newspaper stories, American homemakers and restaurateurs have been warned about the potential dangers of consuming contaminated chickens.

Devine described the effect of Telleen's tenacity as GAP continued to press the campaign:

> We succeeded in getting several corrupt USDA managers forced out of their jobs. That led to another wave of whistleblowers. We got another bunch of plants shut down on the West Coast because there was so much filth. That led to more whistleblowers in the Midwest who started to read about us through the trade journals. Then we had a piece on "60 Minutes" in the spring of 1987 and repeated that summer. That resulted in our doubling the number of statements from inspectors and

workers. Many now in Chicago, San Antonio, Nashville, and New York City all want us to take statements. These people are willing to take the risks, to stick their necks out to get this problem solved.[13]

On 29 March 1987, the issue of contaminated meat and poultry was brought directly into the American home with a dramatic portrayal on television's "60 Minutes." The reporter Diane Sawyer began the segment, entitled "1 out of 3," with some hard-hitting facts:

> Here's a statistic that may startle you. Tomorrow morning, if you buy a chicken at any supermarket, the chances are better than one out of three that the chicken you pick out will be carrying bacteria called salmonella which this year will kill hundreds of people and cause thousands more to come down with a kind of flu or appendicitis or even a perforated colon. And what is the USDA doing about it? Well, we went to some of USDA's own employees to find out and they told us that some chicken producers regularly violate health standards and that the USDA looks the other way.[14]

The "60 Minutes" program was part of a nationwide effort to confront the issue of contaminated poultry. The program was repeated on 6 September 1987. "A Coalition on Food Inspection" has now been spearheaded by the American Federation of Government Employees to initiate further protest against the agency that they believe is "in the pockets" of the processing industry.[15] Officials in the USDA reject allegations that they are allowing contaminated poultry to be sold, and argue that millions of Americans eat chicken daily without any dire consequences. While the debate rages, health advocates urge cooks to take specific steps in the preparation of chicken that will, at least, reduce the likelihood of bacterial infection.

Whistleblowing in the meat industry has united conscientious insiders, public-interest activists, the media, unions, and a myriad of consumer groups. Their alliance has pushed an issue long hidden behind the walls of slaughterhouses to prime-time television. With *The Jungle*, Upton Sinclair's 1906 exposé of filthy conditions in meat-packing plants, as a reference point, contemporary crusaders remind Americans of the nearly century-old battle for safely processed foods and urge the public not to tolerate any slippage into the "bad old days." Despite the reduced health standards in the meat industry, consumer advocates take heart from the knowledge that both USDA inspectors and industry employees continue to speak out despite the risks to their careers. This movement has helped to shut down some of the filthiest plants and keep alive the struggle for clean food.

The Rewards of Heroic Action

The growing impact of ethical resistance has not gone unnoticed by those concerned with public health and safety. Foundations and private donors have supported public-interest groups in their defense of whistleblowers and efforts to publicize the scandals they uncover. In 1987, in a dramatic attempt to recognize the heroism of those who have jeopardized their careers to promote the common good, and to encourage others to speak out, Michael Cavallo, a successful investor, established a foundation to "award three $10,000 prizes annually to people who show courage in business and government":

> I was struck by the contrast between the admirable actions of whistle-blowers and the punishment they often received from their employers and from society. Here are people who are risking their careers and sometimes their lives to defend the stated aims of their organizations, and who are then attacked on the very grounds of disloyalty to their employers. It was this disparity between heroic actions and unjust penalties that prompted me to establish a prize to help redress the balance in some small way.[16]

The first Cavallo Awards, presented in Washington, D.C., on 18 May 1988, included a special award to the resister Ernest Fitzgerald for his continuing commitment to fight for integrity in government and industry (see pages 21–24). Fitzgerald was singled out for his twenty years of service and especially for his most recent act of courage. He is one of only a handful of federal employees who have refused to sign the new security form SF189 that requires government workers not to release "classified or classifiable documents," and believes that such an agreement amounts to an unconstitutional gag order which will make it virtually impossible for anyone to expose illegal actions and cover-ups. Forceful Congressional intervention delayed the enactment of SF189 for one year, thus giving

Fitzgerald a temporary stay. He maintains that SF189 remains a dangerous omen for an open society.[17]

The Cavallo Foundation also made three further awards of $10,000 each: one to Billie Garde for her exposé of sexual exploitation and other corrupt practices in the Muskogee, Oklahoma, Census Bureau (see pages 160–66); and the other two to Leon Bard and John Berter. Bard and Berter had, like other ethical resisters whose stories we have recounted, spoken up about recent abuses in the defense industry and the Veterans Administration.

LEON BARD VERSUS THE BATH IRON WORKS

In 1987, Leon Bard, a quality-control inspector at the Bath Iron Works in Bath, Maine, had charged that his company used uninspected steel in the construction of the Aegis cruiser, considered the navy's most sophisticated air-defense vessel. He feared that if inferior steel were used the ship's hulls might not be strong enough to withstand the impact of combat, and repeatedly tried to alert management to the problem. In return—and shortly after he had received a high evaluation for his work and his commitment to quality—they fired him in September 1986 for "deliberately restricting output" and "committing a nuisance."[18]

Bard contacted the Project on Military Procurement for assistance after he saw its founder, Dina Rasor, publicizing her book about the Project on the Phil Donahue show.[19] The Project assigned a staff member, Danielle Brian-Bland, to investigate the case. In the course of her inquiry, she found ten workers who supported Bard but were afraid to speak up publicly. The Project released several documents supporting Bard's allegations; and the company, realizing that his charges were about to receive national publicity, responded quickly. A Bath Iron Works spokesman totally denied Bard's claim. He acknowledged that a long strike had delayed production, and that BIW was behind schedule and over budget. While conceding that some steel might not have been inspected, the spokesman maintained that "any allegation that Bath Iron Works is using steel that . . . does not meet Navy specification is totally and unequivocally absurd."[20] Within a few days, the navy confirmed the reliability of BIW's quality control.

At the time that he received the Cavallo Award, Bard was doing seasonal excavation work to support his family. He refused to be intimidated by BIW's size or by its influence in the community as one of the state's largest employers and is currently suing the company for wrongful discharge. Bard was shocked when he heard about the Cavallo award. He had been through so many "downs" that he could not believe his fortune might be changing. "The money," he said, "was less important than the thought": "At first I could not figure out what the Cavallo Foundation was all about. Then it started to sink in. But things like that don't happen to me. I told Mr. Cavallo that it sounded too good to be true."[21]

But it was true and not just an act of providence. Bard's recognition was, of course, the culmination of a series of integrated steps. The case did not wither in a small Maine city in part because Dina Rasor's appearance on television inspired Bard to contact the Project on Military Procurement. With the subsequent national publicity, the project staff nominated Bard for the Cavallo award in their eagerness to have an award go to a resister involved in an ongoing case in the defense industry; and the evaluations committee of the Foundation agreed that Bard's "moral courage" should be rewarded. Two senators, the Republican (Iowa) Charles Grassley and the Democrat (Ohio) Howard Metzenbaum, co-sponsored the meeting to honor the resisters.

JOHN BERTER VERSUS THE VETERANS ADMINISTRATION

The third recipient of the Cavallo Award also used a national network to move his case from private oblivion to a public arena. John Berter, a federal police officer in the Veterans Administration hospital in Cincinnati, exposed problems of police brutality and racism anonymously in 1985, then publicly the following year. He and several colleagues claimed that they observed the chief of security assault visitors and patients with little or no provocation. Because of their fear of confronting the chief directly, Berter and three other officers wrote anonymous letters to a variety of agencies, including the Federal Bureau of Investigation. Predictably, the chief learned the identity of his accusers, and Berter's superiors retaliated by chastising him for misspelling in his record books and, in 1987, fired him for spelling and grammar errors and for staying away from work on doctor's orders when the harassment caused excessive stress and an ulcer.[22] Determined not to remain silent, Berter contacted the Government Accountability Project, took his case to the Office of Special

Counsel, testified before Congress on a new bill to protect whistleblowers, and appeared on both radio and television to condemn the assaults perpetrated by his superior. As Berter pointed out, most of the victims were black men, indicating that the case touched the raw nerves of racial bigotry and violence.[23]

The Cavallo Foundation award recognized that Berter had risked career, family security, and personal safety in order to live up to his vision of how federal officers should treat veterans and even unauthorized visitors. The award came at a most opportune time since he had just lost his case before the Office of Special Counsel, which did not find sufficient merit in his allegations of improper dismissal. The OSC report, furthermore, attacked both his credibility and his competence.[24] GAP lawyer Tom Carpenter issued an immediate rejoinder, charging that the OSC misrepresented the testimony of Berter's supporting witnesses, did not review vital information, and refused to disclose the agency's evidence against Berter so he could defend himself. Representative Patricia Schroeder (Democrat-Colorado), chair of the House Civil Service Subcommittee, wrote to the Office of the Special Council that its personal attacks on Berter were unconscionable. As his fight goes on, the recognition he has received makes him feel less lonely and isolated:

> The award makes me feel that the fight with the VA was worth it all, regardless of how the VA and the Office of Special Counsel have responded. I have a warm feeling of pride, knowing that I have been recognized for having the courage to have exposed patient abuse. Over the last year and a half, I have met with criticism and sarcasm from friends and relatives who said that I should hang up the fight. I was constantly reminded that the chief had a paycheck coming in and I didn't. They thought that this was the only issue. It's a very good feeling to be recognized for having moral courage.[25]

While the Cavallo Awards alone cannot change the conditions for whistleblowers, they are a symbol of affirmation for a few of the many whose integrity has led them to take substantial risks. There is an equally important need for ongoing private and foundation support for public-interest groups and legal defense funds. Permanent organizations are necessary to ensure that efforts of ethical resisters are not stymied or their careers automatically ruined. For instance, GAP's budget has grown to

$750,000—a sizable sum for any small nonprofit organization to raise annually. Yet its staff cannot accommodate all the cases whistleblowers bring to them. Since other organizations are in similar straits, many resisters are thrown on their own resources. A range of permanent public-interest groups is essential to sustain the movement for accountability in government and industry.

Protecting Whistleblowers

Resisters serve as bellwethers of emerging social problems. A decade ago when the issue of contaminated meat and poultry was only a subject in history books, a few federal inspectors called attention to this renewed health hazard. As we have benefited from their warnings of salmonella poisoning, we must rely on others to expose future problems of consumer safety, environmental degradation, and public health. To apprise the nation of organizational malfeasance and its dangerous consequences, both government and corporate employees must work to assure adequate compliance with the laws.

There is always a tension in ethical resistance between the severe private costs to an individual and the benefit to the community at large. Because of the significant contributions whistleblowers can make, it is incumbent on society to devise reasonable protections for them and their families. Some whistleblowers, like Frank Serpico or Ernest Fitzgerald, cannot be silenced. They are totally convinced of the seriousness of their charges and of their personal obligation to respond, and they will fight on despite any abuses heaped on them. Most others will come forward in an environment that offers an avenue for disclosure, some hope of effectiveness, and a reasonable degree of personal protection.

Employee protection provided by a range of environmental laws, such as the Toxic Substances Control Act (1976) or the Energy Reorganization Act (1978), far exceeds the protection of most other federal employees. For the larger group, the administrative procedures are among the weakest. Unless the Civil Service Reform Act (1978) is overhauled to revamp the Merit Systems Protection Board and the Office of the Special Counsel, it is extremely unlikely that these laws will be of much assistance to civil service employees who report malfeasance. Several leaders in the

House and the Senate continue to press for this much-needed reform. In 1988, a Whistleblower Protection Bill passed the Senate and House unanimously. Unfortunately, the bill was vetoed by President Reagan. The bill establishes constraints on the OSC's authority to limit the rights of those seeking assistance, establishes more realistic requirements for legal burdens of proof, and expands judicial review. A changed political climate may provide the extra impetus not only to pass a new law but also to enforce it more consistently. Yet it is highly unlikely that problems of protection will disappear. No administration will welcome within its ranks scores of whistleblowers who want to reveal inadequate performance in federal agencies. An improved atmosphere will require ongoing pressure by the various forces that comprise the movement for accountability.

In a reversal of historic trends, whistleblowers in the private sector now appear less vulnerable than civil service employees. Some who work in the nuclear or environmental areas are protected by federal statutes. Others rely on state-court decisions and legislation. In more than half the states, the courts have dramatically expanded the protection for employees in industry by granting a public policy exception to the termination-at-will doctrine. In these states, employers have been barred from firing workers who protest illegal violations by their companies or noncompliance with "a firmly established principle of public policy." State legislatures are also acting to protect their public employees from retaliation. Five states have passed laws covering all workers.[26] (See discussion of California law on pages 188–97.) Nevertheless, litigation will continue to be a lengthy, expensive, and uncertain route.

One new resource that may affect the fate of whistleblowing is the revitalization of the False Claims Act of 1863, a law enacted to prosecute Civil War manufacturers who substituted sawdust for gunpowder in Union army supplies. Those who disclosed information leading to success-ful prosecution were to be awarded 10 percent of any funds returned to the federal treasury. The False Claims Amendment Act of 1986 is the brainchild of the public-interest attorney John R. Phillips, who was seek-ing to devise a way to interdict fraud against the government.[27] Under its provisions, whistleblowers are guaranteed 15 to 30 percent of funds recovered in a successful prosecution, in addition to attorney fees, back pay, and comprehensive protection from retaliation. In the first fourteen months since its inception, forty civil suits were filed, including nineteen against several major defense contractors.[28] In ten of these cases, the

Justice Department joined the plaintiffs. While none has yet been tried, the suits have already raised great concern among their targets. Because it offers a substantial monetary advantage, the new law alters the motivation and may change the character of the people who come forward. Nonetheless, it will provide a shield around prospective whistleblowers and may be a more effective way of protecting them than all previous efforts have been. Its very enactment is a recognition of the scope of the fraud problem and the crucial role insiders may play in the future.

On Taking a Stand

No matter how effective, no social movement can rely exclusively on laws and the courts. Widespread concern with accountability requires commitment from a broad range of social institutions. Educators must continue to socialize students of all ages about the importance of maintaining high ethical standards. There are some early signs that professional schools are beginning to re-evaluate the importance of an education that includes sustained exposure to such issues. A recent multimillion-dollar grant to the Harvard Business School to introduce ethics into all aspects of the curriculum will help propel this trend. Many professional schools that continue to focus exclusively on technical education must rethink their pedagogical goals.

Ethical resisters are contributing to that reformulation. At precisely the same time that the Cavallo Foundation awards have begun to recognize the significant contributions of people of moral courage, engineer Roger Boisjoly has been traveling throughout the United States to speak at colleges and universities about the events leading up to the destruction of the *Challenger* shuttle on 28 January 1986 (see pages 9–11). Boisjoly describes his former duties at Morton Thiokol, his futile attempt to prevent the launch, and his own reaction to the shuttle tragedy: "I had no intention of watching the launch, but was urged to do so by one of my colleagues. After the explosion we all sat in stunned silence. I went to my office and sat there all day, unable to speak to anyone for fear of breaking down completely."[29]

Boisjoly is now a man with a mission. University audiences respond with rapt attention to his call for ethical sensitivity in the training of future professionals. Like other resisters, he argues that technical education is insufficient in the face of the challenges of working in the modern age. Engineers, like other responsible employees, must be ready to speak up inside and outside their companies. According to the profession's own code of ethics which Boisjoly recites, they have a prime responsibility to warn the public of unforeseen dangers. Boisjoly urges all students to protest whenever necessary. If anything good can come from the shuttle disaster, he maintains, it will come from using that case in the teaching of professional ethics.

Boisjoly is not alone in his mission. Sylvia Robins, another whistle-blower in the aerospace industry, is engaged in a similar effort to educate students about ethical issues.[30] Robins was a systems engineer with Rockwell Shuttle Operations Company with ten years of aerospace experience. Like Boisjoly, she has been warmly received by students and has had an influence on their thinking, as one young man recorded in a letter to her:

> You have left quite an impression on the people up here at the University of Wisconsin. . . . You serve as a prime example of someone who stood up for what they thought was right, and I honestly think that your story will positively affect some decisions made by our future graduates. . . . Personally, I now have an ideal to strive for and feel confident that I will never sacrifice my integrity or pride to serve "company policy."[31]

In addition to schools, professional organizations, churches, unions, and community groups must build a far stronger commitment to a safe and honest working environment. They must also provide their members with direct help that goes beyond platitudes about the duties of every doctor, lawyer, or church member. Since so many resisters come from the ranks of professionals, groups like the American Medical Association or the Institute for Electrical and Electronic Engineers must be prepared to assert that their own power to speak as associations of experts rests on their ability to protect members who insist on high standards in the face of management objections.[32]

To date, as we have said, relatively few professionals have turned to their associations for direct help in respect to reprisals; and the professional organizations' willingness to expend their own treasury, energy, or political connections to defend whistleblowers among their members has been woefully inadequate. Far more must be done. There are a few models for future direction, such as the incident that occurred in 1971 when three engineers working for the Bay Area Rapid Transit in metropolitan San

Francisco objected to the safety standards of the automated train controls. When they received no satisfaction, they contacted the California Society of Professional Engineers. In a dramatic reversal of past policy, a professional engineering society "backed its members by criticizing a specific corporation."[33] Subsequently the IEEE, the largest engineering organization in the world, created an award for outstanding service in the public interest and named the three BART engineers as its first recipients. This direct support and recognition aided the dissenting engineers and prevented the destruction of their careers. The affirmation of their colleagues was crucial in sustaining their professional credibility.

Professional organizations stand in a particularly independent relationship with employers of their members. They have the expertise to assess the validity and significance of the dissidents' allegations. Historically, they have always claimed the authority to determine professional standards for training, licensing, and monitoring appropriate activity and have shunned external regulation of their members' conduct. It is entirely in keeping with this tradition of self-regulation for the professional organizations to take responsibility for ensuring fair treatment of those who attempt to maintain their highest standards. In an era when increasing numbers of professionals are employed in large bureaucracies and engaged in highly technical work with significant impact on the health and safety of the population, associations cannot turn their backs if they are to keep their legitimacy as primary spokespersons for professional rights and responsibilities.

While other institutions in the society cannot lay claim to the expertise of professional associations, they, too, have a significant part to play. Churches, in particular, have a long historic association with defending moral behavior. Religious commitments continue to motivate resisters to come forward, and their profound convictions often sustain them during their darkest days. Yet all too often their battles are lonely ones despite the efforts of an occasional priest, minister, or rabbi. The failure of religious organizations to rally around a congregant's struggle for ethical behavior in the workplace is an indictment of their professed willingness to influence the moral climate of a society that stresses deep respect for religious teaching. If influential clergy were to demand an independent investigation, and if members offered financial and emotional support, resisters and their families would not carry the total burden of challenging powerful organizations. Others in the community might join a church that exercises leadership in calling attention to local industries and government agencies that violate safety standards, endanger worker health, or contaminate the environment.

The struggle to create a social climate that supports and defends ethical resisters will be prolonged. As they confront some of the most difficult and deeply entrenched problems in the society, no quick fix is in sight. Government and corporate executives are often subject to pressures to institute policies that are cost-effective, meet tight schedules, and can match foreign competition. In carrying out such policies, managers will inevitably be tempted "to cut corners" to reduce safety margins, and to take greater risks. To rationalize such decisions, they argue that all policies have some risks and that their choices are not outside the reasonable. No one, they assert, has created an accident-proof product, a perfect design, or a plan for a pollution-free environment. A society that wants to benefit from high technology must be prepared to take certain risks. In addition, managers will try to assure themselves and others that empirical evidence is on their side. They will cite the record of a nuclear industry that has had no major accidents, an airline industry that flies millions of passengers with relatively few crashes, or a meat-processing industry where tons of meat are consumed with very limited reports of resultant food poisoning. Employees who disagree have to challenge the judgment that their superiors are determined to defend, and convince others that a Chernobyl or a *Challenger* disaster is more than a remote possibility, but rather a danger serious enough to halt production, increase costs, or disrupt company plans. They must insist on compliance with the laws that set standards to minimize dangerous consequences, some of which may not be readily observable.

As long as these conflicts continue, some ethical employees will feel obligated to speak out publicly when their protests are silenced in the workplace, and will continue to deluge Congress, the media, the courts, and attorneys with evidence of malfeasance. Their struggle to have their objections heard will be long and grueling. A few will feel satisfied that their actions have made a difference; others will despair. But neglect and derision will not stop them from fighting on, especially now that they realize that they are not alone but part of a growing movement committed to bureaucratic accountability. Resisters' families will live under great stress but will continue to support them. Retaliation will simultaneously injure and embolden all of them. For ethical resisters are, indeed, the heart of a national resolve for individual responsibility on behalf of the common good.

Appendix

Who Can Help?

Below is a partial listing of organizations that assist whistleblowers directly or work on behalf of whistleblower-related causes.

Advocacy Institute
1730 Rhode Island Ave., N.W.
Suite 600
Washington, D.C. 20036
202–659–8475
Works to advise organizations that provide direct services to whistleblowers.

Association of Mental Health Specialties
15702 Tasa Pl.
Laurel, Maryland 20707
301–953–7358
Focuses on counseling those who resist organizational lawlessness.

Cavallo Foundation
1 Hancock Pl.
Cambridge, Mass. 02139
617–354–5238
Provides three $10,000 awards each year to employees who exhibit moral courage.

Center for Law in the Public Interest
10951 West Pico Blvd.
Third Floor
Los Angeles, California 90064-2166
800–2–FRAUD–2
Provides attorney services for individuals seeking to bring *Qui tam* actions under the False Claims Act.

Coalition to Stop Government Waste
200 Massachusetts Ave., Suite C1A
Washington, D.C. 20002
202–546–1200
Assists whistleblowers with knowledge of the law, strategies, and networking with others pressing the same issues.

Ethics Resource Center, Inc.
1025 Connecticut Ave., N.W.
Washington, D.C. 20036
202–223–3411
Serves education, government, and business organizations in establishing programs to create a more ethical working environment.

Government Accountability Project
25 E Street, N.W.
Suite 700
Washington, D.C. 20001
202–347–0460
Provides legal counsel for individuals and seeks legislative action to protect whistleblowers.

Project on Military Procurement
422 C Street, N.E.
Washington, D.C. 20002
202–543–0883
Seeks to expose waste, fraud, and abuse in the defense establishment.

Public Citizen
2000 P Street, N.W.
Washington, D.C. 20036
202–293–9142
Lobbies for whistleblower protection and represents whistleblowers in cases brought against government and industry.

Notes

Introduction: A New Tradition of Courageous Dissent

1. For an overview of the most significant cases of corporate malfeasance, see Russell Mokhiber, *Corporate Crime and Violence* (San Francisco: Sierra Club Books, 1988). The dangers of confronting authority are presented in a provocative essay by Deena Weinstein, *Bureaucratic Opposition* (New York: Pergamon Press, 1979). The demand for conformity in industry is discussed in Robert Jackall, *Moral Mazes* (New York: Oxford University Press, 1988).

2. Stanley Milgram, *Obedience to Authority* (New York: Harper & Row, 1974).

3. Norman Bowie, *Business Ethics* (Englewood Cliffs, N.J.: Prentice-Hall, 1982), p. 143.

4. While it is virtually impossible to draw a random sample of whistleblowers, several surveys reveal a similar profile to the group we studied. Karen L. Soeken and Donald R. Soeken, "A Survey of Whistleblowers: Their Stressors and Coping Strategies," in Senate Committee on Governmental Affairs, Hearings on S.508 before the Subcommittee on Federal Services, Post Office, and Civil Service, 100th Cong., 1st sess., 20 and 31 July 1987, pp. 538–48; Lea P. Stewart, " 'Whistle Blowing': Implications for Organizational Communication," *Journal of Communication* 30 (Autumn 1980): 90–101. Bill Bush, the informal archivist of the whistleblower movement, has collected about 1,600 cases of whistleblowers throughout the country, but there is no analysis of this large sample.

5. For an insightful analysis of the lure of the success dream in American society, see Michael Lewis, *The Culture of Inequality* (New York: New American Library, 1979). For a discussion of the requirement to disclose lawless acts, see Kenneth D. Walters, "Your Employees' Right to Blow the Whistle," *Harvard Business Review* 53 (July–August 1975): 26–34, 161–62. Sissela Bok, "Whistleblowing and Professional Responsibility," *New York University Education Quarterly* 11 (Summer 1980): 2–10. Louis Clark, "Blowing the Whistle on Corruption: How to Kill a Career in Washington," *Barrister* 5 (Summer 1978): 10–19.

6. Frederick Elliston, John Keenan, Paula Lockhart, and Jane van Schaick, *Whistleblowing Research: Methodological and Moral Issues* (New York: Praeger, 1985), p. 26; James S. Bowman, "Whistle-Blowing in the Public Service: An Overview of the Issues," *Review of Public Personnel Administration* 1 (Fall 1980): 17. Whistleblowers, in essence, are not alienated from the system when they begin their internal protest. For an important effort to explore that concept, see Ada W. Finifter, ed., *Alienation and the Social System* (New York: Wiley, 1972). Advice to prospective whistleblowers abounds. See Government Accountability Project, *A Whistleblower's Guide to the Federal Bureaucracy* (Washington, D.C.: Institute for Policy Studies, 1977). Peter Raven-Hansen, "Dos and Don'ts for Whistleblowers: Planning for Trouble," *Technology Review* 82 (May 1980): 34–44. Myron Peretz Glazer and Penina Migdal Glazer, "Whistleblowing," *Psychology Today*, August 1986, pp. 36–43.

7. The meaning of community is probed in a powerful study by Kai T. Erikson, *Everything in Its Path* (New York: Simon & Schuster, 1976).

8. Thomas Whiteside, *The Investigation of Ralph Nader* (New York: Arbor House, 1972).

9. A. Ernest Fitzgerald, *The High Priests of Waste* (New York: W. W. Norton, 1972).

Chapter 1. The Beginnings of Ethical Resistance

1. "Report of the Presidential Commission on the Space Shuttle Challenger Accident," Washington, D.C., 6 June 1986, chap. 6, esp. pp. 123–24.

2. Trudy E. Bell and Karl Esch, "The Fatal Flaw in Flight 51-L," *Spectrum* 24 (February 1987): 38. This article is one of the most comprehensive overviews of events leading up to the *Challenger*

disaster; also see David E. Sanger, "NASA Had Warning of Risk to Shuttle in Cold Weather," *New York Times*, 13 May 1986.

3. David E. Sanger, "How See-No-Evil Doomed Challenger," *New York Times*, 29 June 1986; Martin Burkey and Randy Quarles, "Lucas: Launch Process Not Flawed," *Huntsville Times*, 28 February 1986.

4. David E. Sanger, "Engineers Tell of Punishment for Shuttle Testimony," *New York Times*, 11 May 1986.

5. William P. Rogers to James C. Fletcher, 27 May 1986. A 13 May 1986 editorial in the *New York Times*, "Burying the Truth at Morton Thoikol," captured the arrogance created by a noncompetitive market environment.

6. 12 March 1986; also see Philip M. Boffey, "Zeal and Fear Mingle at Vortex of Shuttle Inquiry," *New York Times*, 17 March 1986.

7. Alan Westin, ed., *Whistle Blowing! Loyalty and Dissent in the Corporation* (New York: McGraw-Hill, 1981), pp. 1–14.

8. Ralph Nader, Peter J. Petkas, and Kate Blackwell, eds., *Whistle Blowing* (New York: Bantam, 1972); Michael Pertschuk, *Revolt Against Regulation: The Rise and Pause of the Consumer Movement* (Berkeley: University of California Press, 1982).

9. David Vogel, "The 'New' Social Regulation," in Thomas K. McCraw, ed., *Regulation in Perspective* (Cambridge, Mass.: Harvard University Press, 1981), pp. 160–61. For a discussion of the growth of regulation and the reaction to it, see Larry N. Gerston, Cynthia Fraleigh, and Robert Schwab, *The Deregulated Society* (Pacific Grove, Calif.: Brooks/Cole, 1988), pp. 19–38.

10. Quoted in Stephen M. Kohn and Thomas Carpenter, "Nuclear Whistleblower Protection and the Scope of Protected Activity Under Section 210 of the Energy Reorganization Act," *Antioch Law Journal* 4 (Summer 1986): 76.

11. The following federal acts included employee protection provisions: Toxic Substances Control Act, 15 U.S.C. 2622; Superfund, 42 U.S.C. 9610; Water Pollution Control Act, 33 U.S.C. 1367; Solid Waste Disposal Act, 42 U.S.C. 6971; Clean Air Act, 42 U.S.C. 7622; Energy Reorganization Act, 42 U.S.C. 5851; Safe Drinking Water Act, 42 U.S.C. 300-j-9; Federal Mine Health & Safety Act, 30 U.S.C. 815(c); Fair Labor Standards Act, 29 U.S.C. 215; Occupational Safety & Health Act, 29 U.S.C. 660(c); National Labor Relations Act, 29 U.S.C. 158(a) (4); Surface Transportation Act, 49 U.S.C. 2305; Longshoreman's and Harbor Worker's Compensation Act, 33 U.S.C. 948(a). For a review of these acts, see Stephen M. Kohn and Michael D. Kohn, "An Overview of Federal and State Whistleblower Protections," *Antioch Law Journal* 4 (Summer 1986): 99–152. An expanded treatment of the legal issues can be found in Stephen M. Kohn and Michael D. Kohn, *The Labor Lawyer's Guide to the Rights and Responsibilities of Employee Whistleblowers* (Westport, Conn.: Quorum, forthcoming). There is an abundant literature on the issues of protecting whistleblowers. Among the important early discussions are: John P. Christiansen, "A Remedy for the Discharged Employees Who Refuse to Perform Unethical or Illegal Acts: A Proposal in Aid of Professional Ethics," *Vanderbilt Law Review* 28 (May 1975): 805–40. John Conway, "Protecting the Private Sector At-Will Employee Who 'Blows the Whistle': A Course of Action Based Upon Determinants of Public Policy," *Wisconsin Law Review* 77 (1977): 777–812. Rosemary Chalk and Frank Von Hippel, "Due Process for Dissenting Whistleblowers," *Technology Review* 81 (June–July 1979): 49–55. Alfred G. Feliu, "Discharge of Professional Employees: Protecting Against Dismissal for Acts Within a Professional Code of Ethics," *Columbia Human Rights Law Review* 11 (Fall–Winter 1979–1980): 149–87.

12. Vogel, "The 'New' Social Regulation," p. 165. For a fine history of the struggle for regulation and the attack by business, see Michael D. Reagan, *Regulation: The Politics of Policy* (Boston: Little, Brown, 1987), pp. 85–111.

13. Reagan, *Regulation*, pp. 166–69; Michael Useem, *The Inner Circle* (New York: Oxford University Press, 1984), p. 160; Louis M. Kohlmeier, Jr., *The Regulators* (New York: Harper & Row, 1969), p. 266; Francis T. Cullen, William J. Maakestad, and Gray Cavender, *Corporate Crime under Attack* (Cincinnati: Anderson Publishing, 1987), p. 130; Vogel, "The 'New' Social Regulation," pp. 166–67.

14. Vogel, "The 'New' Social Regulation," p. 161; Useem, *Inner Circle*, p. 161.

15. Useem, *Inner Circle*, p. 162.

16. Nancy Frank and Michael Lombness, *Controlling Corporate Illegality* (Cincinnati: Anderson Publishing, 1988), p. 3.

17. Useem, *Inner Circle*, p. 161, 163.

18. Ibid., p. 151. Vogel, "The 'New' Social Regulation," p. 164; the "attack on social regulation" is cogently argued by Reagan, *Regulation,* pp. 105–9.

19. Useem, *Inner Circle,* p. 164.

20. Frank Donner and James Ledbetter, "Deregulation by Sleaze," *The Nation,* 6 February 1988, pp. 162–66; also see Gerston, Fraleigh, and Schwab, *Deregulated Society,* pp. 40–61, for a detailed discussion of the intense conflict over OSHA and its ultimate weakening under Ronald Reagan.

21. Vogel, "The 'New' Social Regulation," p. 177; Pertschuk, *Revolt,* pp. 51–60.

22. Jameson W. Doig, Douglas E. Phillips, and Tycho Manson, "Deterring Illegal Behavior by Officials of Complex Organizations," *Criminal Justice Ethics* (Winter/Spring 1984) : 27–56; Marshall B. Clinard and Peter C. Yeager, *Corporate Crime* (New York: Free Press, 1980), pp. 110–32; and "Corporate Crime. The Untold Story," *U.S. News and World Report,* 6 September 1982, pp. 25–29.

23. Clinard and Yeager, *Corporate Crime,* p. 11.

24. See, for example, Arthur M. Louis, "Lessons from the Firestone Fracas," *Fortune,* 28 August 1978, pp. 44–48; "Total Recall," *Time,* 25 June 1979, p. 58; Stuart A. Feldstein, "How Not to React to Safety Controversy," *Business Week,* 6 November 1978, p. 65; Ralph E. Winter, "Firestone Tests in 1975 Showed Some Tire Flaws," *Wall Street Journal,* 24 July 1978; Alfonso A. Narvaez, "State Issues Warning on Firestone 500 Radial Tire," *New York Times,* 29 July 1978; Subcommittee on Oversight and Investigations of the Committee on Interstate and Foreign Commerce, "The Safety of Firestone 500 Steel Belted Radial Tires," 95th Cong., 2d sess., 16 August 1978.

25. Westin, *Whistle Blowing!* p. 12; Michael Brown, *Laying Waste* (New York : Pantheon Books, 1979), pp. 1–27; Adeline Gordon Levine, *Love Canal: Science, Politics, and People* (Lexington, Mass.: D. C. Heath, 1982).

26. Donald G. McNeil, Jr., "Study at Hooker Plant Found 75 Emissions Dangerous to Health," *New York Times,* 17 April 1979; Greg Mitchell, *Truth . . . and Consequences* (New York: Dembner Books, 1981), p. 223.

27. Robert Jackall, *Moral Mazes* (New York: Oxford University Press, 1988), pp. 101–5.

28. Ibid., p. 160.

29. David R. Simon and D. Stanley Eitzen, *Elite Deviance* (Boston: Allyn & Bacon, 1982), pp. 26–27.

30. Jackall, *Moral Mazes,* p. 105.

31. Simon and Eitzen, *Elite Deviance,* p. 92.

32. Frank Camps, "Warning an Auto Company About an Unsafe Design," in Westin, *Whistle Blowing!,* pp. 119–29. Quotation on p. 120.

33. Frank Camps, interview with authors, 26 August 1983, and phone conversations and correspondence, 1982–88.

34. Jackall, *Moral Mazes,* p. 118.

35. Francis T. Cullen, William J. Maakestad, and Gray Cavender, "The Ford Pinto Case and Beyond: Corporate Crime, Moral Boundaries, and the Criminal Sanction," in Ellen Hochstedler, ed., *Corporations as Criminals* (Beverly Hills: Sage Publications, 1984), pp. 107–30. For a detailed account of the airbag controversy, see Gerston, Fraleigh, and Schwab, *Deregulated Society,* pp. 142–69.

36. Camps, interview with authors.

37. Camps, "Warning," p. 123.

38. The first article to raise public consciousness about the dangers of the Pinto was Mark Dowie, "Pinto Madness," *Mother Jones,* September-October 1977, pp. 18–30. The fullest discussion of the Ford Pinto case appears in Cullen, Maakestad, and Cavender, *Corporate Crime,* pp. 145–308. For an insider's explanation defending Ford, see Lee Iacocca, *Iacocca* (New York: Bantam, 1984), pp. 161–62. Ford's defense and the financial and reputational costs to the company of the Pinto litigation are spelled out in Brent Fisse and John Braithwaite, *The Impact of Publicity on Corporate Offenders* (Albany: State University of New York Press, 1983), pp. 41–54.

39. A. Ernest Fitzgerald, *The High Priests of Waste* (New York: W. W. Norton, 1972).

40. Dina Rasor, *The Pentagon Underground* (New York: Times Books, 1985), p. 144.

41. Ibid., pp. 137–41.

42. Berkeley Rice, *The C-5A Scandal* (Boston: Houghton Mifflin, 1971), p. 21; Nader, Petkas, and Blackwell, *Whistle Blowing,* pp. 40–43.

43. Nader, Petkas, and Blackwell, *Whistle Blowing,* p. 46; Subcommittee on Economy in Government of the Joint Economic Committee, 90th Cong., 2d sess., 11, 12, 13 November 1968, 16 January

1969. Also see Senate Committee on Governmental Affairs, *The Whistleblowers: A Report on Federal Employees Who Disclose Acts of Governmental Waste, Abuse, and Corruption,* 95th Cong., 2d sess., February 1978, p. 6; Fitzgerald, *High Priests,* p. 224.

44. Rasor, *Pentagon,* pp. 154, 207–30; Stewart Toy, "The Defense Scandal," *Business Week,* 4 July 1988, pp. 28–30.

45. John Braithwaite, *Corporate Crime in the Pharmaceutical Industry* (Boston: Routledge & Kegan Paul, 1984), pp. 65–74.

46. Frank Graham, Jr., *Since Silent Spring* (Greenwich, Conn.: Fawcett Publications, 1970), pp. 63–72.

47. Bernard Barber, *The Logic and Limits of Trust* (New Brunswick, N.J.: Rutgers University Press, 1983), pp. 68–100.

48. Mark Hertsgaard, *Nuclear Inc.* (New York: Pantheon Books, 1983), pp. 15–16; Paul Boyer, *By the Bomb's Early Light* (New York: Pantheon Books, 1985), pp. 49–106.

49. Harold L. Rosenberg, *Atomic Soldiers* (Boston: Beacon Press, 1980).

50. Hertsgaard, *Nuclear Inc.,* p. 27.

51. Ibid., p. 33; William C. Wood, *Nuclear Safety: Risks and Regulations* (Washington, D.C.: American Enterprise Institute for Public Policy Research, 1983), pp. 15–16.

52. Hertsgaard, *Nuclear Inc.,* p. 52.

53. Rosenberg, *Atomic Soldiers,* pp. 150–51.

54. Hertsgaard, *Nuclear Inc.,* pp. 49–50.

55. Richard Rashke, *The Killing of Karen Silkwood* (Boston: Houghton Mifflin, 1981). For a critical view of Silkwood, see Nick Thimmesch, "Karen Silkwood Without Tears," *Saturday Evening Post* (November 1979): 14ff.

56. Rashke, *Karen Silkwood,* pp. 120–28.

57. Janet Raloff, "Silkwood—The Legal Fallout," *Science News* 125 (February 4, 1984): 74ff.

58. For a discussion, see Matthew L. Wald, "Troubles Infest System for Making Plutonium," *New York Times,* 14 December 1986, and "Nuclear Arms Plants: A Bill Long Overdue," *New York Times,* 23 October 1988. Section 4.

59. Westin, *Whistle Blowing!,* pp. 39–54.

60. Leslie J. Freeman, *Nuclear Witnesses* (New York: W. W. Norton, 1982), pp. xxiii, 258–68.

61. Ibid., p. 267.

62. Ibid., pp. 279–80; Senate Committee, *Whistleblowers,* pp. 16–18, 324–25. Pollard's concerns were later included in a volume dealing with nuclear plant safety: Robert D. Pollard, ed., *The Nugget File* (Cambridge, Mass.: Union of Concerned Scientists, 1979).

63. Freeman, *Nuclear Witnesses,* p. 281.

64. Vivian Weil, "Moral Responsibility and Whistleblowing in the Nuclear Industry: Browns Ferry and Three Mile Island," in Frederick Elliston, ed., *Conflicting Loyalties in the Workplace* (South Bend, Ind.: University of Notre Dame Press), forthcoming.

65. Jackall, *Moral Mazes,* pp. 118–19.

66. Hertsgaard, *Nuclear Inc.,* p. 4.

67. Todd La Porte and Daniel Metlay, "They Watch and Wonder: Public Attitudes Toward Advanced Technology," Institute of Governmental Studies, University of California, Berkeley, California, December 1975, pp. 323–27.

68. Ellyn R. Weiss, "Three Mile Island: The Loss of Innocence," in Environmental Action Foundation, *Accidents Will Happen* (New York: Harper & Row, 1979), pp. 17–42.

69. David Burnham, "U.S. Orders Construction Halt on Ohio Atom Plant," *New York Times,* 13 November 1982, p. 1; Robert T. Grives, "A $1.6 Billion Nuclear Fiasco," *Time,* 31 October 1983, p. 96.

70. Grives, *Nuclear Fiasco,* pp. 96–97; Geraldine Brooks, "Nuclear Plant Poses Dilemma at Ohio Utility," *Wall Street Journal,* 14 October 1983.

71. Kohn and Kohn, "An Overview," p. 126.

72. See, for example, Charles R. Morris, *A Time of Passion* (New York: Penguin Books, 1986), pp. 143–51; William H. Chafe, *The Unfinished Journey* (New York: Oxford University Press, 1986), pp. 289–301, 388–404.

73. Neil Sheehan, Hedrick Smith, E. W. Kenworthy, and Fox Butterfield, *The Pentagon Papers* (New York: Bantam Books, 1971), p. x.

74. Ibid., p. 308.

75. Interview with Daniel Ellsberg in Charles Peters and Taylor Branch, *Blowing the Whistle* (New York: Praeger, 1972), pp. 248–51; John Stockwell, *In Search of Enemies* (New York: W. W.

Norton, 1978); Victor Marchetti and John D. Marks, *The CIA and the Cult of Intelligence* (New York: Knopf, 1974); Philip Agee, *Inside the Company: CIA Diary* (New York: Stonehill, 1975); Frank Snepp, *Decent Interval* (New York: Random House, 1977).

76. Peters and Branch, *Blowing the Whistle*, pp. 248, 252.

77. Ibid., p. 267.

78. Sheehan et al., *Pentagon Papers*, p. i; Peters and Branch, *Blowing the Whistle*, pp. 238–39; Jonathan Schell, *A Time of Illusion* (New York: Vintage Books, 1976), pp. 151–55. For a collection of pertinent essays, see John C. Merrill and Ralph Barney, eds., *Ethics and the Press* (New York: Hastings House, 1975).

79. Senate Testimony by John W. Dean III, in Jack D. Douglas and John M. Johnson, eds., *Official Deviance* (Philadelphia: J. P. Lippincott, 1977), pp. 109–11; John Dean, *Blind Ambition* (New York: Simon & Schuster, 1976), pp. 277–306.

80. Jack D. Douglas, "Watergate: Harbinger of the American Prince," in Douglas and Johnson, *Official Deviance*, pp. 112–20; for an excellent discussion of the Watergate affair, see Schell, *Time of Illusion*, pp. 309–34.

81. Jim Pope, interview with authors, 5 June 1984.

82. Fitzgerald, *High Priests*. For an insider's view of the Nixon administration's decision to support the air force's firing of Fitzgerald, see Clark R. Mollenhoff, *Game Plan for Disaster* (New York: W. W. Norton, 1976), pp. 65–73. For a discussion of the Carter administration's ineffectiveness in protecting Fitzgerald and other whistleblowers, see idem, *The President Who Failed* (New York: Macmillan, 1980), particularly pp. 147–59.

83. Civil Service Reform Act of 1978, P.L. No. 95–454, 92 Stat. 1111 (1978) (codified in scattered sections of 5 U.S.C.).

84. Rasor, *Pentagon*.

85. The issue of loyalty has been a focal point in the analysis of the whistleblower's dilemma. See Albert O. Hirschman, *Exit, Voice, and Loyalty* (Cambridge, Mass.: Harvard University Press, 1970); Alan F. Westin and Stephan Salisbury, eds., *Individual Rights in the Corporation: A Reader on Employee Rights* (New York: Pantheon Books, 1980); Myron Glazer, "Ten Whistleblowers and How They Fared," *Hastings Center Report* 13 (December 1983): 33–41; Andrew Hacker, "Loyalty and the Whistle Blower," *Across the Board* 15 (November 1979): 4–9, 67; Richard Reeves, "The Last Angry Men," *Esquire*, March 1978, pp. 41–48; Albert Robbins, "Dissent in the Corporate World: When Does an Employee Have the Right to Speak Out?" *Civil Liberties Review* 5 (September/October 1978): 6–10, 15–17; J. Patrick Dobel, "Doing Good by Staying In?" *Public Personnel Management Journal* 11 (Summer 1982): 126–39. Phillip I. Blumberg, "Corporate Responsibility and the Employee's Duty of Loyalty and Obedience: A Preliminary Inquiry," *Oklahoma Law Review* 24 (August 1971): 297–318. For some members of government the price of loyalty is too high. For a comparison of the American and English systems, see Edward Weisband and Thomas M. Frank, *Resignation in Protest* (New York: Grossman, 1975).

Chapter 2. The Legitimation of Public Disclosure

1. Richard Harris, *The Real Voice* (New York: Macmillan, 1964).

2. Console testified twice, once in 1960 and again in 1969. See ibid., pp. 78, 85–86; also Senate Select Committee on Small Business, Hearings before the Subcommittee on Monopoly, Present Status of Competition in the Pharmaceutical Industry, 91st Cong., 1st sess., 26 March 1969, part II pp. 4477–4506; Ralph Nader, Peter J. Petkas, and Kate Blackwell, eds., *Whistle Blowing* (New York: Bantam, 1972), pp. 118–25.

3. Nader, Petkas, and Blackwell, *Whistle Blowing*, pp. 12–19.

4. James Boyd, *Above the Law* (New York: New American Library, 1968).

5. Peter Maas, *Serpico* (New York: Viking, 1973).

6. David Burnham, "Graft Paid to Police Said to Run into Millions," *New York Times*, 25 April 1970.

7. New York City, *The Knapp Commission Report on Police Corruption* (New York: George Braziller, 1973).

8. Barbara Gelb, *The Varnished Brass: The Decade after Serpico* (New York: G. P. Putnam, 1983).

9. Senate Committee on Governmental Affairs, The Whistleblowers: A Report on Federal Employees Who Disclose Acts of Governmental Waste, Abuse, and Corruption, 95th Cong., 2d sess., February 1978, p. 6.

10. Among the important works studying the rise and impact of whistleblowing are: Nader, Petkas, and Blackwell, *Whistle Blowing;* Alan Westin, ed., *Whistle Blowing! Loyalty and Dissent in the Corporation* (New York: McGraw-Hill, 1981); Charles Peters and Taylor Branch, *Blowing the Whistle* (New York: Praeger, 1972); Robert M. Anderson, Robert Perucci, Dan D. Schendel, and Leon E. Tractman, *Divided Loyalties: Whistle-Blowing at BART* (West Lafayette, Ind.: Purdue University Press, 1980); Greg Mitchell, *Truth . . . and Consequences* (New York: Dembner Books, 1981); David E. Ewing, *Do It My Way or You're Fired: Employee Rights and the Changing Role of Management Prerogatives* (New York: John Wiley, 1983); Frederick Elliston, John Keenan, Paula Lockhart, and Jane van Schaick, *Whistleblowing: Managing Dissent in the Workplace* (New York: Praeger, 1985).

11. Nader, et al., *Whistle Blowing,* p. 119.

12. Senate Select Committee on Small Business, p. 4496.

13. Letter from Mrs. A. Dale Console to authors, 11 August 1982.

14. Ibid.

15. Ibid.

16. Quoted in Nader, Petkas, and Blackwell, *Whistle Blowing,* p. 123.

17. Ray H. Hilling, "The Political Economy of International Health with a Focus on the Capitalist World-System," in Michael Lewis, ed., *Social Problems and Public Policy,* vol. II (Greenwich, Conn.: JAI Press, 1982), pp. 97–148.

18. John Braithwaite, *Corporate Crime in the Pharmaceutical Industry* (Boston: Routledge & Kegan Paul, 1984), pp. 165, 224, 227, 255.

19. Boyd, *Above the Law,* pp. 79–86.

20. Marjorie Carpenter, interview with authors, 17 July 1984.

21. James Boyd, interview with authors, 17 July 1984.

22. Boyd, *Above the Law,* p. 116.

23. William V. Shannon, "Prelude to Censure," *New York Times Book Review,* 31 March 1968, pp. 12ff.

24. Boyd, interview with authors.

25. Boyd, *Above the Law,* pp. 130–40; Drew Pearson and Jack Anderson, *The Case Against Congress* (New York: Simon & Schuster, 1968), part I.

26. Carpenter, interview with authors.

27. See, for example, "The Acceptance Factor," *Time,* 6 May 1966, pp. 23–24.

28. Senate Select Committee on Standards and Conduct, Report on the Investigation of Senator Thomas J. Dodd of Connecticut to Accompany S. Res. 112. 90th Cong., 1st sess., 1967, Report No. 193; "Senate Censures Dodd for Misuse of Political Funds," *Congressional Quarterly Almanac,* 90th Cong., 1st sess., 1967, vol. XXIII, 239–55. For a summary of how the Dodd case, among others, led to the enactment of a code of ethics for the U.S. Senate, see Bruce Jennings, "The Institutionalization of Ethics in the U.S. Senate," *Hastings Center Report* 11 (February 1981): 5–9.

29. Boyd, *Above the Law,* p. 302.

30. "Revising the U.S. Senate Code of Ethics, A Special Supplement," *The Hastings Center Report* 11 (February 1981): 1–28. For a set of essays on many aspects of legislative ethics, see Bruce Jennings and Daniel Callahan, *Representation and Responsibility* (New York: Plenum Press, 1985).

31. Robert Yoakum, "Alive and Well in Washington," *The New Republic,* 10 February 1968, 23–28; Shannon, "Prelude to Censure," 12ff.

32. Boyd, *Above the Law,* pp. 264–66.

33. Ibid., p. 267.

34. See Joel L. Fleishman, "The Disclosure Model and Its Limitations," *Hastings Center Report* 11 (February 1981): 15–17.

35. Maas, *Serpico,* p. 297.

36. Knapp Commission Report, pp. 1–3.

37. William A. Westley, "Secrecy of the Police," *Social Forces* 34 (March 1956): 254–57.

38. Lawrence W. Sherman, "Becoming Bent: Moral Careers of Corrupt Policemen," in Lawrence W. Sherman, ed., *Police Corruption* (Garden City, N.Y.: Doubleday, 1974), pp. 191–208.

39. Rupert Wilkinson, *American Tough: The Tough-Guy Tradition and American Character* (New York: Harper & Row, 1984).

40. Bob Ellis, interview with authors, 27 June 1984.

41. Robert Daley, *Prince of the City* (New York: Houghton Mifflin, 1978), pp. 17–22.

42. Bob Leuci, interview with authors, 12 March 1982; conversations and telephone calls, 1982–88.

43. For a severe critique of Leuci, see Alan M. Dershowitz, *The Best Defense* (New York: Random House, 1982), pp. 321–83.

44. Leuci, interview with authors.

45. Daley, *Prince of the City;* the movie of the same title was released in 1981.

46. Gelb, *Varnished Brass.*

47. Ralph Nader, *Unsafe at Any Speed* (New York: Grossman Publishers, 1965); Thomas White-side, *The Investigation of Ralph Nader* (New York: Arbor House, 1972).

48. Charles McCarry, *Citizen Nader* (New York: Saturday Review Press, 1972), pp. xii–xiii, 186–211.

49. Ibid. Nader and his associates published, among others, books on old age, water pollution, corruption in Congress, and defective automobiles.

50. Nader, Petkas, and Blackwell, *Whistle Blowing.*

51. Inderjit Badhwar, "GAP Right for the Times," *Federal Times,* 12 June 1978, p. 9.

52. Unpublished transcript, June 1977; shortly after, Louis Clark, then staff attorney for GAP, published an article on GAP's views on whistleblowing, "The Sound of Professional Suicide," *Barrister,* Summer 1978, pp. 10–13f.

53. Louis Clark, conversation with authors, 6 April 1988.

54. See, for example, Paul Roberts, "Callaway Plant Inquiry Draws Mixed Reviews," *Columbia Daily Tribune,* Columbia, Mo., 11 March 1984; Julie Morrison, "Consumers, GAP Vie for Public Opinion," *Midland Daily News,* Midland, Mich., 14 March 1984; Cindy Skrzycki, "A Whistle Blower's Voice," *Fort-Worth Star-Telegram,* 27 February 1983. GAP has been accused by its opponents of taking an antinuclear stand. See Rael Jean Isaac, "Games Anti-Nukes Play," *The American Spectator* (November 1985): pp. 12–16.

55. For a discussion of the Project on Military Procurement, see Francis X. Clines, "Perhaps the Pentagon's Enemy No. 1," *New York Times,* 27 March 1985.

56. Senate Commitee on Governmental Affairs, Establishment of Offices of Inspector and Auditor General in Certain Executive Departments and Agencies, 95th Cong., 2d sess., 1978. For a discussion of the Inspectors General offices, see Frederick Elliston, John Keenan, Paula Lockhart, and Jane van Schaick, *Whistleblowing Research* (New York: Praeger Publishers, 1985), pp. 109–12.

57. P.L. 95–452; Senate Committee on Governmental Affairs, Establishment of Offices of Inspector and Auditor General, pp. 35–37.

58. Ibid., pp. 36–37.

59. Elliston et al., *Whistleblowing Research,* pp. 106–9; Civil Service Reform Act, 5 U.S.C. 2302; Stephen M. Kohn and Michael D. Kohn, "An Overview of Federal and State Whistleblower Protections," *Antioch Law Journal* (Summer 1986): 104–5.

60. A Report of the U.S. Merit Systems Protection Board, Office of Merit Systems Review and Studies, *Whistleblowing and the Federal Employee* (Washington, D.C.: U.S. Government Printing Office, 1981), pp. 43–47; John M. Palguta, "Federal Agency Mechanisms That Encourage Dissent," *IEEE Technology and Society Magazine* 3 (September 1985): 23–30.

61. Elliston et al., *Whistleblowing Research,* pp. 99–102; Kohn and Kohn, "An Overview," pp. 107–12; Alfred G. Feliu, "Discharge of Professional Employees: Protecting Against Dismissal for Acts Within a Professional Code of Ethics," *Columbia Human Rights Law Review,* 11 (Fall–Winter 1979–80): 149–87.

62. Kohn and Kohn, "An Overview," pp. 102–6.

63. Ibid., pp. 107–11.

Chapter 3. Professionals as Ethical Resisters

1. Several important interpretations of the professionalization process are: Magali S. Larson, *The Rise of Professionalism* (Berkeley: University of California Press, 1977); J. A. Jackson, ed., *Professions and Professionalization* (Cambridge: Cambridge University Press, 1970); Burton Bledstein, *The Culture of Professionalism* (New York: W. W. Norton, 1976), esp. chap. 3; Bernard Barber, "Control

and Responsibility in the Powerful Professions," *Political Science Quarterly* 93 (Winter 1978): 599–615. For a discussion of several professions, see "The Public Duties of the Professions," *Hastings Center Report Special Supplement* 17 (February 1987): 1–20; Albert Flores, ed., *Professional Ideals* (Belmont, Calif.: Wadsworth, 1988); Michael D. Bayles, *Professional Ethics* (Belmont, Calif.: Wadsworth, 1981).

2. Rosemary Stevens, *Medicine and the Public Interest* (New Haven: Yale University Press, 1971); Eliot Freidson, *Profession of Medicine* (New York: Dodd, Mead, 1972), pp. 82–84, 359–82; Penina Migdal Glazer and Miriam Slater, *Unequal Colleagues* (New Brunswick, N.J.: Rutgers University Press, 1987), pp. 227–31.

3. Paul Starr, *The Social Transformation of American Medicine* (New York: Basic Books, 1982), pp. 3–29, 351.

4. Freidson, *Profession of Medicine*, pp. 29–30.

5. Glazer and Slater, *Unequal Colleagues*, pp. 224–27; Jerold S. Auerbach, *Unequal Justice* (New York: Oxford University Press, 1976), p. 61.

6. Freidson, *Profession of Medicine*, pp. 359–82; Larson, *Rise of Professionalism*, p. 56; Starr, *Social Transformation*, pp. 299–306.

7. Glazer and Slater, *Unequal Colleagues*, pp. 229–31.

8. John H. Ehrenreich, *The Altruistic Imagination: A History of Social Work and Social Policy in the United States* (Ithaca, N.Y.: Cornell University Press, 1985), deals with the growth of bureaucratic controls in the social work profession.

9. Freidson, *Profession of Medicine*, p. 88.

10. Ralph Nader, Peter J. Petkas, and Kate Blackwell, eds., *Whistle Blowing* (New York: Bantam, 1972), p. 121.

11. Joseph Rose, telephone interview with authors, 10 July 1982.

12. Deena Weinstein, *Bureaucratic Opposition* (New York: Pergamon, 1979), esp. pp. 36–52.

13. Frank von Hippel, "Protecting the Whistleblowers," *Physics Today* (October 1977): 8–13; Kenneth T. Bogen, "Managing Technical Dissent in Private Industry: Societal and Corporate Strategies for Dealing with Whistle-blowing Professionals," *Industrial and Labor Relations Forum* 13 (1979): 3–32; Stephen H. Unger, *Controlling Technology: Ethics and the Responsible Engineer* (New York: Holt, Rinehart & Winston, 1982); Stephen H. Unger, "Would Helping Ethical Professionals Get Societies Into Trouble?" *IEEE Technology and Society Magazine* (September 1987): 17–21. For a discussion warning auditors about the dangers of exposing corporate illegality, see Gil Courtemanche, "The Ethics of Whistle Blowing," *Internal Auditor* (February 1988): 36–41. For a strong rejoinder drawing upon his own experiences, see the response by Arthur L. Suchodolski in the letters column in *Internal Auditor* (April 1988): 4, 6; Arthur L. Suchodolski blew the whistle in 1976. He is discussed by Alan Westin in *Whistle Blowing!* (New York: McGraw-Hill, 1981), pp. 83–94.

14. Demetrios Basdekas, interview with authors, 3 June 1984; phone conversations and correspondence, 1984–88.

15. Ibid.

16. Ibid.

17. Ibid.

18. Mark Hertsgaard, *Nuclear Inc.* (New York: Pantheon Books, 1983), pp. 50–51.

19. Ibid., 51; William C. Wood, *Nuclear Safety: Risks and Regulation* (Washington, D.C.: American Enterprise Institute for Public Policy Research, 1983), pp. 14–19.

20. Hertsgaard, *Nuclear Inc.*, pp. 51–52.

21. Ibid., p. 69. For a pro-nuclear point of view, see Irvin C. Bupp and Jean-Claude Derian, *Light Water* (New York: Basic Books, 1978), pp. 3–11, 132–36.

22. Rita Basdekas, interview with authors, 3 June 1984.

23. For an astute analysis of the concept of trust, see Bernard Barber, *The Logic and Limits of Trust* (New Brunswick, N.J.: Rutgers University Press, 1983), particularly pp. 1–25.

24. D. Basdekas, interview with authors.

25. Hertsgaard, *Nuclear Inc.*, pp. 53–55. For another discussion of safety in the civilian reactor program, see Elizabeth S. Ralph, *Nuclear Power and the Public Safety* (Lexington, Mass.: D.C. Heath, 1979), pp. 21–29.

26. Hertsgaard, *Nuclear Inc.*, pp. 53–55, 86–95.

27. D. Basdekas, interview with authors.

28. Stanley Milgram, *Obedience to Authority* (New York: Harper & Row, 1974), p. 6.

29. D. Basdekas, interview with authors.

30. Hearing before the Senate Committee on Government Operations, Nuclear Regulatory Commission's Safety and Licensing Procedures, 94th Cong., 2d sess., 13 December 1976, 161–65. The issue of autonomy is central to the responsible actions of whistleblowers. For a discussion of this issue and its significance in the education of children, see Constance Kamii, "Autonomy: The Aim of Education Envisioned by Piaget," *Phi Delta Kappan* 65 (February 1984): 410–15. Whistleblowers often invoke their values and act upon them despite the rational calculation that they may pay a price. "Absolute ends" and "affectual sentiments" take priority over immediate self-interest. Deena Weinstein, "Bureaucratic Opposition: The Challenge to Authoritarian Abuses at the Workplace," *Canadian Journal of Political and Social Theory* 1 (Spring–Summer 1977): 38.

31. Milgram, *Obedience*, p. 10.

32. Leslie J. Freeman, *Nuclear Witnesses* (New York: W. W. Norton, 1982), pp. 258–92.

33. D. Basdekas, interview with authors.

34. For the testimony of Ronald M. Fluegge, a colleague of Basdekas, see Senate Committee on Governmental Affairs, *The Whistleblowers: A Report on Federal Employees Who Disclose Acts of Governmental Waste, Abuse, and Corruption*, 95th Cong., 2d sess., February 1978, 327–32. For further discussion of the responsibilities of engineers and engineering societies, see Rosemary Chalk, "Ethical Dilemmas in Modern Engineering," *Technology and Society* 9 (March 1981): 1, 8–12. Albert Flores, "The Professional Rights of Engineers," *Technology and Society* (December 1980): 3–18. Albert Flores, "Engineers' Professional Rights," *Engineering Issues* 106 (October 1980): 389–96. Vivian Weil, ed., *Beyond Whistle-Blowing* (Chicago: Illinois Institute of Technology, 1983).

35. Milgram, *Obedience*, p. 121.

36. Public Meeting, Nuclear Regulatory Commission, Briefing on Pressurized Thermal Shock, 4 May 1982, pp. 100, 119; Basdekas's concerns were clearly delineated in an Op-Ed article: Demetrios L. Basdekas, "The Risk of a Meltdown," *New York Times*, 29 March 1982. For a rejoinder by Denwood F. Ross, Jr., deputy director, Office of Nuclear Regulatory Research, N.R.C., see *New York Times*, 8 April 1982. For an exchange between Basdekas and Nunzio J. Palladino, chairman of the N.R.C., see *New York Times*, 22 May 1985.

37. Nuclear Regulatory Commission, Briefing of Chairman John F. Ahearne, Washington, D.C., 17 December 1979, p. 14.

38. Dr. Mary McAnaw, interview with authors, 21 October 1984.

39. Starr, *Transformation*, pp. 348, 351.

40. McAnaw, interview with authors.

41. Ibid.

42. Dr. Arthur Shaw, interview with authors, 20 October 1984.

43. An excellent history appears in James H. Jones, *Bad Blood* (New York: Free Press, 1981). For a discussion of the use and abuse of subjects in other forms of behaviorial research, see Bernard Barber, "The Ethics of Experimentation with Human Subjects," *Scientific American* 234 (February 1976): 25–31; Stanley Milgram, "Subject Reaction in Social Psychology: The Neglected Ethical Factor," *Hastings Center Report* 7 (October 1977): 19–23 (the *Hastings Center Report* frequently covers the work of ethics committees dealing with both clinical and research issues); Myron Glazer, "Controlling Ourselves: Deviant Behavior in Social Science Research," in Michael Lewis, ed., *Research in Social Problems and Public Policy* (Greenwich, Conn.: JAI Press, 1979), pp. 43–64.

44. Dr. Mike Brigg, interview with authors, 21 October 1984.

45. Weinstein, *Bureaucratic Opposition*, pp. 59–60.

46. McAnaw, interview with authors.

47. Robert Klein, *Wounded Men, Broken Promises* (New York: Macmillan, 1981), pp. 21–22.

48. William A. Gamson, Bruce Fireman, and Steven Rytina, *Encounters with Unjust Authority* (Homewood, Ill.: Dorsey Press, 1982), pp. 113, 124.

49. Dr. Betsy Brothers, interview with authors, 21 October 1984; telephone conversations and correspondence, 1984–88.

50. Ibid.

51. M. E. Brothers, M.D., to Allan Reynolds, Inspector General of the Veterans Administration, 1 August 1980.

52. Shaw, interview with authors.

53. Ibid.

54. W. J. Jacoby, Jr., M.D., to Honorable Bob Dole, undated 1981. For a discussion of the conflict, see Keith Sinzinger, "Nightmare in Leavenworth," *Federal Times*, 1 November 1982.

55. John Petterson, "Judge's Ruling Places Limits on VA Surgeon's Bias Suit," *Kansas City Times,* 1 July 1983; Ron Ostroff, "Transferred VA Doctor Assigned To Surgery Staff in Surprise Move," *Kansas City Times,* 2 April 1983.

56. Dr. Betsy Brothers, telephone interview with authors, 15 April 1988.

57. Dr. Betsy Brothers, letter to authors, 26 June 1988.

58. In addition to our own interview, the case of Dr. Grace Pierce has been recorded in Westin, *Whistle Blowing!* pp. 107–17.

59. Dr. Grace Pierce, interview with authors, 14 August 1982.

60. Ibid.

61. Alfred G. Feliu, "Discharge of Professional Employees: Protecting Against Dismissal for Acts Within a Professional Code of Ethics," *Columbia Human Rights Law Review* 11 (Fall–Winter 1979–80): esp. 186–87.

62. Stephen M. Kohn and Michael D. Kohn, "An Overview of Federal and State Whistleblower Protections," *Antioch Law Journal* 4 (Summer 1986): 107–8.

Chapter 4. The Power of Belief Systems for Ethical Resisters

1. Bert Berube, interview with authors, 5 June 1984; telephone conversations and correspondence, 1984–88.

2. Pat Berube, interview with authors, 18 July 1984; telephone conversations, 1984–88.

3. B. Berube, interview with authors.

4. Ibid.

5. Ibid.

6. Ibid.

7. Ibid.

8. Ibid.

9. Robert Jackall, *Moral Mazes* (New York: Oxford University Press, 1988), p.6.

10. David W. Ewing, *Do It My Way or You're Fired!* (New York: John Wiley, 1983), pp.202–10.

11. Senate Committee on Governmental Affairs, *GSA Contract Fraud Investigation,* Hearings before the Subcommittee on Federal Spending Practices and Open Government, 95th Cong., 2d sess., 23 June 1978, pp. 133–43.

12. Memo to Chuck Lewis for ABC's "20/20" from Louis Clark, 28 January 1981.

13. Senate Committee on Governmental Affairs, pp. 168–69; letter from Louis Clark to David A. Stockman, 13 February 1981. The efforts of Jay Solomon to root out GSA corruption is discussed in Clark Mollenhoff, *The President Who Failed* (New York: Macmillan, 1980), pp. 134–46; for an analytical account of corruption in government, see Jerome B. McKinney, "Viewing Fraud, Waste and Abuse in Government," in James S. Bowman and Frederick A. Elliston, eds., *Ethics, Government and Public Policy* (Westport, Conn.: Greenwood Press, forthcoming).

14. Clark to Stockman; also Berube, interview with authors.

15. James Crawford, "Former 'Hero' at GSA Now Rides Toboggan," *Federal Times,* 4 July 1983.

16. Bertrand Berube to deputy administrator, General Services Administration, 16 May 1983.

17. Crawford, "Former 'Hero' "; also James Crawford, "GSA Regional Chief Backs Berube Claims," *Federal Times,* 26 March 1984.

18. Crawford, "Former 'Hero.' " Several articles appeared in the Washington newspapers in 1983 and 1984 citing reports showing negligent maintenance, as Berube had charged: see, for example, Myron Struck, "Study of Archives Finds 567 Hazards and Deficiencies," *Washington Post,* 27 October 1983; Gene Goltz, "GSA Maintenance Termed Negligent," *Washington Times,* 16 August 1983.

19. B. Berube, interview with authors.

20. P. Berube, interview with authors.

21. B. Berube, interview with authors.

22. Ibid.

23. P. Berube, interview with authors.

24. Mark Price, interview with authors, 15 June 1984; telephone conversations and correspondence, 1984–88.

25. Ibid.

26. Judy Jones and Alice Allred Pottmyer, "Whistleblower," *Utah Holiday*, July 1987, p. 21.

27. Bill Lambrecht, "Misconduct Alleged As Illinois Battles for School Cash," *St. Louis Post-Dispatch*, 1 April 1984. The inspector general's report criticizing the appeals board is also referred to in a memorandum from Price's superior to Earl Ingram, director, Equal Employment Opportunity Office, 20 December 1983.

28. Memorandum of Agreement, Mark Price v. U.S. Department of Education, 30 January 1984.

29. Ruth Marlow, "Ex-Education Attorney, Now in Jail, to Get 'Patriot' Award," *Federal Times*, 13 October 1986; memorandum from Price's former superior to Ingram.

30. Price, interview with authors, 15 June 1984; also Mark Price, affidavit, Washington, D.C., 30 January 1984. The same kinds of charges are made in Illinois State Board of Education and Board of Education of the City of Chicago District 200 v. Terrell H. Bell, James B. Thomas, U.S. Department of Education, Hunter Harrison, U.S. Department of Education, and David S. Pollen, Case no. 84-0337, filed 31 January 1984; also appears in affidavit of Mark Price, 84-0337, 8 June 1984.

31. Price, interview with authors. Similar charges of politicized unfair conduct are stated in an affidavit by David Rich, assistant attorney general for the State of Arizona, 9 April 1984.

32. Price, interview with authors.

33. Ibid.

34. Ibid.; also Jones and Pottmyer, "Whistleblower," p. 40; Mark Urry Price v. Terrell H. Bell, A. Wayne Roberts, Thomas J. Burns, David S. Pollen, Richard I. Slippen, verified complaint before the Office of Special Counsel, Merit Systems Protection Board, District of Columbia, 22 February 1984.

35. Price, interview with authors.

36. Lambrecht, "Misconduct Alleged," 1 April 1984; Jones and Pottmyer, "Whistleblower," pp. 37–39.

37. Price, interview with authors.

38. Jackall, *Moral Mazes*, pp. 109–10. The issue of management decision making is also dealt with by J. Scott Armstrong, "Social Irresponsibility in Management," *Journal of Business Research* 5 (September 1977): 185–213. For a review of the literature that confirms the development and reinforcement of "moral numbness," see James W. Coleman, *The Criminal Elite* (New York: St. Martin's Press, 1985), pp. 212–17. For an insightful analysis of the pressure to conform in government service, see J. Patrick Dobel, "Doing Good by Staying In?" *Public Personnel Management Journal* 11 (Summer 1982): 126–39.

39. Jackall, *Moral Mazes*, p. 110. There is substantial literature on the issue of corporate ethics, responsibility, and ideology. For a fine recent collection of essays, see S. Prakash Sethi and Cecilia M. Falbe, eds., *Business and Society* (Lexington, Mass.: Lexington Books, 1987). The articles in that volume by Michael Novak, "Toward a Theology of the Corporation," pp. 1–21, and Gerald F. Cavanagh, "Values and Morality in Corporate America," pp. 21–38, merit special attention. Other pertinent writings on these issues include: Jerome H. Skolnick and Elliot Curie, eds., *Crisis in American Institutions* (Glenview, Ill.: Scott, Foresman, 1988); Richard T. DeGeorge and Joseph A. Pickler, eds., *Ethics, Free Enterprise, and Public Policy* (New York: Oxford University Press, 1978); Thomas Donaldson, *Corporations and Morality* (Englewood Cliffs, N.J.: Prentice-Hall, 1982); Norman Bowie, *Business Ethics* (Englewood Cliffs, N.J.: Prentice-Hall, 1982); Joseph R. Des Jardins and John M. McCall, *Contemporary Issues in Business Ethics* (Belmont, Cal.: Wadsworth, 1985); and Tom L. Beauchamp, *Case Studies in Business, Society and Ethics* (Englewood Cliffs, N.J.: Prentice-Hall, 1983).

40. Illinois State Board of Education and Board of Education of the City of Chicago District No. 200 v. Terrell H. Bell et al.

41. Price, interview with authors.

42. Donald G. Gill to Honorable William French Smith, Attorney General of the United States, 12 April 1984.

43. Eugene M. Daly, telephone interview with authors, June 1988.

44. Settlement Agreement, Illinois State Board of Education v. William J. Bennett, Secretary of Education et al., 84-0337, 1986.

45. Price, interview with authors; Jones and Pottmyer, "Whistleblower," p. 28.

46. Gary Hanna to Mark Price, 17 April 1984.

47. Price, interview with authors; Jones and Pottmyer, "Whistleblower," pp. 29–30.

48. Judge Quin S. Elson, transcript of Proceedings before U.S. District Court, Eastern District of Virginia, 24 September 1984, p. 88.

49. Bill Lambrecht, "Whistle-Blower Imprisoned on Misdemeanors," *St. Louis Post-Dispatch*, 10 September 1986; Marlow, "Ex-Education Attorney." The activities of psychiatrists in organizational settings that could lead to conflicting loyalties were explored in detail in a symposium sponsored by The Hastings Center: "In the Service of the State: The Psychiatrist as Double Agent," *The Hastings Center Report*, A Special Supplement 8 (April 1978): 1–23.

50. Jones and Pottmyer, "Whistleblower," p. 35; letter from Mark Price to Bernard S. Grimm (public defender), 16 August 1986.

51. Jones and Pottmyer, "Whistleblower," p. 35.

52. Lambrecht, "Whistle-Blower Imprisoned"; Marlow, "Ex-Education Attorney"; Jones and Pottmyer, "Whistleblower," pp. 35–36.

53. Jones and Pottmyer, "Whistleblower," p. 26; Bill Lambrecht, "Education Agency Replaces Officer Assailed by Illinois," *St. Louis Post-Dispatch*, 18 November 1984.

54. Price, interview with authors.

55. Ibid.

56. Ibid.

57. David S. Pollen v. Mark U. Price, Stipulation of Settlement, Civil Action 84-0892, U.S. District Court, District of Columbia, 2 February 1988.

58. Criminal Case 48517, State of Maryland, 25 April 1988.

59. Dr. Zalman Magid, interview with authors, 10 April 1988; correspondence and telephone calls, 1986–88.

60. Ibid.

61. Ibid.

62. Ibid.

63. Material prepared by Rabbi Jeffrey Wohlgelerntner, Congregation Adat Jeshurun, La Jolla, California, at the request of Dr. Zalman Magid and the authors, October 1987.

64. Robert N. Bellah, Richard Madsen, William M. Sullivan, Ann Swidler, and Steven M. Tipton, *Habits of the Heart* (New York: Harper & Row, 1985), pp. 63–65; Charles E. Silberman, *A Certain People* (New York: Summit Books, 1985), pp. 177–81.

65. The importance of community has long been emphasized by social science researchers; for an excellent study, see Kai T. Erikson, *Everything in Its Path* (New York: Simon & Schuster, 1976).

66. For a discussion of the absence of the concept of the common good in modern society, see Manfred Stanley, "The Mystery of the Commons: On the Indispensability of Civic Rhetoric," *Social Research* 50 (Winter 1983): 851–83.

67. 10 CFR 2.206 Petition of Government Accountability Project on behalf of nuclear workers and Citizens Association for Sound Energy (CASE), filed 19 March 1984 with the Nuclear Regulatory Commission, and attached affidavits of disclosure.

68. Dobie Hatley, interview with authors, 23 August 1984; telephone conversations, 1984–88.

69. Cass Peterson, "In the War on Drugs, You Don't Always Win the Medal of Honor," *Washington Post*, National Weekly Edition, 20 October 1986; also Representative Edward J. Markey, "Drug and Alcohol Use at the Seabrook Nuclear Power Plant," U.S. House of Representatives, January 1988.

70. Bob Messerly, interview with authors, 24 August 1984.

71. See newspaper articles regarding testimony of Charles Atchison to the Atomic Safety and Licensing Board, *Dallas Times Herald* and *Dallas Morning News*. Mary Barrineau, "Blowing the Whistle," *Dallas Times Herald*, Westward Section, 9 January 1983.

72. Victor Gilinsky, "Comanche Peak Licensing Delay," A Report to Brazos Electric Power Cooperative Tex-La Electric Cooperative of Texas, 15 February 1988; Report of Texas Utilities to the Nuclear Regulatory Commission on 10CFR50.55E, 11 February 1988.

73. Hatley, interview with authors.

74. Ibid.

75. Ibid.

76. Testimony of Frank Strand, 12 February 1985, deposition in Hatley v. Brown and Root, 84-ERA-23.

77. Department of Labor complaint and affidavit of Sue Neumeyer, 16 March 1984, and March 1984 affidavit to the NRC.

78. Sue Neumeyer, interview with authors, 25 August 1984.

79. Ibid.

80. Stan Miles, interview with authors, 24 August 1984.

81. Neumeyer, telephone interview with authors, 12 July 1988; Miles, telephone interview with authors, 20 June 1988.

82. Juanita Ellis, founder of Citizens Association for Sound Energy, interview with authors, 22 August 1984. Ellis has dedicated almost a decade to the struggle against the nuclear plant.

83. Report of Texas Utilities to NRC on 10CFR50.55E; Gilinsky, "Comanche Peak Licensing Delay."

Chapter 5. Retaliation: Management's Effort to Destroy the Ethical Resister

1. Linda Rose, interview with authors, 26 August 1984.

2. Vincent Laubach, interview with authors, 3 June 1984.

3. The issue of retaliation is discussed in most of the major sources on whistleblowing (see chap. 2, note 10). For some particularly relevant articles on retaliation, see Marcia A. Parmerlee, Janet P. Near, and Tamila C. Jensen, "Correlates of Whistleblowers' Perceptions of Organizational Retaliation," *Administrative Science Quarterly* 27(1982):17–34; The U.S. Merit Systems Protection Board, *Whistle Blowing and the Federal Employee* (Washington, D.C.: U.S. Government Printing Office, October 1981). For some popular sources, see Clyde Farnsworth, "Survey of Whistle Blowers Finds Retaliation but Few Regrets," *New York Times,* 22 February 1987; Don Oldenburg, "Whistle Blower's Anguish," *Washington Post,* 31 March 1987; N. R. Kleinfeld, "The Whistle Blowers' Morning After," *New York Times,* 9 November 1986, Business Section.

4. Dr. Anthony Morris, letter to authors, 13 November 1985.

5. Karen L. Soeken and Donald R. Soeken, "A Survey of Whistleblowers: Their Stressors and Coping Strategies," in Senate Committee on Governmental Affairs, Hearings on S.508 before Subcommittee on Federal Services, Post Office, and Civil Service, 100th Cong., 1st sess., 20 and 31 July 1987, pp. 537–48. For an insightful and general account of repression in American society, see Alan Wolfe, *The Seamy Side of Democracy* (New York: Longman, 1978).

6. For a discussion of how "mutual pretense" safeguards the social order, see Myra Bluebond-Langer, *The Private Worlds of Dying Children* (Princeton: Princeton University Press, 1978), pp. 198–230. The continuation of self-deception is often dependent on mutual pretense and insulates leadership from the consequences of their decisions. The results are often disastrous, as in Lyndon Johnson's policies in Vietnam. J. Patrick Dobel, "Doing Good by Staying In?" *Public Personnel Management Journal* 11 (Summer 1982): 126–39.

7. Kaufman's battle with the bureaucracy began in the mid-1970s and intensified during the early Reagan years. For a thorough account of Kaufman's early confrontations, see Greg Mitchell, *Truth . . . and Consequences* (New York: Dembner Books, 1981), pp. 267–312. Kaufman's later battles and vindication are recorded in the press: see, for example, David Burnham, "Paper Chase of a Whistle-Blower," *New York Times,* 16 October 1982; Cass Peterson, "A Nagging Voice from EPA Depths Now Singing from the Catbird Seat," *Washington Post,* 14 February 1983; Maureen Dowd, "Extra! Extra! Extra! Shredder Update," *Time,* 28 February 1983.

8. Richard Campbell, interview with authors, 19 June 1983. Mr. Campbell's affidavit (15 December 1982) attests to the facts.

9. Hugh Kaufman, interview and telephone conversations with authors, June 1983.

10. Myron Peretz Glazer and Penina Migdal Glazer, "This Witness Must Be Destroyed: The Fate of Whistleblowers in Government and Industry," in James S. Bowman and Frederick A. Elliston, eds., *Ethics, Government, and Public Policy* (Westport, Conn.: Greenwood Press, forthcoming).

11. For a functionalist approach to the study of social issues, see Robert K. Merton, *Social Theory and Social Structure* (Glencoe, Ill.: Free Press, 1957), pp. 19–84.

12. See Victor Navasky, *Naming Names* (New York: Viking, 1980); William H. Chafe, *The Unfinished Journey* (New York: Oxford University Press, 1986), pp. 130–33; Nancy Lynn Schwartz, *The Hollywood Writers' Wars* (New York: Alfred A. Knopf, 1982).

13. For a discussion of anger, its derivatives and consequences, see Willard Gaylin, *The Rage Within* (New York: Simon & Schuster, 1984).

14. David Peretz, "Reaction to Loss," in Bernard Schoenberg, Arthur C. Carr, David Peretz, and Austin H. Kutscher, eds., *Loss and Grief: Psychological Management in Medical Practice* (New York: Columbia University Press, 1970), pp. 20–35.

15. In addition to our discussion, the Rose case is examined in Alan F. Westin, *Whistle Blowing! Loyalty and Dissent in the Corporation* (New York: McGraw-Hill, 1981), pp. 31–38. The legal problems of the Associated Milk Producers are presented by the Watergate prosecutor Leon Jaworski, *The Right and the Power* (New York: Reader's Digest Press, 1976), pp. 17, 260, 263–64, 267–68.

16. Linda Rose, interview with authors, 26 August 1984.

17. Joseph Rose, telephone interview with authors, 10 July 1982; interview, 26 August 1984; additional telephone calls and correspondence, 1984–88.

18. Ibid.

19. Ibid.

20. Ibid.

21. Ibid.

22. Ibid.

23. See Jaworski, *The Right and the Power,* pp. 263, 287.

24. L. Rose, interview with authors.

25. Frederick Elliston, "Anonymous Whistleblowing: An Ethical Analysis," *Business and Professional Ethics* 1 (Winter 1982): 39–59.

26. NRC Inspection Report no. 82-14, issued 29 September 1982.

27. Ibid.

28. Charles A. Atchison v. Brown & Root, Inc., Department of Labor Case no. 82-ELA-9, Recommended Decision (3 December 1982) and Decision and Final Order (10 June 1983); Brown & Root, Inc. v. Raymond J. Donovan, U.S. Court of Appeals, Fifth Circuit, no. 83-4486 (29 December 1984).

29. Deposition of Robert R. Taylor, "Texas Utilities Electric et al., before the Atomic Safety & Licensing Board, Nuclear Regulatory Commission (17 June 1984).

30. Chuck Atchison, interview with authors, 23 August 1984.

31. Mary Barrineau, "Blowing the Whistle," *Dallas Times Herald,* 9 January 1983, Westward Section.

32. Barrineau, "Blowing the Whistle," p. 8.

33. Charles A. Atchison v. Tompkins-Beckwith, Inc., Department of Labor Case no. 82-ERA-12, 22 February 1985.

34. Atchison, interview with authors.

35. Adam Condo, "Whistleblower Says Officials Apathetic," *Cincinnati Post,* 10 March 1987, p. 5B; Anne Laurent, "Hill Seeks Probe into Charges by Fired VA Whistleblower," *Federal Times,* 30 March 1987, pp. 2, 18; Jack Anderson and Joseph Spear, "Complaints About VA Police Official Grow," *Washington Post,* 2 June 1987.

36. "Gore Letter Urges FBI to Investigate N-Worker's Death," *Tennessean,* 10 October 1985, p. 4; Neil Karlen and Ginny Carroll, "Nuclear-Powered Murder?" *Time,* 4 November 1985, p. 29.

37. See CASE's Preliminary Proposed Findings of Fact of Harassment and Intimidation, 4 September 1984.

38. Atchison, interview with authors.

39. For an insightful analysis of factors leading to a different outcome, see Rick Fantasia, *Cultures of Solidarity* (Berkeley: University of California Press, 1988).

40. Victor Gilinsky, "Comanche Peak Licensing Delay," A Report to Brazos Electric Power Cooperative Tex-La Electric Cooperative of Texas, 15 February 1988.

41. Mary Howard, interview with authors, 16 August 1984; telephone conversations, additional visits, and correspondence, 1984–88.

42. The material for Terry Howard's case derives from a personal interview conducted on 21 June 1984 and his affidavit, prepared July 1982 and issued, according to Howard, to the Nuclear Regulatory Commission, the U.S. attorney general, the Illinois attorney general, and the Michigan attorney general; also Albert T. Howard and Sharon L. Marello v. Zack Company in the Circuit Court of Cook County, Ill., case no. 86L 20025, filed 5 September 1986.

43. M. Howard, interview with authors.

44. Ibid.

45. T. Howard, interview with authors; telephone conversations, additional visits, and correspondence, 1984–88.

46. Harold Garfinkel, "Conditions of Successful Degradation Ceremonies," *American Journal of Sociology* 61 (January 1956): 420–24; Victor W. Turner, *The Ritual Process* (Chicago: Aldine, 1969), pp. 168–203.

47. M. Howard, interview with authors.

48. Ibid.

49. Carroll M. Brodsky, *The Harassed Worker* (Lexington, Mass.: Lexington Books, 1976), pp. 43–46; Bernard Barber, *The Logic and Limits of Trust* (New Brunswick, N.J.: Rutgers University Press, 1985), pp. 7–25.

50. M. Howard, interview with authors.

51. "The Nuclear Plant Papers: Profits Before Public Safety," Channel 5 News (NBC), Chicago, 22 and 23 July 1982.

52. David Everett, "Not the Best of Times for Us," *Detroit Free Press*, 29 January 1984.

53. Billie Garde of the Government Accountability Project provided this information in a telephone interview with authors, 5 July 1988.

54. Confidential interview with authors, 12 January 1986.

55. Soeken and Soeken, "A Survey of Whistleblowers."

56. J. Rose, interview with authors.

57. "Probe of TCAS," *Aviation Digest*, January 1986, section B, pp. 5–7; Don Alpin and Tom Devine, "Is the FAA Perpetuating Jet Crashes?" *Sacramento Bee*, 21 September 1986, Forum, pp. 1–2.

58. "Probe TCAS," section B, p. 5; John Doherty, "Collision Course," *Reason*, June 1982, p. 37.

59. "Memorandum in Support of James C. Pope's Request for Return to Active Status in the Department of Transportation," A Presentation to Department of Transportation, Office of General Counsel, 16 December 1983, p. 2.

60. Jim Pope, interview with authors, 5 June 1984.

61. Dick Cleaver, "Exile in Seattle," *Seattle Times*, 30 October 1980; "Portrait of a 'Whistle-Blower,'" *Aviation Consumer*, 1 January 1981, pp. 8–13; Doherty, "Collision Course," pp. 37–42.

62. Doherty, "Collision Course," pp. 37–39.

63. "Memorandum in Support of James C. Pope," p. 48.

64. Florence Pope, interview with authors, 6 June 1984.

65. "Memorandum in Support of James C. Pope," p. 49.

66. Alpin and Devine, "Is the FAA Perpetuating Jet Crashes?"

67. "Probe TCAS," section B, p. 6.

68. Susan Kellam, "Former FAA Employee Says Agency Ignoring Anti-Collision Device," *Federal Times*, 7 July 1986.

69. Peter Maas, *Marie* (New York: Random House, 1983).

70. Billie Pirner Garde, interview with authors, 16 June 1984; telephone conversations and additional visits, 1984–88.

71. Ibid.

72. Clifford Terry, "Census Worker Fought for Right but Didn't Count on Such a War," *Chicago Tribune*, 3 June 1982, Tempo section. Charges against Hudson are reported in "Final Decision by the Department of Commerce in the Discrimination Complaint of Billie P. Garde," 8 October 1984.

73. Garde, interview with authors.

74. Ibid.

75. Ibid.

76. Ibid.

77. Article in *Muskogee Daily Phoenix*, 26 June 1980; Billie Pirner Garde, "Whistleblower: 'Go Pound Sand,'" *Muskogee Daily Phoenix*, 20 August 1981.

78. "Discrimination Complaint of Billie P. Garde," 11 October 1984, pp. 17–27.

79. Garde, interview with authors.

80. For other cases of sexual discrimination and harassment, see Cristine Colt, "Protesting Sex Discrimination Against Women," and Adriene Tompkins, "Resisting Sexual Demands on the Job," in Alan F. Westin, *Whistle Blowing! Loyalty and Dissent in the Corporation* (New York: McGraw-Hill, 1981); for a current case at the SEC, see Sharon W. Walsh, "The One-Woman War at the SEC," *Washington Post*, 6 June 1988.

81. "Discrimination Complaint of Billie P. Garde," pp. 15–16.

82. Terry, "Census Worker."

83. Jack Anderson, "Case Angering Reagan Stymied by Bureaucrat," *Washington Post,* 22 February 1984.

Chapter 6. Allies in the Struggle: The Press, Legislators, and Public-Interest Groups

1. Stephan Landsman, "The Triumph of Justice," *Michigan Law Review* 85 (April/May 1987): 1101. Landsman's statement is part of his review of Jean-Denis Bredin, *The Affair: The Case of Alfred Dreyfus* (New York: George Braziller, 1986).
2. Irwin Levin, interview with authors, 26 June 1984; Sydney H. Schanberg, "Adult Abuse," *New York Times,* 28 April 1984; editorial, *New York Times,* 28 April 1984; Bruce Lambert, Jr., "Koch Restores Whistle-Blower," *Newsday,* 3 May 1984; "Whistle-Blower Vindicated," *New York Times,* 6 May 1984; James Lemoyne, "City May Take Punitive Action on Caseworkers," *New York Times,* 10 May 1984; for a discussion of the journalist's craft, see Clark R. Mollenhoff, *Investigative Reporting* (New York: Macmillan, 1981).
3. Richard A. Serrano, "VA Hospital Being Probed," *Kansas City Times,* 29 May 1981; Richard A. Serrano, "VA Inspector Denies That Dispute Affects Overall Health Care at Center," *Kansas City Times,* 2 June 1981; Richard A. Serrano, "VA Drug Study Leads to Patient Abuse Charges," *Kansas City Times,* 20 March 1982; Richard A. Serrano, "FDA Says Doctor Mishandled Drug Studies at VA Hospital," *Kansas City Times,* 18 May 1982.
4. Dina Rasor, *The Pentagon Underground* (New York: Times Books, 1985), pp. 193–99.
5. C. Wright Mills, *The Sociological Imagination* (New York: Oxford University Press, 1959).
6. Eric Nalder, "Hanford Auditor Breaks His Silence," *Seattle Times,* 8 October 1986.
7. Eric Nalder, "Audits Say Hanford Plants Unsafe," *Seattle Times,* 4 October 1986.
8. Eric Nalder, interview with authors, 28 November 1986; telephone conversations, 1986–88.
9. Hill Williams and Eric Nalder, "Hanford N Reactor Also Uses Graphite," *Seattle Times,* 29 April 1986; William D. Marbach, "A Chernobyl in the Making?" *Newsweek,* 3 November 1986, p. 29.
10. Nalder, "Audits Say Hanford Plants Unsafe."
11. Eric Nalder, "Audit Finds More Faults at Hanford," *Seattle Times,* 5 October 1986.
12. Eric Nalder and Eric Pryne, "Security Flaw at Hanford Is Revealed," *Seattle Times,* 7 October 1986.
13. Nalder, "Hanford Auditor Breaks His Silence."
14. Casey Ruud, telephone interview with authors, February 1987.
15. Nalder, "Hanford Auditor Breaks His Silence."
16. Elouise Schumacher and Eric Nalder, "Fears of Lethal Chain Reaction Led to Closure," *Seattle Times,* 9 October 1986.
17. Nalder, interview with authors.
18. David L. Altheide, *Media Power* (Beverly Hills, Calif.: Sage Publications, 1985), pp. 256–60.
19. Ruud, telephone interview with authors.
20. Eric Nalder and Eric Pryne, "Audits Reveal Still More Problems at Hanford," *Seattle Times,* 10 October 1986.
21. Ibid.
22. Eric Nalder, "Rockwell Kept Audit Details under Wraps," *Seattle Times,* 15 October 1986.
23. Casey Ruud, telephone interview with authors, June 1988.
24. Eric Nalder, "House Probers to Keep an Eye on Whistle-Blowers," *Seattle Times,* 2 June 1988; Chris Sivula, "Westinghouse Says It Will Appeal Ruling on Whistleblower," *Tri-City Herald,* 7 June 1988; Eric Pryne, "DOE: 'We Failed' in Harassment Case," *Seattle Times,* 12 May 1988.
25. Dr. J. Milton Clark, interview with authors, 25 August 1983; telephone conversations and correspondence, 1983–88.
26. House Committee on Science and Technology, Hearing before the Subcommittee on Natural Resources, Agriculture Research, and Environment, 98th Cong., 1st sess., 23 March 1983, p. 222. Newspaper articles appeared cautioning readers about the dangers of eating fish contaminated by

dioxin. Robert Reinhold, "New York Area Is Receiving Carp from Toxin-Tainted Michigan Bay," *New York Times*, 28 March 1983; Robert Reinhold, "E.P.A.'s Dow Tests Find High Toxicity," *New York Times*, 31 March 1983. For a discussion of the strengths and weaknesses of congressional oversight, see Lawrence C. Dodd and Richard L. Schott, *Congress and the Administrative State* (New York: Wiley, 1979), pp. 155–211.

27. Clark, interview with authors.

28. Valdas Adamkus, interview with authors, 25 August 1983; telephone conversations and correspondence, 1983–88.

29. Maureen Dowd with Jay Branegan, "Down in the Dumps at EPA," *Time*, 28 March 1983, p. 18.

30. Ibid.

31. Jim Greene, interview with authors, 20 June 1983.

32. Cass Peterson, "A Whistle Blower's Controversial Ascent," *Washington Post*, 16 February 1983; Melinda Black, "Stalking EPA's Whistle Blower," *Newsweek*, 26 July 1982, p. 24.

33. Clark, interview with authors.

34. House Committee on Congress, Hearings before the Subcommittee on Oversight and Investigations, 98th Cong., 1st sess., 18 March 1983, pp. 541–42; Howard Kurtz, "EPA Officials Testify about Pressure to Alter Report on Chemical," *Washington Post*, 19 March 1983; Leslie Maitland, "E.P.A. Aides Recall Pressure to Alter Dow Dioxin Study," *New York Times*, 19 March 1983.

35. Hearings before Subcommittee on Natural Resources, Agriculture Research, and Environment, p. 148.

36. Ibid., p. 150.

37. Ibid., p. 156.

38. Carolyn Phillips, "Morale, Enforcement in EPA Office Improve since Burford Resignation," *Wall Street Journal*, 28 July 1983.

39. Clark, interview with authors.

40. Adamkus, interview with authors.

41. Hugh Kaufman, interview with authors, 6 June 1983; telephone conversations and correspondence, 1983–88.

42. Letter from James C. Pope to the *Washington Post*, 1 April 1987 (unpublished).

43. Dr. Martin Schorr, interviews with authors, 8 and 10 April 1988; telephone conversations and correspondence, 1986–88.

44. Betsy Bates, "Mikey's Dad Went Berserk," *San Diego Tribune*, 29 March 1985.

45. Schorr, interviews with authors.

46. Ibid.

47. Ibid.

48. Report by the Auditor General of California, Review of Two Health Care Facilities in San Diego County, Sacramento, California, 26 June 1985, p. 7; Report by the State Department of Health Services, Review of San Diego County Hillcrest Mental Health Facility, August 1985; Betsy Bates, "Man's Suicide May Be Linked to CMH Woes," *San Diego Tribune*, 27 August 1985.

49. Report by the Auditor General, pp. 7–8; Report by the State Department of Health Services; Claude Walbert, "Parents Sue County in Son's Death," *San Diego Tribune*, 19 July 1985.

50. Report by the Auditor General, pp. 9–10. Betsy Bates and Claude Walbert, reporters for the *San Diego Tribune*, wrote an important review article of problems at CMH: "CMH Crowding: A Tragic Toll," *San Diego Tribune*, 29 March 1985.

51. Dr. Zalman Magid, letter to authors, 15 October 1987; interview with authors, 10 April 1988.

52. Larry Stirling, telephone interview with authors, 25 April 1987; interview with authors, 6 April 1988.

53. The problems of that facility can be found in Report by the Auditor General, pp. 13–15.

54. Art Letter, interview with authors, 15 April 1987; telephone conversations and correspondence, 1987–88.

55. Art Letter, telephone conversations with authors during January, February, and March 1987. Memorandum from Larry Stirling to all members of the San Diego Legislative Delegation, 29 September 1986.

56. Schorr, interviews with authors.

57. Letter, interview with authors.

58. Memorandum from Larry Stirling.

59. Letter, interview with authors.

60. Memorandum from Larry Stirling; Report by the State Department of Health Services; editorial, "Let UCSD Care for Mentally Ill," *San Diego Tribune,* 4 February 1986.

61. Memorandum from Larry Stirling; Betsy Bates, "Close CMH, Stirling Says," *San Diego Tribune,* 15 August 1985.

62. "Action Against Psychiatrist Called Reprisal," *San Diego Union,* 21 November 1985.

63. Stirling, telephone interview with authors.

64. Report by the State Department of Health Services.

65. Sid Rhodes, interview with authors, 10 April 1988.

66. Letter, interview with authors.

67. Dr. Jim Hardison, interview with authors, 10 April 1988.

68. California A.B. 1916, 1986; Daniel M. Weintraub, "State Probes Sex Incident at County Mental Hospital," *Los Angeles Times,* 28 November 1985; Claude Walbert, "State Is Probing CMH Incident of Woman on Fire," *San Diego Tribune,* 25 December 1985; Bill Boyarsky, "Bradley to Urge Stronger Shield for Whistle-Blowers," *Los Angeles Times,* 6 August 1987.

69. There were frequent stories in the *San Diego Tribune.* See also Kenneth F. Bunting, "4 Honored for Blowing Whistle on Hospital," *Los Angeles Times,* 28 January 1986. Opposition to the bill came from such groups as the Board of Supervisors of San Diego County and from the Orange County Board of Supervisors. (Letters from Patricia Gayman to Governor George Deukmejian, 15 July 1986; letter from Karen M. Cohen to Senator Dan McCoquodale, 14 April 1986.) Support came from California State Employees Association. (Letter from Gerald Gress to Larry Stirling, 3 April 1986.)

70. Magid, letter to authors.

71. Letter from Dr. Zalman Magid to Larry Stirling, 8 March 1987.

72. Letter from Larry Stirling to Michael O'Connor, 24 March 1987.

73. Ron Roach, "Hiring Bias Against CMH Whistle-Blower Alleged," *San Diego Tribune,* 28 March 1987; "Whistle-Blower Job Bias Claim Probed," *San Diego Union,* 31 March 1987.

74. Stirling, interview with authors.

75. Dave Longest, "Louis Clark, 'Campus Rebel,' Is Not Without a Cause," *University of Evansville Campus Newspaper,* 26 January 1968.

76. Louis Clark, interview with authors, 29 May 1984; telephone conversations and correspondence, 1984–88.

77. Ibid.

78. Ibid.

79. Vince Laubach, interview with authors, 3 June 1984; telephone conversations and correspondence, 1984–88.

80. Bob Jensen, "Right but Painful Describes Laubach's Battle against Fraud," *St. John's University Magazine,* Fall 1985, pp. 4–5.

81. See U.S. Department of Interior, "Abandoned Mine Reclamation Fund, Fee Collection Program," March 1981; Phillip Shabecoff, "Former Aide Says U.S. Ignores Mining Violations," *New York Times,* 24 April 1983; this was later confirmed by GAO review officials. See House Committee on Government Operations, Statement of Pasquale L. Esposito at Hearings before the Subcommittee on Environment, Energy, and Natural Resources, 98th Cong., 2nd sess., 13 June 1984.

82. V. Laubach, interview with authors.

83. Myron Peretz Glazer and Penina Migdal Glazer, "Whistleblowing," *Psychology Today,* August 1986, pp. 36–43.

84. See, for example, Keith Sinzinger, "Pushing Too Hard," *Federal Times,* 6 June 1983.

85. Kathy Laubach, interview with authors, 3 June 1984; telephone conversations, 1984–88.

86. Letter from Louis Clark to John Trezise, U.S. Department of the Interior, 5 June 1985.

87. "Committee on Government Operations, Breakdowns in the Department of the Interior, Civil Penalty Assessment, and Collections Program Have Adversely Affected the Enforcement of the Surface Mining Control and Reclamation Act of 1977," House Report 98–1146, 98th Cong., 2nd sess., 5 October 1984; p. 42; Ben A. Franklin, "Many Strip Miners Play Without Rules," *New York Times,* 14 October 1984; the National Wildlife Federation issued a report on the chaos in the Office of Surface Mining. See "Failed Oversight," a report by Surface Mining Project, Public Lands and Energy Division, National Wildlife Federation, Washington, D.C., October 1985; Cass Peterson, "Report Cites Problems at Mine Agency," *Washington Post,* 2 October 1985, describes this report by the National Wildlife Federation.

88. U.S. Department of the Interior, Grievance of Vincent Laubach, PG 83-22.

89. Clark, interview with authors.

90. For an analysis of the strengths and limits of the public-interest movement, see David Vogel, "The Public-Interest Movement and the American Reform Tradition," *Political Science Quarterly* 95 (Winter 1980–81): 607–27.

Chapter 7. Remaking One's Life: Aftermath of Retaliation

1. Al Louis Ripskis's response to authors' query concerning whistleblower's advice to people considering public disclosure of lawless acts, undated 1985.

2. William Sanjour, ibid., undated 1985.

3. Al Louis Ripskis, telephone interview with authors, 15 July 1988.

4. Florence Heffeon, "Protection of the Constitutional Rights of Federal Employees: The Impact of Bush v. Lucas," *Cooley Law Review* 3 (Trinity Term 1985): 297–323.

5. Bill Bush's response to authors' query concerning whistleblower's advice to people considering public disclosure of lawless acts, 24 May 1985.

6. Four resisters in the sample are not included in these figures: three retired and one died.

7. James Boyd, interview with authors, 17 July 1984. See James Boyd, "The Tragedy of Thomas Dodd," *Saturday Evening Post* (part I), 13 January 1968, pp. 19–25; James Boyd, "The Tragedy of Thomas Dodd," *Saturday Evening Post* (part II), 27 January 1968, pp. 58–64; James Boyd, "The Tragedy of Thomas Dodd," *Saturday Evening Post* (part III), 10 February 1968, pp. 26–37.

8. Boyd, interview with authors.

9. Jack Anderson, with James Boyd, *Fiasco* (New York: Times Books, 1983).

10. Boyd, interview with authors.

11. "The Dodd Case," *Newsweek*, 4 July 1966, pp. 17–18.

12. Marjorie Carpenter, interview with authors, 17 July 1984.

13. Ibid.

14. John Emshwiller, "Suit by Ford Engineer Claims Firm Built Over Million Cars Below Safety Standard," *Wall Street Journal*, 25 July 1977.

15. Frank Camps, telephone interview with authors, 15 June 1982.

16. Frank Camps, interview with authors, 26 August 1983. General Motors was required to pay compensation to the victims of the crash. See Ronda Pempleton, "Accident Victims Win $4 Million Award from Jury," *San Antonio Express*, 16 September 1983.

17. Ibid.

18. "Anne Jennings," interview with authors, 23 August 1984.

19. Ibid.

20. Matthew L. Wald, "For Nuclear Industry, Harm Is Already Done," *New York Times*, 27 May 1986.

21. Dr. Grace Pierce, letter to authors, 12 November 1982.

22. Dr. Betsy Brothers, letter to authors, 26 June 1988.

23. Senate Committee on Governmental Affairs, Hearings before the Subcommittee on Federal Services, Post Office, and Civil Service, 100th Cong., 1st sess., S.508, 20 and 31 July 1987, p. 34.

24. Summary of Whistleblower Protection Act of 1988, passed in October 1988.

25. Rich Jaroslovski, "Blowing the Whistle Begins a Nightmare for Lawyer Joe Rose," *Wall Street Journal*, 10 December 1981.

26. Joseph Rose, telephone interview with authors, 10 July 1982.

27. Joseph Rose, letter to authors, 28 June 1982.

28. Leonard Orland, "Reflections on Corporate Crime: Law in Search of Theory and Scholarship," *American Criminal Law Review* 17 (1980): 514–18.

29. Rose, interview with authors.

30. For a discussion of "make-do's" in a hospital setting, see Erving Goffman, *Asylums* (New York: Anchor Books, 1961), pp. 207–38.

31. Bert Berube, interview with authors, 5 June 1984.

32. Ibid.

33. U.S. Merit Systems Protection Board, *Bertrand G. Berube v. General Services Administration Agency*, Docket no. DC07528410055, 31 October 1984.

34. Pat Berube, telephone interview with authors, May 1986.

35. Bertrand Berube, "A Whistleblower's Perspective of Ethics in Engineering," *Engineering Education*, February 1988, pp. 294–95.

36. U.S. Merit Systems Protection Board, *Bertraud G. Berube v. General Services Administration Agency*, Docket no. DC07528410055, 14 July 1988; U.S. Court of Appeals for the Federal Circuit, *Bertrand G. Berube, Petitioner v. General Services Administration, Respondent*, Appeal no. 86-1584, 2 June 1987; news release from Government Accountability Project, 2 September 1988.

37. Dobie Hatley, telephone interview with authors, May 1988.

38. Chuck Atchison, telephone interview with authors, 14 July 1988.

39. Juanita Ellis, telephone interview with authors, 16 July 1988.

40. Letter from W. G. Counsil to Juanita Ellis, 28 June 1988, read into record of public hearing. See also Settlement Agreement between CASE, Mrs. Juanita Ellis, and Texas Utilities Electric Company, 13 July 1988; Nuclear Regulatory Commission before the Atomic Safety and Licensing Board, in the Matter of Texas Utilities Electric Company et al., Docket nos. 50-445-OL, 50-446-OL, 50-445 CPA, 13 July 1988.

41. Ellis, interview with authors.

42. Greg Mitchell, *Truth . . . and Consequences* (New York: Dembner Books, 1977), pp. 87–127. For a discussion of the Agent Orange issue, see Fred A. Wilcox, *Waiting for an Army to Die* (New York: Vintage Books, 1983).

43. Jacob V. Lamar, "Winning Peace with Honor," *Time*, 21 May 1984.

44. "Ruling Ends Challenge to Agent Orange Fund," *New York Times*, 1 July 1988.

45. Ralph Blumenthal, "Agent Orange: How Fund Will Work," *New York Times*, 9 May 1984; editorial, "Justice, Mercy and Agent Orange," *New York Times*, 9 May 1984; the settlement was later disputed in an appeals court. See Arnold Lubasch, "200-Million Agent Orange Award Is Upheld by U.S. Appeals Court," *New York Times*, 22 April 1987.

46. Mitchell, *Truth . . . and Consequences*, p. 122.

47. Maude DeVictor, telephone interview with authors, April 1985; interview with authors, 20 February 1988.

48. Maude DeVictor, telephone interview with authors, October 1985.

49. Ibid.

50. Terry Howard, interview with authors, 21 June 1984.

51. Ibid.

52. Mary Howard, interview with authors, 16 August 1984.

53. "Tom Sinon," interview with authors, 6 March 1988.

54. Chuck Atchison's response to authors' query concerning whistleblower's advice to people considering public disclosure of lawless acts, 31 May 1985.

Chapter 8. The Fight Goes On

1. Sid Rhodes and Terri Richardson, interview with authors, 10 April 1988.

2. Michael Isikoff, "Grassley to Civil Servants: Ignore Secrecy Pledge," *Washington Post*, 16 October 1987.

3. Tom Devine, interview with authors, 21 March 1988.

4. Dina Rasor, *The Pentagon Underground* (New York: Times Books, 1985), pp. 148–66.

5. Transcript from videotape of General Counsel of Systems Management Group of Major Defense Contractor, "Fraud, Waste, and Abuse," anonymous, 1986.

6. Letter from Wallace H. Robinson, Jr., president of National Security Industrial Association, to the Honorable David Packard, chairman of the President's Blue Ribbon Commission on Defense Management, 6 June 1986.

7. Philip Shenon, "FBI in Surprise Search of Pentagon and Suppliers," *New York Times*, 15 June 1988; Stephen Engelberg, "Inquiry into Bribery Began with a Telephone Call," *New York Times*, 19 June 1988; Stewart Toy, "The Defense Scandal," *Business Week* 4 (July 1988): 28–30.

8. For a detailed discussion of John Coplin's career, see Wayne Swanson and George Schultz, *Prime Rip* (Englewood Cliffs, N.J.: Prentice-Hall, 1982).

9. Devine, interview with authors.

10. Bill Andronicos, "Meaty Charges Spoil His Record," *Federal Times*, 29 October 1984; Ward Sinclair, "Whistle Blower, at Age 71, Won't Leave USDA Alone," *Washington Post*, 13 December 1984; *Consumer Newsweekly* 14 (19 August 1985): 47.

11. Paul Rauber, "How to Stop Salmonella," *Bay Area Coop News*, 23 September 1987; Sean Ford, "Food Inspectors Face Renewed Call to Clean Up Poultry," *Federal Times*, 3 August 1987.

12. Diane Sawyer, quoted in *Food Chemical News*, 6 April 1987, p. 53.

13. Devine, interview with authors.

14. Sawyer, *Food Chemical News*, p. 53; see also Ward Sinclair, "Inspectors Petition for Meat Inquiry," *Washington Post*, 6 June 1986.

15. Ford, "Food Inspectors," p. 5.

16. Michael Cavallo, interview with authors, 21 March 1988; conversations, 1987–88.

17. Ernest Fitzgerald, conversation with authors, 18 May 1988.

18. Bryan Brumley, "Steel Uninspected, Documents Show," *Portland Press Herald*, 13 March 1987; Kendall Holmes, "Charges 'Absurd' Spokesman Says," *Portland Press Herald*, 13 March 1987.

19. Rasor, *The Pentagon Underground*.

20. Brumley, "Steel Uninspected."

21. Leon Bard, telephone interview with authors, 8 May 1988; interview with authors, 18 May 1988.

22. Affidavit by John Berter, 11 February 1987; also Request for an Investigation Pursuant to the Inspector General Act of 1978 before the Office of Inspector General, Veterans Administration, 17 March 1987, p. 2. This request was brought by the Government Accountability Project.

23. House Committee, Post Office, and Civil Service, Hearings before the subcommittee on Civil Service. H.R. 25, Whistleblower Protection Act of 1987, 100th Cong., 1st sess., 10 March 1987. See also Bob Musselman, "Testimony Rekindles Interest in VA Probe," *Cincinnati Post*, 18 March 1987. An excellent article on the case can be found in Karen Franklin, "Fear and Loathing at the Cincinnati VA Medical Center," *Veteran*, February 1988, pp. 13–17.

24. Office of the Special Counsel, U.S. Merit Systems Protection Board, OSC File 10-6-00991, 31 March 1988.

25. John Berter, telephone interview with authors, 10 May 1988; interviews and correspondence, 1987–88.

26. Stephen M. Kohn and Michael D. Kohn, "An Overview of Federal and State Whistleblower Protections," *Antioch Law Journal* 4 (Summer 1986): 108–10. The states that have recognized the public policy exception include: Arizona, California, Connecticut, Florida, Hawaii, Idaho, Illinois, Kansas, Kentucky, Maryland, Massachusetts, Michigan, Montana, Nevada, New Hampshire, New Jersey, New Mexico, North Carolina, Oregon, Pennsylvania, Tennessee, Texas, Virginia, Washington, West Virginia, and Wisconsin.

27. Tamar Lewin, "Business and the Law," *New York Times*, 27 January 1987; interview with John R. Phillips, *Corporate Crime Reporter*, 9 November 1987, pp. 5–12. The False Claims Amendments Act of 1986 is 31 U.S.C. 37-29 to 37-33.

28. Michael Isikoff, "Profit Motive Helps Revive Use of 1863 Antifraud Law," *Washington Post*, 8 November 1987.

29. Talk by Roger Boisjoly at the University of Massachusetts at Amherst, 28 March 1988.

30. Robins's case is described in Ed Magnuson, "Putting Schedule over Safety," *Time*, 1 February 1988, pp. 2–21; also Peter Applebome, "Four Say Problems in Space Shuttle Are Continuing," *New York Times*, 25 September 1987.

31. Letter from Charles W. Hansen to Sylvia Robins, 5 April 1988.

32. Stephen H. Unger, "Would Helping Ethical Professionals Get Professional Societies into Trouble?" *IEEE Technology and Society Magazine*, September 1987, pp. 17–21.

33. Robert M. Anderson, Robert Perrucci, Dan D. Schendel, and Leon E. Tractman, *Divided Loyalties: Whistle-Blowing at BART* (West Lafayette, Ind.: Purdue University Press, 1980); Carl Mitcham, "Schools for Whistle Blowers: Educating Ethical Engineers," *Commonweal*, 10 April 1987, p. 204.

Index